Rick Steves®

SNAPSHOT

Copenhagen
& the Best of Denmark

CONTENTS

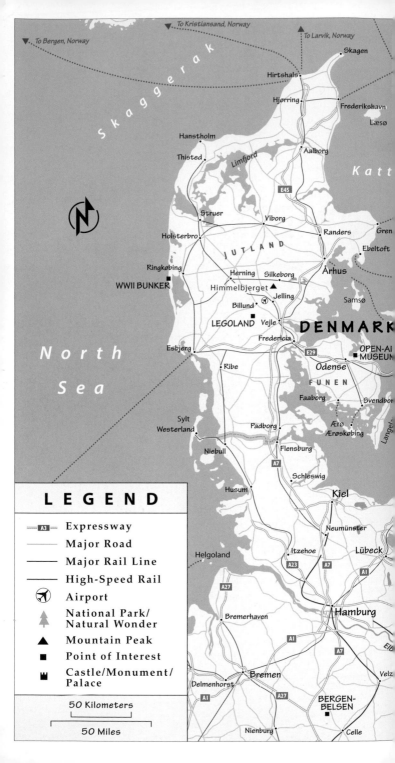

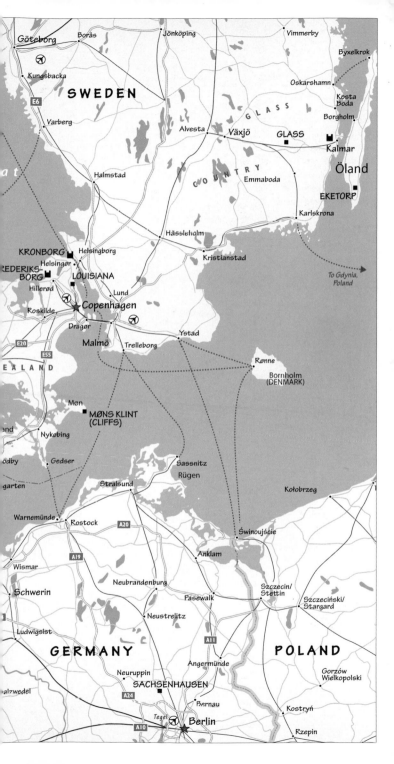

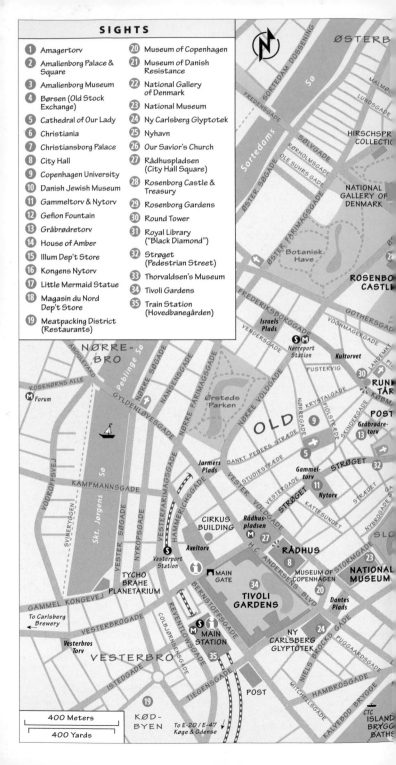

SIGHTS

1. Amagertorv
2. Amalienborg Palace & Square
3. Amalienborg Museum
4. Børsen (Old Stock Exchange)
5. Cathedral of Our Lady
6. Christiania
7. Christiansborg Palace
8. City Hall
9. Copenhagen University
10. Danish Jewish Museum
11. Gammeltorv & Nytorv
12. Gefion Fountain
13. Gråbrødretorv
14. House of Amber
15. Illum Dep't Store
16. Kongens Nytorv
17. Little Mermaid Statue
18. Magasin du Nord Dep't Store
19. Meatpacking District (Restaurants)
20. Museum of Copenhagen
21. Museum of Danish Resistance
22. National Gallery of Denmark
23. National Museum
24. Ny Carlsberg Glyptotek
25. Nyhavn
26. Our Savior's Church
27. Rådhuspladsen (City Hall Square)
28. Rosenborg Castle & Treasury
29. Rosenborg Gardens
30. Round Tower
31. Royal Library ("Black Diamond")
32. Strøget (Pedestrian Street)
33. Thorvaldsen's Museum
34. Tivoli Gardens
35. Train Station (Hovedbanegården)

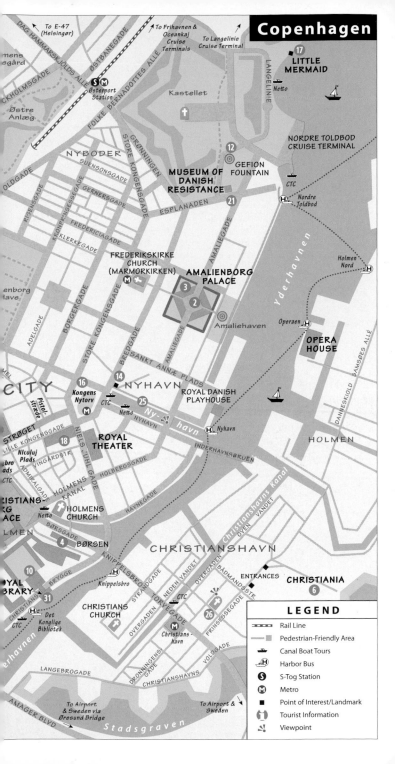

Copenhagen

LITTLE MERMAID 17

Kastellet

To E-47 (Helsingør)

To Frihavnen & Oceankaj Cruise Terminals

To Langelinie Cruise Terminal

ØSTBANEGADE

DAG HAMMARSKJÖLDS ALLÉ

mens egård

Østerport Station

Østre Anlæg

CKHOLMSGADE

LANGELINIE

Netto

NORDRE TOLDBOD CRUISE TERMINAL

NYBODER

STORE KONGENSGADE

GRØNNINGEN

FOLKE BERNADOTTES ALLÉ

SUENSONSGADE

GERNERSGADE

FREDERICIAGADE

KØKKENPENGEGADE

KØKLERKEGADE

RYGENGADE

OLDGADE

MUSEUM OF DANISH RESISTANCE

GEFION FOUNTAIN 12

CTC

Nordre Toldbod

ESPLANADEN

21

AMALIEGADE

Holmen Nord

FREDERIKSKIRKE CHURCH (MARMORKIRKEN)

AMALIENBORG PALACE

3

2

Amaliehaven

Yderhavnen

enborg lave

BORGERGADE

ADELGADE

BREDGADE

STORE KONGENSGADE

AMALIEGADE

Operaen

OPERA HOUSE

SANKT ANNÆ PLADS

CITY

NYHAVN 14 16

Kongens Nytorv

CTC

Netto 25

ROYAL DANISH PLAYHOUSE

Ny- havn NYHAVN

Nyhavn

DANESKJOLD SAMSØES ALLÉ

Pistol-stræde

STRØGET

LILLE KONGENSGADE

18

Niculaj Plads

ROYAL THEATER

NIELS JUHL GADE

VINGÅRDSTR

ADMIRALGADE

HOLBERGSGADE

INDERHAVNSBRUEN

HOLMEN

bro ads

CTC

HOLMENS KANAL

HAVNEGADE

CRISTIANS-RG ACE

Netto

HOLMENS CHURCH

Christianshavns Kanal

OVEN VANDET

CHRISTIANSHAVN

LMEN

4

BØRSGADE

BØRSEN

KNIPPELSBRO

STRANDGADE

OVERGADEN NEDEN VANDET

OVERGADEN OVEN VANDET

BÅDMANDSSTR.

ENTRANCES

CHRISTIANIA 6

YAL BRARY

10

BRYGGE

Knippelsbro

CTC

PRINSESSEGADE

31

CTC

Det Kongelige Bibliotek

CHRISTIANS CHURCH

26

erhavnen

Christians-havn

M

rhavnen

LANGEBROGADE

DRONNINGENS GADE

CHRISTIANSHAVNS

VOLDGADE

To Airport & Sweden via Øresund Bridge

To Airport & Sweden

Stadsgraven

LEGEND

▪▪▪▪	Rail Line
▬	Pedestrian-Friendly Area
⛴	Canal Boat Tours
⚓	Harbor Bus
Ⓢ	S-Tog Station
Ⓜ	Metro
■	Point of Interest/Landmark
⛨	Tourist Information
⌄!	Viewpoint

INTRODUCTION

This Snapshot guide, excerpted from my guidebook *Rick Steves Scandinavia*, introduces you to one of the most technologically advanced, yet traditional and welcoming nations in Europe—Denmark. There's a lot more here than just Hans Christian Andersen stories, sweet breakfast pastries, and rolling farmlands. Start with the livable Danish capital, Copenhagen, where you can experience the classic Tivoli Gardens amusement park, Europe's first pedestrian shopping mall, a warrior-king's Renaissance castle, and a free-spirited squatters' colony. You can side-trip to nearby Roskilde to see millennium-old Viking ships, or head to Frederiksborg Castle to tour Denmark's Versailles.

Beyond the capital, make time for the rest of Denmark—rugged islands, salty harbors, and windswept sandy coasts. The isle of Ærø is your time-warp experience back into a cozy 18th-century town and a chance to unwind in an utterly authentic Danish environment. To complete your visit, check out Hans Christian Andersen's house in Odense and stop in Denmark's "second city"—Aarhus—with its open-air folk museum and wildly contemporary art museum.

To help you have the best trip possible, I've included the following topics in this book:

- **Planning Your Time,** with advice on how to make the most of your limited time
- **Orientation,** including tourist information (abbreviated as TI), tips on public transportation, local tour options, and helpful hints
- **Sights** with ratings:
  - ▲▲▲—Don't miss
  - ▲▲—Try hard to see
  - ▲—Worthwhile if you can make it
  - **No rating**—Worth knowing about

• **Sleeping** and **Eating,** with good-value recommendations in every price range

• **Connections,** with tips on trains, buses, boats, and driving

Practicalities, near the end of this book, has information on money, staying connected, hotel reservations, transportation, and more.

To travel smartly, read this little book in its entirety before you go. It's my hope that this guide will make your trip more meaningful and rewarding. Traveling like a temporary local, you'll get the absolute most out of every mile, minute, and dollar.

God rejse! Happy travels!

Rick Steves

DENMARK

DENMARK

Danmark

Denmark is by far the smallest of the Scandinavian countries, but in the 16th century, it was the largest: At one time, Denmark ruled all of Norway and the three southern provinces of Sweden. Danes are proud of their mighty history and are the first to remind you that they were a lot bigger and a lot stronger in the good old days. And yet, they're a remarkably mellow, well-adjusted lot—organized without being uptight, and easygoing with a delightfully wry sense of humor.

In the 10th century, before its heyday as a Scan-superpower, Denmark was, like Norway and Sweden, home to the Vikings. More than anything else, these fierce warriors were known for their great shipbuilding, which enabled them to travel far. Denmark's Vikings journeyed west to Great Britain and Ireland (where they founded Dublin) and brought back various influences, including Christianity.

Denmark is composed of many islands, a peninsula (Jutland) that juts up from northern Germany, Greenland, and the Faroe Islands. The two main islands are Zealand (*Sjælland* in Danish), where Copenhagen is located, and Funen (*Fyn* in Danish), where Hans Christian Andersen (or, as Danes call him, simply "H. C.") was born. Out of the hundreds of smaller islands, ship-in-bottle-cute Ærø is my favorite. The Danish landscape

is gentle compared with the dramatic fjords, mountains, and vast lakes of other Scandinavian nations. Danes (not to mention Swedes and Norwegians) like to joke about the flat Danish landscape, saying that you can stand on a case of beer and see from one end of the country to the other. Denmark's highest point in Jutland is only 560 feet above sea level, and no part of the country is more than 30 miles from the sea.

In contrast to the rest of Scandinavia, much of Denmark is

arable. The landscape consists of rolling hills, small thatched-roof farmhouses, beech forests, and whitewashed churches with characteristic stairstep gables. Red brick, which was a favorite material of the nation-building King Christian IV, is everywhere—especially in major civic buildings such as city halls and train stations.

Like the other Scandinavian countries, Denmark is predominantly Lutheran, but only a small minority attend church regularly. The majority are ethnic Danes, and many (but certainly not all) of them have the stereotypical blond hair and blue eyes. Two out of three Danes have last names ending in "-sen." The assimilation of ethnic groups into this homogeneous society, which began in earnest in the 1980s, is a source of some controversy. But in general, most Danes have a live-and-let-live attitude and enjoy one of the highest standards of living in the world. Taxes are high in this welfare state, but education is free and medical care highly subsidized. Generous parental leave extends to both men and women.

Denmark Almanac

Official Name: Kongeriget Danmark—the Kingdom of Denmark—or simply Denmark.

Population: Denmark's 5.6 million people are mainly of Scandinavian descent, with immigrants—mostly Turkish, Polish, Syrian, German, and Iraqi—making up 12 percent of the population. Greenland is home to the indigenous Inuit, and the Faroe Islands to people of Nordic heritage. Most Danes speak both Danish and English, with a small minority speaking German, Inuit, or Faroese. The population is 76 percent Protestant (mostly Evangelical Lutheran), 4 percent Muslim, and 20 percent "other."

Latitude and Longitude: 56°N and 10°E, similar latitude to northern Alberta, Canada.

Area: 16,600 square miles, roughly twice the size of Massachusetts.

Geography: Denmark includes the Jutland peninsula in northern Europe. Situated between the North Sea and the Baltic Sea, it shares a 42-mile border with Germany. In addition to Greenland and the Faroe Islands, Denmark also encompasses over 400 islands (78 of which are inhabited). Altogether Denmark has 4,544 miles of coastline. The mainland is mostly flat, and nearly two-thirds of the land is cultivated.

Biggest Cities: Denmark's capital city, Copenhagen (pop. 1.2 million), is located on the island of Zealand (Sjælland). Aarhus (on the

Denmark, one of the most environmentally conscious European countries, is a front-runner in renewable energy, recycling, and organic farming. You'll see lots of modern windmills dotting the countryside. Wind power accounts for 36 percent of Denmark's energy today, with a goal of 50 percent by 2020. By 2050, the country hopes to free itself completely from its dependence on fossil fuels. About 60 percent of waste is recycled. In grocery stores, organic products are shelved right alongside nonorganic ones—for the same price.

Denmark's Queen Margrethe II is a very popular and talented woman who, along with her royal duties, has designed coins, stamps, and book illustrations. Danes gather around the TV on New Year's Eve to hear her annual speech to the nation and flock to the Royal Palace in Copenhagen on April 16 to sing her "Happy Birthday." Her son, mainland) has 310,000, and Odense (on Funen/Fyn) has 170,000.

Economy: Denmark's modern economy is holding its own, with a gross domestic product of just over $306 billion. Denmark's top exports include pharmaceuticals, machinery, and food products. It is also one of the world's leaders in exports of wind turbine technology. The GDP per capita is about $48,000.

Currency: 6 Danish kroner (DKK) = about $1.

Government: Denmark is a constitutional monarchy. Queen Margrethe II is the head of state, but the head of government is the prime minister, a post held since June 2015 by Lars Løkke Rasmussen. The 179-member parliament (Folketinget) is elected every four years.

Flag: Red with a white cross.

The Average Dane: He or she is 42 years old, has 1.7 children, and will live to be 79. Danes get five weeks of paid vacation per year, and their most popular vacation destination is Spain. Despite the cozy lifestyle, no European nation consumes more antidepressants per capita except Iceland.

Crown Prince Frederik, married Australian Mary Donaldson in 2004. Their son Christian's birth in 2005 was cause for a national celebration (the couple now have four children).

The Danes are proud of their royal family and of the flag, a white cross on a red background. Legend says it fell from the sky during a 13th-century battle in Estonia, making it Europe's oldest continuously used flag. You'll see it everywhere—decorating cakes, on clothing, or fluttering in the breeze atop government buildings. It's as much a decorative symbol as a patriotic one.

You'll also notice that the Danes have an odd fixation on two animals: elephants and polar bears, both of which are symbols of national (especially royal) pride. The Order of the Elephant is the highest honor that the Danish monarch can bestow on someone; if you see an emblematic elephant, you know somebody very important is involved. And the polar bear represents the Danish protectorate of Greenland—a welcome reminder to Danes that their nation is more than just Jutland and a bunch of flat little islands.

From an early age, Danes develop a passion for soccer. You may see red-and-white-clad fans singing on their way to a match. Despite the country's small size, the Danish national team does well in international competition. Other popular sports include sailing, cycling, badminton, and team handball.

The Danish language, with its three extra vowels (Æ, Ø, and Å), is notoriously difficult for foreigners to pronounce. Even seemingly predictable consonants can be tricky. For example, the letter "d" is often dropped, so the word *gade* (street)—which you'll see, hear, and say constantly— is pronounced "gah-eh." Luckily for us, most Danes also speak English and are patient with thick-tongued foreigners. Danes have playful fun teasing tourists who make the brave attempt to say Danish words. The hardest phrase, *rød grød med fløde* (a delightful red fruit porridge topped with cream), is nearly impossible for a non-Dane to pronounce. Ask a local to help you.

Sample Denmark's sweet treats at one of the many bakeries you'll see. The pastries that we call "Danish" in the US are called *wienerbrød* in Denmark. Bakeries line their display cases with several varieties of *wienerbrød* and other delectable sweets. Try *kringle, snegle,* or *Napoleonshatte,* or find your own favorite.

(Chances are it will be easier to enjoy than to pronounce.)

For a selection of useful Danish survival phrases, see page 10. Two important words to know are *skål* ("cheers," a ritual always done with serious eye contact) and *hyggelig* (pronounced HEW-geh-lee), meaning warm and cozy. Danes treat their home like a sanctuary and spend a great deal of time improving their gardens and houses—inside and out. Cozying up one's personal space (a national obsession) is something the Danes do best. If you have the opportunity, have some Danes adopt you during your visit so you can enjoy their warm hospitality.

Heaven to a Dane is returning home after a walk in a beloved beech forest to enjoy open-faced sandwiches washed down with beer among good friends. Around the *hyggelig* candlelit table, there will be a spirited discussion of the issues of the day, plenty of laughter, and probably a few good-natured jokes about the Swedes or Norwegians. *Skål!*

Danish Survival Phrases

The Danes tend to say words quickly and clipped. In fact, many short vowels end in a "glottal stop"—a very brief vocal break immediately following the vowel. While I haven't tried to indicate these in the phonetics, you can listen for them in Denmark...and (try to) imitate.

Three unique Danish vowels are æ (sounds like the e in "egg"), ø (sounds like the German ö—purse your lips and say "oh"), and å (sounds like the o in "bowl"). The letter r is not rolled—it's pronounced farther back in the throat, almost like a w. A d at the end of a word sounds almost like our th; for example, mad (food) sounds like "math." In the phonetics, ī sounds like the long i sound in "light," and bolded syllables are stressed.

English	Danish	Pronunciation
Hello. (formal)	Goddag.	goh-**day**
Hi. / Bye. (informal)	Hej. / Hej-hej.	hī / hī-hī
Do you speak English?	Taler du engelsk?	**tay**-lehr doo **eng**-elsk
Yes. / No.	Ja. / Nej.	yah / nī
Please. (May I?)*	Kan jeg?	kahn yī
Please. (Can you?)*	Kan du?	kahn doo
Please. (Would you?)*	Vil du?	veel doo
Thank you (very much).	(Tusind) tak.	(**too**-sin) tack
You're welcome.	Selv tak.	sehl tack
Can I help (you)?	Kan jeg hjælpe (dig)?	kahn yī **yehl**-peh (dī)
Excuse me. (to pass)	Undskyld mig.	**oon**-skewl mī
Excuse me. (Can you help me?)	Kan du hjælpe mig?	kahn doo **yehl**-peh mī
(Very) good.	(Meget) godt.	(**mī**-ehl) goht
Goodbye.	Farvel.	fah-**vehl**
zero / one / two	nul / en / to	nool / een / toh
three / four	tre / fire	tray / feer
five / six	fem / seks	fehm / sehks
seven / eight	syv / otte	syew / **oh**-deh
nine / ten	ni / ti	nee / tee
hundred	hundred	**hoo**-nuh
thousand	tusind	**too**-sin
How much?	Hvor meget?	vor **mī**-ehl
local currency: (Danish) crown	(Danske) kroner	(**dahn**-skeh) **kroh**-nah
Where is...?	Hvor er...?	vor ehr
...the toilet	...toilettet	toy-**leh**-teht
men	herrer	**hehr**-ah
women	damer	**day**-mah
water / coffee	vand / kaffe	van / **kah**-feh
beer / wine	øl / vin	uhl / veen
Cheers!	Skål!	skohl
Can I have the bill?	Kan jeg få regningen?	kahn yī foh **rī**-ning-ehn

*Because Danish has no single word for "please," they approximate that sentiment by asking "May I?", "Can you?", or "Would you?", depending on the context.

COPENHAGEN

København

Copenhagen, Denmark's capital, is the gateway to Scandinavia. It's an improbable combination of corny Danish clichés, well-dressed executives having a business lunch amid cutting-edge contemporary architecture, and some of the funkiest counterculture in Europe. And yet, it all just works so tidily together. With the Øresund Bridge connecting Sweden and Denmark (creating the region's largest metropolitan area), Copenhagen is energized and ready to dethrone Stockholm as Scandinavia's powerhouse city.

A busy day cruising the canals, wandering through the palace, and taking an old-town walk will give you your historical bearings. Then, after another day stroll-ing the Strøget (STROY-et, Europe's first and greatest pedestrian shopping mall), biking the canals, and sampling the Danish good life (including a gooey "Danish" pastry), you'll feel right at home. Live it up in Scandinavia's cheapest and most fun-loving capital.

PLANNING YOUR TIME

A first visit deserves a minimum of two days. Note that many sights are closed on Monday year-round or in the off-season.

Budget Itinerary Tip: Kamikaze sightseers on tight budgets see Copenhagen as a useful Scandinavian bottleneck. They sleep heading into town by train, tour the city during the day, and sleep on a boat or train as they travel north to their next destination. At the end of their Scandinavian travels, they do the same thing in reverse. The result is two days and no nights in Copenhagen (you can check your bag and take a shower at the train station). Considering the joy of Oslo and Stockholm, this isn't all that crazy if you have limited time (and can sleep on a moving train or boat). Consider taking a night train to Sweden with connections to Stockholm, or cruise up to Oslo on a night boat.

Day 1

Catch a 9:30 city walking tour with Richard Karpen (Mon-Sat mid-May-mid-Sept). After lunch, catch the relaxing canal-boat tour out to *The Little Mermaid* and back. Enjoy the rest of the afternoon tracing Denmark's cultural roots in the National Museum and visiting the Ny Carlsberg Glyptotek art gallery (Impressionists and Danish artists). Spend the evening following my "Copenhagen City Walk" and strolling with Copenhageners at the same time.

Day 2

At 10:00, go Neoclassical at Thorvaldsen's Museum, and tour the royal reception rooms at the adjacent Christiansborg Palace. After a *smørrebrød* lunch, spend the afternoon seeing Rosenborg Castle, with Denmark's crown jewels. Spend the evening at Tivoli Gardens.

Christiania—the hippie squatters' community—is not for everyone. But it's worth considering if you're intrigued by alternative lifestyles, or simply want a break from museums. During a busy trip, Christiania fits best in the evening.

Orientation to Copenhagen

Copenhagen is huge (with 1.2 million people), but for most visitors, the walkable core is the diagonal axis formed by the train station, Tivoli Gardens, Rådhuspladsen (City Hall Square), and the Strøget pedestrian street, ending at the colorful old Nyhavn sailors' harbor. Bubbling with street life, colorful pedestrian zones, and most of the city's sightseeing, the Strøget is fun. But also be sure to get off the main drag and explore. By doing things by bike or on foot, you'll stumble upon some charming bits of Copenhagen that many travelers miss. The city feels pretty torn up, as they are deep into a multiyear Metro expansion project, which will add 17 stations to their already impressive system.

Outside of the old city center are three areas of interest to tourists:

• To the north are Rosenborg Castle and Amalienborg Palace, with *The Little Mermaid* nearby.

• To the east, across the harbor, are Christianshavn (Copen-

The Story of Copenhagen

If you study your map carefully, you can read the history of Copenhagen in today's street plan. København ("Merchants' Harbor") was born on the little island of Slotsholmen—today

home to Christiansborg Palace—in 1167. What was Copenhagen's medieval moat is now a string of pleasant lakes and parks, including Tivoli Gardens. You can still make out some of the zigzag pattern of the moats and ramparts in the city's greenbelt.

Many of these fortifications— and several other landmarks—were built by Denmark's most memorable king. You need to remember only one character in Copenhagen's history: Christian IV. Ruling from 1588 to 1648, he was Denmark's Renaissance king and a royal party animal (see the "King Christian IV" sidebar, later). The personal energy of this "Builder King" sparked a Golden Age when Copenhagen prospered and many of the city's grandest buildings were erected. In the 17th century, Christian IV extended the city fortifications to the north, doubling the size of the city, while adding a grid plan of streets and his Rosenborg Castle. This "new town" was the district around the Amalienborg Palace.

In 1850, Copenhagen's 140,000 residents all lived within this defensive system. Building in the no-man's-land outside the walls was only allowed with the understanding that in the event of an attack, you'd burn your dwellings to clear the way for a good defense.

Most of the city's historic buildings still in existence were built within the medieval walls, but conditions became too crowded, and outbreaks of disease forced Copenhagen to spread outside the walls. Ultimately those walls were torn down and replaced with "rampart streets" that define today's city center: Vestervoldgade (literally, "West Rampart Street"), Nørrevoldgade ("North"), and Østervoldgade ("East"). The fourth side is the harbor and the island of Slotsholmen, where København was born.

hagen's "Little Amsterdam" district) and the alternative enclave of Christiania.

• To the west (behind the train station) is Vesterbro, a young and trendy part of town with lots of cafés, bars, and boutiques; the hip Meatpacking District (Kødbyen); and the Carlsberg Brewery (plus the picnic-friendly Frederiksberg Park).

Most of these sights are walkable from the Strøget, but taking a bike, bus, or taxi is more efficient. I rent a bike for my entire

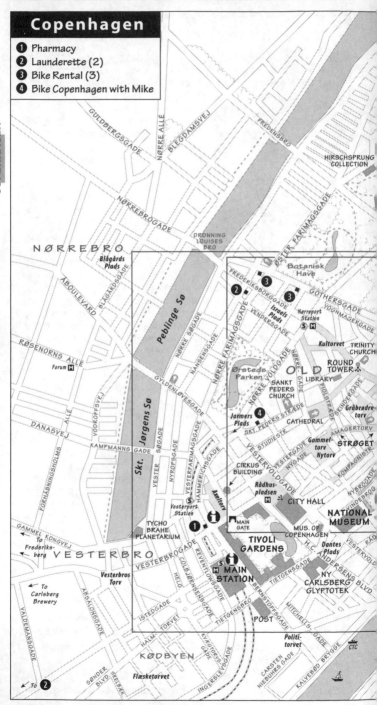

COPENHAGEN

Copenhagen

1. Pharmacy
2. Launderette (2)
3. Bike Rental (3)
4. Bike Copenhagen with Mike

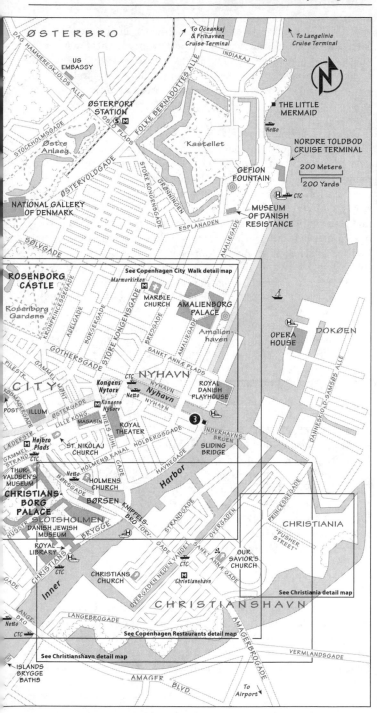

visit (for about the cost of a single cab ride per day) and park it safely in my hotel courtyard. I get anywhere in the town center faster than by taxi (nearly anything is within a 10-minute pedal). In good weather, the city is an absolute delight by bike (for more on biking in Copenhagen, see "Getting Around Copenhagen: By Bike," later).

TOURIST INFORMATION

Copenhagen's questionable excuse for a TI, which bills itself as "Wonderful Copenhagen," is actually a blatantly for-profit company. As in a (sadly) increasing number of big European cities, it provides information only about businesses that pay a hefty display fee of thousands of dollars each year. This colors the advice and information the office provides. While they can answer basic questions, their two most convenient offices—at the train station (daily 9:00-17:00) and on Vesterbrogade—are worthwhile mostly for their big racks of advertising brochures—you can pick up the free map at many hotels and other places in town (main TI: May-June Mon-Sat 9:00-18:00, Sun until 14:00; July-Aug daily 9:00-19:00; Sept-April Mon-Fri 9:00-17:00, Sat until 16:00, closed Sun, Vesterbrogade 4A, just up the street from the main exit of train station—across from the towering Radisson Blu Royal Hotel, good Lagkagehuset bakery in building; tel. 70 22 24 42, www.visitcopenhagen.com).

Copenhagen Card: This card includes entry to many of the city's sights (including expensive ones, like Tivoli and Rosenborg Castle) and all local transportation in all zones of the greater Copenhagen area. It can save busy sightseers some money and the hassle of choosing the right transportation pass. If you're planning on visiting a lot of attractions (especially ones with steep entry prices) and are going to travel to outlying sights such as Kronborg Castle and Roskilde Cathedral, do the arithmetic to see if buying this pass adds up (389 DKK/24 hours, 550 DKK/48 hours, 660 DKK/72 hours, 890 DKK/120 hours—sold at the TI, online, and some hotels; www.copenhagencard.com).

Alternative Sources of Tourist Information: As the TI's bottom line competes with its mission to help tourists, you may want to seek out other ways to inform yourself. The weekly English-language newspaper, *The Copenhagen Post*, has good articles about what's going on in town. Read it online at www.cphpost.dk (also available in print, sometimes free at TI or some hotels, or buy it at a 7-Eleven or newsstand). The witty alternative website, www.aok.dk, has several articles in English (and many more in Danish—readable and very insightful if you translate them online).

ARRIVAL IN COPENHAGEN
By Train

The main train station is called Hovedbanegården (HOETH-bahn-gorn; look for *København H* on signs and schedules). It's a temple of travel and a hive of travel-related activity (and 24-hour thievery). Kiosks and fast-food eateries cluster in the middle of the main arrivals hall. From the main entrance, the **ticket office** is at the back of the station (Mon-Fri 7:00-20:00; Sat-Sun 8:00-18:00). If you need to make reservations for an upcoming high-speed train trip (required even of rail-pass holders), you could do it here.

Within the station, you'll find **baggage storage** (go down stairs at back of station marked *Bagagebokse;* lockers and check-room/*garderobe* both open long hours daily); pay **WCs** (right side of station; a branch of the recommended **Lagkagehuset** bakery (front of station); and lots more. At both the front and the back of the station, you'll find **ATMs.**

The tracks at the back of the station (tracks 9-10 and 11-12) are for the suburban train (S-tog).

Getting into Town: If you want to get right to sightseeing, you're within easy walking distance of downtown. Just walk out the front door and you'll run into one of the entrances for Tivoli amusement park; if you go around its left side and up a couple of blocks, you'll be at Rådhuspladsen, where my "Copenhagen City Walk" begins.

Hotels are scattered far and wide around town. It's best to get arrival instructions from your hotelier, but if you're on your own, here are some tips:

To reach hotels **behind the station,** slip out the back door—just go down the stairs at the back of the station marked *Reventlowsgade.*

For hotels **near Nørreport** (Ibsens and Jørgensen), ride the S-tog from the station two stops to Nørreport, within about a 10-minute walk of the hotels. Bus #14 also runs from near the train station to Nørreport.

For hotels **near Nyhavn** (71 Nyhavn and Bethel Sømandshjem), you can take the S-tog to Nørreport, then transfer to the Metro one stop to Kongens Nytorv, within a few minutes' walk of Nyhavn. Or you can take bus #66 to Nyhavn (or #26 from around the corner to Kongens Nytorv).

Note: If you're staying near Nørreport (or near Nyhavn, an easy Metro connection from Nørreport), check the train schedule carefully; many local trains (such as some from Roskilde and those from the airport) continue through the main train station to Nørreport Station, saving you an extra step.

By Plane
Copenhagen Airport (Kastrup)

Copenhagen's international airport is a traveler's dream, with a TI, baggage check, bank, ATMs, post office, shopping mall, grocery store, bakery, and more (airport code: CPH, airport tel. 32 31 32 31, www.cph.dk). The three check-in terminals are within walking distance of each other (departures screens tell you which terminal to go to). On arrival, all flights feed into one big lobby in Terminal 3. When you pop out here, a TI kiosk is on your left, taxis are out the door on your right, trains are straight ahead, and shops and eateries fill the atrium above you. You can use dollars or euros at the airport, but you'll get change back in kroner.

Getting Between the Airport and Downtown: Your options include the Metro, trains, and taxis. There are also buses into town, but the train/Metro is generally better.

The **Metro** runs directly from the airport to Christianshavn, Kongens Nytorv (near Nyhavn), and Nørreport, making it the best choice for getting into town if you're staying in any of these areas (36-DKK three-zone ticket, yellow M2 line, direction: Vanløse, 4-10/hour, 11 minutes to Christianshavn). The Metro station is located at the end of Terminal 3 and is covered by the roof of the terminal.

Convenient **trains** also connect the airport with downtown (36-DKK three-zone ticket, covered by rail pass, 4/hour, 12 minutes). Buy your ticket from the ground-level ticket booth (look for *DSB: Tickets for Train, Metro & Bus* signs) before riding the escalator down to the tracks. Track 2 has trains going into the city (track 1 is for trains going east, to Sweden). Trains into town stop at the main train station (signed *København H;* handy if you're sleeping at my recommended hotels behind the train station), as well as the Nørreport and Østerport stations. At Nørreport, you can connect to the Metro for Kongens Nytorv (near Nyhavn) and Christianshavn.

With the train/Metro trip being so quick, frequent, and cheap, I see no reason to take a taxi. But if you do, **taxis** are fast, civil, accept credit cards, and charge about 300 DKK for a ride to the town center.

By Boat or Cruise Ship

For information on Copenhagen's cruise terminals, see the end of this chapter.

HELPFUL HINTS

Pharmacy: Steno Apotek is across from the train station (open 24 hours, Vesterbrogade 6C, tel. 33 14 82 66, see the Copenhagen map, earlier, for location).

Blue Monday: As you plan, remember that most sights close on Monday, but these attractions remain open: Amalienborg Museum, Christiansborg Palace (closed Mon Oct-April), City Hall, Rosenborg Castle (generally closed Mon Jan-April and Nov-Dec), Round Tower, Royal Library, Our Savior's Church, Tivoli Gardens (generally closed late Sept-late March), both Harbor Baths (closed Oct-May), and various tours (canal, bus, walking, and bike). You can explore Christiania, but Monday is its rest day so it's unusually quiet and some restaurants are closed.

Laundry: Møntvask is a good coin-op laundry near Nørreport (daily 6:00-21:00, 50 yards from Ibsens Hotel at 86 Nansensgade). Another **Møntvask** is several blocks west of my train-station-area hotel listings (daily 7:00-21:00, Flensborggade 20). For both locations, see the Copenhagen map, earlier. *Vaskel* is wash, *tørring* is dry, and *sæbe* is soap.

Ferries: While in Copenhagen, book any ferries that you plan to take in Scandinavia. Visit a travel agent or book directly with the ferry company. For the Copenhagen-Oslo overnight ferry, contact **DFDS** or visit the **DSB Rejsebureau** at the main train station (see page 96 for details).

Jazz Festival: The Copenhagen Jazz Festival—10 days in early July—puts the town in a rollicking slide-trombone mood. The Danes are Europe's jazz enthusiasts, and this music festival fills the town with happiness. The TI prints up an extensive listing of each year's festival events, or get the latest at www. jazz.dk. There's also a winter jazz festival in February.

GETTING AROUND COPENHAGEN
By Public Transit

It's easy to navigate Copenhagen, with its fine buses, Metro, and S-tog (a suburban train system with stops in the city). Be sure to pick up the *Bus, Train & Metro Guide* map at the TI for an overview of all your public transportation options. For a helpful website that covers public transport (nationwide) in English, consult www. rejseplanen.dk.

Tickets: The same tickets are used throughout the system. A 24-DKK, **two-zone ticket** gets you an hour's travel within the center—pay as you board buses, or buy from station ticket offices, convenience stores, or vending machines for the Metro. (Ticket machines should accept American credit cards with a chip, and most machines also take Danish cash; if the machine won't take your credit card, find a cashier.) Assume you'll be within the middle two zones unless traveling to or from the airport, which requires a **three-zone ticket** (36 DKK).

If you plan to ride transit in Copenhagen and to the outlying sights in one day, consider a **"24-hour ticket"** that covers all travel zones for 130 DKK.

If you're traveling exclusively in central Copenhagen, the **City Pass** is a good value (80 DKK/24 hours, 200 DKK/72 hours, covers travel within zones 1-4, including the airport). You can buy a pass at some train and Metro stations or use www.dinoffentligetransport. dk; it will be sent as a text message to your mobile phone. To travel throughout the greater Copenhagen region—including side-trips to Roskilde, Frederiksborg Castle, Louisiana Art Museum, and Kronborg Castle—you'll need to pay more (buy supplementary tickets at ticket machines or station ticket office).

For some visitors, the **Copenhagen Card** will be the best choice for its sheer convenience. It covers all public transportation in the greater Copenhagen area (including to Roskilde, Frederiksborg Castle, Louisiana Art Museum, etc.), canal boat tours, and admission to nearly all the major sights (see "Tourist Information," earlier).

Buses: While the train system is slick (Metro and S-tog, described later), its usefulness is limited for the typical tourist—but buses serve all of the major sights in town every five to eight minutes during daytime hours. If you're not riding a bike everywhere, get comfortable with the buses. Bus drivers are patient, have change, and speak English. City maps list bus routes. Locals are usually friendly and helpful. There's also a floating "Harbor Bus" (described on page 22).

Bus lines that end with "A" (such as #1A) use quiet, eco-friendly, electric buses that are smaller than normal buses, allowing access into the narrower streets of the Old Town. Designed for tourists, these provide an easy overview to the city center. Among these, the following are particularly useful:

Bus **#1A** loops from the train station up to Kongens Nytorv (near Nyhavn) and then farther north, to Østerport.

Bus **#2A** goes from Christianshavn to the city center, then onward to points west.

Bus **#6A** connects the station to Nørreport, but you'll need to catch it up around the corner on Vesterbrogade.

Other, non-"A" buses, which are bigger and tend to be more direct, can be faster for some trips:

Bus **#5C** connects the station more or less directly to Nørreport.

Bus **#14** runs from Nørreport (and near my recommended hotels) down to the city center, stopping near the Strøget, and eventually going near the main train station.

Bus **#26** runs a handy route right through the main tourist zone: train station/Tivoli to Slotsholmen Island to Kongens Nytorv (near Nyhavn) to the Amalienborg Palace/*Little Mermaid* area. It continues even farther north to one of the city's main cruise ports, but the line splits, so check with the driver to make sure you're on the right bus.

Bus **#66** goes from Nyhavn to Slotsholmen Island to Tivoli.

Metro: Copenhagen's Metro line, while simple, is super-futuristic and growing. For most tourists' purposes, only the airport and three consecutive stops within the city matter: Nørreport (connected every few minutes by the S-tog to the main train station), Kongens Nytorv (near Nyhavn and the Strøget's north end), and Christianshavn. Nearly all recommended hotels are within walking distance of the main train station or these three stops.

The city is hard at work on its Cityringen (City Circle) Metro line, which will intersect with its two existing lines. Eventually, the Metro will become far handier for tourists—linking the train station, Rådhuspladsen, Gammel Strand (near Slotsholmen Island), and Kongens Nytorv (near Nyhavn). In the meantime, expect to see massive construction zones at each of those locations. For the latest on the Metro and route maps, see www.m.dk.

S-tog Train: The S-tog is basically a commuter line that links stations on the main train line through Copenhagen; for those visiting the city, the most important stops are the main train station and Nørreport (where it ties into the Metro system). Note that while rail passes are valid on the S-tog, it's probably not worth using a travel day. The S-tog is very handy for reaching many of the outlying sights described in the Near Copenhagen chapter.

By Boat

The hop-on, hop-off "Harbor Bus" (Havnebus) boat stops at the "Black Diamond" library, Christianshavn (near Knippels Bridge), Nyhavn, the Opera House, and the Nordre Toldbod cruise-ship pier, which is a short walk from *The Little Mermaid* site. The boat is part of the city bus system (lines #991 and #992) and covered by the tickets described earlier. Taking a long ride on this boat, from the library to the end of the line, is the "poor man's cruise"—without commentary, of course (runs

6:00-19:00). Or, for a true sightseeing trip, consider a guided harbor cruise (described later, under "Tours in Copenhagen").

By Taxi

Taxis are plentiful, easy to call or flag down, and pricey (35-DKK pickup charge and then about 15 DKK/kilometer—higher in evenings and on weekends). For a short ride, four people spend about the same by taxi as by bus. Calling 35 35 35 35 will get you a taxi within minutes...with the meter already well on its way.

By Bike

Cyclists see more, save time and money, and really feel like locals. With a bike, you have Copenhagen at your command. I'd rather have a bike than a car and driver at my disposal. Virtually every street has a dedicated bike lane (complete with bike signal lights). Warning: Police routinely issue hefty tickets to anyone riding on sidewalks or through pedestrian zones. Note also that bikes can't be parked just anywhere. Observe others and park your bike among

other bikes. The simple built-in lock that binds the back tire is adequate.

Renting a Bike: Your best bet for renting a bike is often your hotelier: Many rent (or loan) decent bikes at fair rates to guests.

For an (often) better-quality bike and advice from someone with cycle expertise, consider one of these rental outfits in or near the city center (see the Copenhagen map, earlier, for locations).

Københavns Cyklebørs, near Nørreport Station, has a good selection of three-gear bikes (90 DKK/1 day, 170 DKK/2 days, 240 DKK/3 days, 450 DKK/week; Mon-Fri 10:00-17:30, Sat-Sun until 14:00, closed all day Sun in off-season; Gothersgade 157, tel. 33 14 07 17, www.cykelborsen.dk).

Cykelbasen, even closer to Nørreport, rents three- and seven-gear bikes (90 DKK/day, 450 DKK/week, includes lock; Mon-Fri 9:00-17:30, Sat until 14:30, closed Sun; Gothersgade 137, tel. 35 12 06 00, www.cykel-basen.dk, select "Info").

Copenhagen Bicycles, at the entrance to Nyhavn by the Inderhavnsbroen pedestrian/bicycle bridge, rents basic three-gear bikes (90 DKK/3 hours, 110 DKK/6 hours, 120 DKK/24 hours, includes lock, helmet-40 DKK, daily 8:30-17:30, Nyhavn 44, tel. 35 43 01 22, www.copenhagenbicycles.dk). They also offer guided tours in English and Danish (100 DKK, not including bicycle, April-Sept daily at 11:00, 2.5 hours).

Using City Bikes: The city's public bike-rental program **Bycyklen** lets you ride white, three-gear "smart bikes" (with GPS

and an electric motor) for 30 DKK/hour. You'll find them parked in racks near the train station, on either side of City Hall, and at many locations around town. Use the touch-screen on the handlebars to create an account. At their website (http://bycyklen.dk), you can locate docking stations, reserve a bike at a specific station, and create an account in advance. I'd use these bikes for a short hop here or there, but for more than a couple of hours, it's more cost-efficient to rent a regular bicycle.

Tours in Copenhagen

ON FOOT

Copenhagen is an ideal city to get to know by foot. You have several good options:

▲▲Hans Christian Andersen Tours by Richard Karpen

Once upon a time, American Richard Karpen visited Copenhagen and fell in love with the city. Now, dressed as writer Hans Christian

Andersen in a 19th-century top hat and long coat, he leads 1.5-hour tours that wander in and out of buildings, court-yards, back streets, and un-usual parts of the old town. Along the one-mile route, he gives insightful and humor-

ous background on the history, culture, and contemporary life of Denmark, Copenhagen, and the Danes—their core values, gender and economic equality, treatment of the elderly and children, health care, Vikings, royal family—along with the life and work of H. C. Andersen (140 DKK, kids under 12 free; departs from outside the TI, up the street from the main train station at Vesterbrogade 4A; mid-May-mid-Sept Mon-Sat at 9:30, none on Sun; Richard departs promptly—if you miss him try to catch up with the tour at the next stop at Rådhuspladsen).

Richard also gives excellent one-hour tours of **Rosenborg Castle** while in the role of Hans Christian Andersen (100 DKK, doesn't include castle entry, mid-May-mid-Sept Mon and Thu at 12:00, meet outside castle ticket office). No reservations are needed for any of Richard's scheduled tours—just show up.

You can also hire Richard for 1.5-hour private tours of the city or of Rosenborg Castle (price depends on number of participants, May-Sept, mobile 91 61 95 02, www.copenhagenwalks. com, copenhagenwalks@yahoo.com).

▲Daily City Walks by Red Badge Guides

Five local female guides work together, giving two-hour English-language city tours. Their walks mix the city's highlights, back lanes, history, art, and contemporary social issues, and finish at Amalienborg Palace around noon for the changing of the guard (100 DKK, daily mid-April-Sept at 10:00, departs from TI at Vesterbrogade 4A, just show up, pay direct, small groups, tel. 20 92 23 87, www.redbadgeguides.dk, redbadgeguides@gmail.com). They also offer private guided tours year-round upon request.

▲▲Copenhagen History Tours

Christian Donatzky, a charming Dane with a master's degree in history, runs a walking tour on Saturday mornings. In April and May, the theme is "Old Copenhagen" (covering the period from 1100-1600); in June and July, "King's Copenhagen" (1600-1800); and in August and September, "Hans Christian Andersen's Copenhagen" (1800-present). Those with a serious interest in Danish history will find these tours time well spent (90 DKK, Sat at 10:00, approximately 1.5 hours, small groups of 5-15 people, tours depart from statue of Bishop Absalon on Højbro Plads between the Strøget and Christiansborg Palace, English only, no reservations necessary—just show up, tel. 28 49 44 35, www.historytours.dk, info@historytours.dk).

BY BOAT

For many, the best way to experience the city's canals and harbor is by canal boat. Two companies offer essentially the same live, three-language, one-hour cruises. Both boats leave at least twice an hour from Nyhavn and Christiansborg Palace, cruise around the palace and Christianshavn area, and then proceed into the wide-open harbor. Best on a sunny day, it's a relaxing way to see *The Little Mermaid* and munch on a lazy picnic during the slow-moving narration.

▲Netto-Bådene

These inexpensive cruises cost about half the price of their rival, Canal Tours Copenhagen. Go with Netto; there's no reason to pay nearly double (40 DKK, mid-March-mid-Oct daily 10:00-17:00, runs later in summer, shorter hours in winter, sign at dock shows next departure, generally every 30 minutes, dress warmly—boats are open-top until Sept, tel. 32 54 41 02, www.havnerundfart.dk). Netto boats often make two stops where passengers can get off, then hop back on a later boat—at the bridge near *The Little Mermaid,* and at the Langebro bridge near Danhostel. Not every boat makes these stops; check the clock on the bridges for the next departure time.

Don't confuse the cheaper Netto and pricier Canal Tours Copenhagen boats: At Nyhavn, the Netto dock is midway down the canal (on the city side), while the Canal Tours Copenhagen dock is at the head of the canal. Near Christiansborg Palace, the Netto boats leave from Holmen's Bridge in front of the palace, while Canal Tours Copenhagen boats depart from Gammel Strand, 200 yards away. Boats leaving from Christiansborg are generally less crowded than those leaving from Nyhavn.

Canal Tours Copenhagen

This more expensive option does the same cruise as Netto for 75 DKK (daily March-late Oct 9:30-18:00, runs later in summer, shorter hours in winter, no tours Jan-Feb, boats are sometimes covered if it's raining, tel. 32 96 30 00, www.stromma.dk).

Canal Tours Copenhagen also runs audioguided hop-on, hop-off boat tours (99 DKK/48 hours, daily late May-mid-Sept 9:30-19:00), 1.5-hour evening **jazz cruises** (see "Nightlife in Copenhagen," page 76), and other theme cruises.

BY BUS

Hop-On, Hop-Off Bus Tours

Several buses with recorded narration circle the city for a basic 1.25- to 1.5-hour orientation, allowing you to get on and off as you like at the following stops: Tivoli Gardens, Gammel Strand near Christiansborg Palace, *The Little Mermaid,* Rosenborg Castle, Nyhavn sailors' quarter, and more. Cruise passengers arriving at

COPENHAGEN

Hans Christian Andersen (1805-1875)

The author of such classic fairy tales as *The Ugly Duckling* was an ugly duckling himself—a misfit who blossomed. Hans Christian Andersen (called H. C., pronounced "hoe see" by the Danes) was born to a poor shoemaker in Odense. As a child he was gangly, high-strung, and effeminate. He avoided school because the kids laughed at him, so he spent his time in a fantasy world of books and plays. When his father died, the 11-year-old was on his own, forced into manual labor. He loved playing with a marionette theater that his father had made for him, sparking a lifelong love affair with the theater. In 1819, at the age of 14, he moved to Copenhagen to pursue an acting career and worked as a boy soprano for the Royal Theater. When his voice changed, the director encouraged him to return to school. He dutifully attended—a teenager among boys—and eventually went on to the university. As rejections piled up for his acting aspirations, Andersen began to shift his theatrical ambitions to playwriting.

After graduation, Andersen won a two-year scholarship to travel around Europe, the first of many trips he'd make and write about. His experiences abroad were highly formative, providing inspiration for many of his tales. Still in his 20s, he published an obviously autobiographical novel, *The Improvisatore*, about a poor young man who comes into his own while traveling in Italy. The novel launched his writing career, and soon he was hobnobbing with the international crowd—Charles Dickens, Victor Hugo, Franz Liszt, Richard Wagner, Henrik Ibsen, and Edvard Grieg.

the Langelinie Pier can catch a hop-on, hop-off bus there; those arriving at the Oceankaj Pier can take a free shuttle provided by the hop-on, hop-off tour companies (or their own cruise shuttle) to *The Little Mermaid*, where they can pick up a hop-on, hop-off bus.

The same company runs **City Sightseeing**'s red buses and Strömma's green **Hop-On, Hop-Off** buses. Both offer a Mermaid route: City Sightseeing tickets, 195 DKK, are valid 72 hours, and Hop-On, Hop-Off tickets, 175 DKK, are good for 48 hours; other routes include the Carlsberg Brewery and Christiania area (pay driver, 2/hour, May-mid-Sept daily 9:30-18:00, shorter hours off-season, buses depart near the TI in front of the Radisson Blu Royal Hotel and at many other stops throughout city, www.city-sightseeing.dk or www.stromma.dk). Strömma's Hop-On, Hop-

Despite his many famous friends, Andersen remained a lonely soul who never married. He had very close male friendships and journaled about unrequited love affairs with several women, including the famous opera star of the day, Jenny Lind, the "Swedish Nightingale." Without a family of his own, he became very close with the children of his friends—and, through his fairy tales, with a vast extended family of kids around the world.

Though he wrote novels, plays, and travel literature, it was his fairy tales, including *The Ugly Duckling, The Emperor's New Clothes, The Princess and the Pea, The Little Mermaid, The Snow Queen,* and *The Red Shoes,* that made him famous in Denmark and abroad. They made him Denmark's best-known author, the "Danish Charles Dickens." Some stories are based on earlier folk tales, and others came straight from his inventive mind, all written in an informal, conversational style that was considered unusual and even surprising at the time.

Andersen's compelling tales appeal to children and adults alike. They're full of magic and touch on strong, universal emotions—the pain of being different, the joy of self-discovery, and the struggle to fit in. The ugly duckling, for example, is teased by his fellow ducks before he finally discovers his true identity as a beautiful swan. In *The Emperor's New Clothes,* a boy is derided by everyone for speaking the simple, self-evident truth that the emperor is fooling himself. J. K. Rowling said, "The indelible characters he created are so deeply implanted in our subconscious that we sometimes forget that we were not born with the stories." (For more on Andersen's famous story *The Little Mermaid*—and what it might tell us about his life—see page 43.)

By the time of his death, the poor shoemaker's son was wealthy, cultured, and had been knighted. His rise through traditional class barriers mirrors the social progress of the 19th century.

Off also offers a 245-DKK ticket that includes all tour routes and a cruise on their hop-on, hop-off canal boat.

Another operation—called **Red Buses**—does a similar Mermaid route (every 30-40 minutes, shorter hours off-season; 210 DKK/24 hours, www.redbuses.com).

BY BIKE

▲Bike Copenhagen with Mike

Mike Sommerville offers three-hour guided bike tours of the city. A Copenhagen native, Mike enjoys showing off his city to visitors, offering both historic background and contemporary cultural insights along the way (April-Sept daily at 10:00, second departure Fri-Sat at 14:30, must book all tours in advance; 300 DKK includes bike rental, price same with or without a bike, 50-DKK discount with this book—maximum 2 discounts per book and must have book with you, cash only; participants must have good urban biking skills). All tours are in English and depart from his bike shop at Sankt Peders Straede 47, in the Latin Quarter (see the Copenhagen map in the Orientation section, earlier, for location). Mike also offers evening tours (19:00, 2.5 hours) and private tours; details at www.bikecopenhagenwithmike.dk.

Copenhagen City Walk

This self-guided walk takes about two hours. It starts at Rådhuspladsen (City Hall Square) and heads along the pedestrian street, the Strøget, through the old city, onto "Castle Island" (home of Christiansborg Palace), along the harbor promenade, and through Nyhavn, the sailors' quarter with the city's iconic canalfront houses. The walk officially ends at Kongens Nytorv ("King's New Square"), though you can continue another 10 minutes to Amalienborg Palace and then another 15 minutes beyond that to *The Little Mermaid*.

❶ Rådhuspladsen

Start from Rådhuspladsen, the bustling heart of Copenhagen, dominated by the tower of the City Hall. Today this square always

seems to be hosting some lively community event, but it was once Copenhagen's fortified west end. For 700 years, Copenhagen was contained within its city walls. By the mid-1800s, 140,000 people were packed inside. The overcrowding led to hygiene problems. (A cholera outbreak killed 5,000.) It was clear: The walls needed to come down...and they did. Those formidable town walls survive today only in echoes—a circular series of roads and the remnants of moats, which are now people-friendly city lakes (see the sidebar on page 13).

• *Stand 50 yards in front of City Hall and turn clockwise for a...*

Rådhuspladsen Spin-Tour: The **City Hall,** or Rådhus, is worth a visit (described on page 46). Old **Hans Christian Andersen** sits to the right of City Hall, almost begging to be in another photo (as he used to in real life). Climb onto his well-worn knee. (While up there, you might take off your shirt for a racy photo, as many Danes enjoy doing.)

He's looking at ❷ **Tivoli Gardens** (across the street), which he loved and which inspired him when writing some of his stories. Tivoli Gardens was founded in 1843, when magazine publisher

Georg Carstensen convinced the king to let him build a pleasure garden outside the walls of crowded Copenhagen. The king quickly agreed, knowing that happy people care less about fighting for democracy. Tivoli became Europe's first great public amusement park. When the train lines came, the station was placed just beyond Tivoli.

The big, glassy building with the *DI* sign is filled with the offices of Danish Industry—a collection of Danish companies whose logos you can see in the windows (plus the Irma grocery store at street level).

The big, broad boulevard is **Vesterbrogade** ("Western Way"), which led to the western gate of the medieval city (behind you, where the pedestrian boulevard begins). Here, in the traffic hub of this huge city, you'll notice...not many cars. Denmark's 180 percent tax on car purchases makes the bus, Metro, or bike a sweeter option. In fact, the construction messing up this square is part of a huge expansion of the Metro system.

Down Vesterbrogade towers the **Radisson Blu Royal Hotel,** Copenhagen's only skyscraper. Locals say it seems so tall because the clouds hang so low. When it was built in 1960, Copenhageners took one look and decided—that's enough of a skyline. Notice there are no other buildings taller than the five-story limit in the old center.

The golden ❸ **weather girls** (on the corner, high above Vesterbrogade) indicate the weather: on a bike (fair weather) or with an umbrella (foul). These two have been called the only women in Copenhagen you can trust, but for years they've been stuck in the almost-sunny mode...with the bike just peeking out. Notice that the red temperature dots max out at 28° Celsius (that's 82° Fahrenheit...a good memory aid: transpose 28 to get 82).

To the right, just down the street, is the Tiger Store (a popular local "dollar store"...nearly everything is super affordable). The next street (once the local Fleet Street, with the big newspapers) still has the offices for *Politiken* (the leading Danish newspaper) and the best bookstore in town, Boghallen.

As you spin farther right, three fast-food joints stand at the entry to the Strøget (STROY-et), Copenhagen's grand pedestrian boulevard— where we're heading next. Just beyond that and the Art Deco-style Palace Hotel (with a tower to serve as a sister to the City Hall) is the *Lur Blowers* **sculpture,** which honors the earliest warrior Danes. The *lur* is a curvy, trombone-sounding horn that was used to call soldiers to battle or to accompany pagan religious processions. The earliest bronze *lurs* date

Copenhagen City Walk

1 Rådhuspladsen
2 Tivoli Gardens
3 Weather Girls
4 Strøget
5 Sankt Peders Church
6 Cathedral of Our Lady
7 Copenhagen University
8 Gammeltorv & Nytorv
9 Amagertorv
10 Gråbrødretorv
11 Royal Copenhagen Store & Illums Bolighus
12 Bishop Absalon Statue
13 Christiansborg Palace Chapel
14 Frederik VII Statue

15 Børsen
16 Havnegade Promenade
17 Inderhavnsbroen Sliding Bridge
18 View of Nyhavn
19 Kongens Nytorv
20 Hviids Vinstue
21 Amalienborg Palace & Square
22 To Little Mermaid

as far back as 3,500 years ago. Later, the Vikings used a wood version of the *lur*. The ancient originals, which still play, are displayed in the National Museum.

• *Now head down the pedestrian boulevard (pickpocket alert).*

❹ The Strøget

The American trio of Burger King, 7-Eleven, and KFC marks the start of this otherwise charming pedestrian street. Finished in 1962, Copenhagen's experimental, tremendously successful, and much-copied pedestrian shopping mall is a string of lively (and

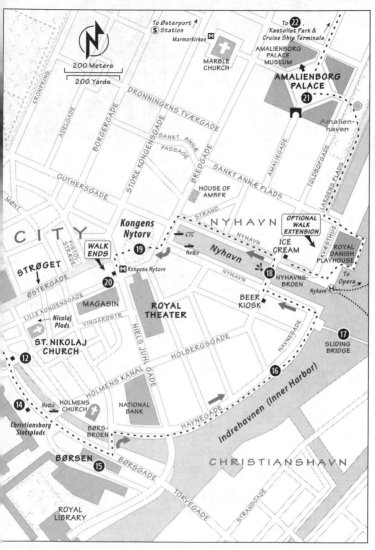

individually named) streets and lovely squares that bunny-hop through the old town from City Hall to the Nyhavn quarter, a 20-minute stroll away. Though the Strøget has become hamburger-ized, historic bits and attractive pieces of old Copenhagen are just off this commercial can-can.

As you wander down this street, remember that the commercial focus of a historic street like the Strøget drives up the land value, which generally trashes the charm and tears down the old buildings. Look above the modern window displays and street-level advertising to discover bits of 19th-century character that still sur-

vive. This end of the Strøget is young
and cheap, while the far end has the
high-end designer shops. Along the
way, wonderfully quiet and laid-back
areas are just a block or two away on
either side.

After one block (at Kattesundet),
make a side-trip three blocks left into
Copenhagen's colorful **university
district.** Formerly the old brothel neighborhood, later the heart of
Copenhagen's hippie community in the 1960s, today this "Latin
Quarter" is SoHo chic. Enjoy the colorful string of artsy shops
and cafés. Because the old town was densely populated and built of
wood, very little survived its many fires. After half-timbered and
thatched buildings kept burning down, the city finally mandated
that new construction be made of stone. But because stone was so
expensive, many people built half-timbered structures, then dis-
guised their facades with stucco, which made them look like stone.
Exposed half-timbered structures are seen in courtyards and from
the back sides. At Sankt Peders Stræde, turn right and walk to the
end of the street. Notice the old guild signs (a baker, a key maker,
and so on) identifying the original businesses here.

Along the way, look for large mansions that once circled ex-
pansive **courtyards.** As the population grew, the city walls con-
stricted Copenhagen's physical size. The courtyards were gradually
filled with higgledy-piggledy secondary buildings. Today throughout the old center, you can step off a busy pedestrian mall and back
in time in these characteristic, half-timbered, time-warp courtyards. Replace the parked car with a tired horse and the bikes with
a line of outhouses, and you're in 19th-century Copenhagen. If you
see an open courtyard door, you're welcome to discreetly wander in
and look around.

You'll also pass funky shops and the big brick **❺ Sankt Peders
Church**—the old German merchant community's church, which
still holds services in German. Its fine 17th-century brick grave
chapel (filling a ground-floor building out back due to the boggy
nature of the soil) is filled with fancy German tombs (open Wed-
Sat 11:00-15:00).

• *When Sankt Peders Stræde intersects with Nørregade, look right to find
the big, Neoclassical...*

❻ Cathedral of Our Lady (Vor Frue Kirche)

The obelisk-like **Reformation Memorial** across the street from
the cathedral celebrates Denmark's break from the Roman Catholic Church to become Lutheran in 1536. Walk around and study
the reliefs of great Danish reformers protesting from their pulpits.

The relief facing the church shows King Christian III presiding over the pivotal town council meeting when they decided to break away from Rome. As a young man, Prince Christian had traveled to Germany, where he was influenced by Martin Luther. He returned to take the Danish throne by force, despite Catholic opposition. Realizing the advantages of being the head of his own state church, Christian confiscated church property and established the state Lutheran Church. King Christian was crowned inside this cathedral. Because of the reforms of 1536, there's no Mary in the Cathedral of Our Lady. The other reliefs show the popular religious uprising, with people taking control of the word of God by translating the Bible from Latin into their own language.

COPENHAGEN

Like much of this part of town, the church burned down in the British bombardment of 1807 and was rebuilt in the Neoclassical style. The cathedral's **facade** looks like a Greek temple. (Two blocks to the right, in the distance, notice more Neoclassicism—the law courts.) You can see why Golden Age Copenhagen (early 1800s) fancied itself a Nordic Athens. Old Testament figures (King David and Moses) flank the cathedral's entryway. Above, John the Baptist stands where you'd expect to see Greek gods. He invites you in...into the New Testament.

The **interior** is a world of Neoclassical serenity (free, open daily 8:00-17:00). It feels like a pagan temple that now houses Christianity. The nave is lined by the 12 apostles, clad in classical robes—masterpieces by the great Danish sculptor Bertel Thorvaldsen (see sidebar, page 54). Each strikes a meditative pose, carrying his identifying symbol: Peter with keys, Andrew with the X-shaped cross of his execution, Matthew and John writing their books, and so on. They lead to a statue of the *Risen Christ* (see photo), standing where the statue of Zeus would have been: inside a temple-

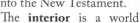

like niche, flanked by columns and topped with a pediment. Rather than wearing a royal robe, Jesus wears his burial shroud, opens his arms wide, and says, "Come to me." (Mormons will recognize this statue—a replica stands in the visitors center at Salt Lake City's Temple Square and is often reproduced in church publications.) The marvelous acoustics are demonstrated in free organ concerts Saturdays in July and August at noon. Notice how, in good Protestant style, only the front half of the pews are "reversible," allowing the congregation to flip around and face the pulpit (in the middle of the church) to better hear the sermon.

• *Head back outside. If you face the church's facade and look to the left (across the square called Frue Plads), you'll see...*

❼ Copenhagen University

Now home to nearly 40,000 students, this university was founded by the king in the 15th century to stop the Danish brain drain to

Paris. Today tuition is free (but room, board, and beer are not). Locals say it's easy to get in, but given the wonderful student lifestyle, very hard to get out.

Step up the middle steps of the university's big building; if the doors are open, enter a colorful lobby, starring Athena and Apollo. The frescoes celebrate high thinking, with themes such as the triumph of wisdom over barbarism. Notice how harmoniously the architecture, sculpture, and painting work together.

Outside, busts honor great minds from the faculty, including (at the end) Niels Bohr, a professor who won the 1922 Nobel Prize for theoretical physics. He evaded the clutches of the Nazi science labs by fleeing to America in 1943, where he helped develop the atomic bomb.

• *Rejoin the Strøget (one block downhill from the Reformation Memorial to the black-and-gold fountain) at the twin squares called...*

❽ Gammeltorv and Nytorv

This was the old town center. In Gammeltorv ("Old Square"), the Fountain of Charity (Caritas) is named for the figure of Charity on top. It has provided drinking water to locals since the early 1600s. Featuring a pregnant woman squirting water from her breasts next to a boy urinating, this was just too much for people of the Victorian Age. They corked both figures and raised the statue to what they hoped would be out of view. The exotic-looking kiosk was one of the city's first community telephone centers from the days before phones were privately owned. Look at the reliefs ringing its top: an airplane with bird wings (c. 1900) and two women talking on a newfangled telephonic device. (It was thought business would popularize the telephone, but actually it was women.)

While Gammeltorv was a place of happiness and merriment, Nytorv ("New Square") was a place of severity and judgment. Walk to the small raised area 20 yards in front of the old ancient-Greek-style former City Hall and courthouse. Do a 360. The square is Neoclassical (built mostly after the 1807 British bombardment). Read the old Danish on the City Hall facade: "With Law Shall

Man Build the Land." Look down at the pavement and read the plaque: "Here stood the town's *Kag* (whipping post) until 1780."

• *Now walk down the next stretch of the Strøget—called Nygade—to reach...*

❾ Amagertorv

This is prime real estate for talented street entertainers. Walk to the stately brick Holy Ghost Church (Helligåndskirken). The fine spire is typical of old Danish churches. Under the stepped gable was a medieval hospital run by monks (one of the oldest buildings in town, dating from the 12th century). Today the hospital is an antiques hall. In summer the pleasant courtyard is shared by a group of charities selling light bites and coffee.

Walk behind the church, down Valkendorfsgade—the street just before the church—and through a passage under the reddish-colored building at #32 (if locked, loop back and go

down Klosterstræde); here you'll find the leafy and beer-stained ❿ **Gråbrødretorv.** Surrounded by fine old buildings, this "Grey Friars' Square"—a monastic square until the Reformation made it a people's square—is a popular place for an outdoor meal or drink in the summer. At the end of the square, the street called Niels Hemmingsens Gade returns (past the recommended Copenhagen Jazz House, a good place for live music nightly) to the Strøget.

Once back on busy Strøget, turn left and continue down Amagertorv, with its fine inlaid Italian granite stonework, to the next square with the "stork" fountain (actually three herons). The Victorian WCs here (free, steps down from fountain) are a delight.

This square, Amagertorv, is a highlight for shoppers, with the

Copenhagen at a Glance

▲▲▲**Tivoli Gardens** Copenhagen's classic amusement park, with rides, music, food, and other fun. **Hours:** Late March-mid-Sept daily 11:00-23:00, Fri-Sat until 24:00, also open daily 11:00-22:00 for a week in mid-Oct and mid-Nov-New Year's Day. See page 44.

▲▲▲**National Museum** History of Danish civilization with tourable 19th-century Victorian Apartment. **Hours:** Museum—Tue-Sun 10:00-17:00, closed Mon; Victorian Apartment—English tours June-Sept Sat at 14:00, Danish tours Sat-Sun at 11:00, 12:00, and 13:00 year-round. See page 48.

▲▲▲**Rosenborg Castle and Treasury** Renaissance castle of larger-than-life "warrior king" Christian IV. **Hours:** Mid-June-mid-Sept daily 9:00-17:00; mid-April-mid-June and mid-Sept-Oct daily 10:00-16:00, except closed Mon in April; shorter hours and generally closed Mon rest of year. See page 58.

▲▲▲**Christiania** Colorful counterculture squatters' colony. **Hours:** Guided tours at 13:00 and 15:00 (daily July-Aug, only Sat-Sun rest of year). See page 67.

▲▲**Christiansborg Palace** Royal reception rooms with dazzling tapestries. **Hours:** Reception rooms, castle ruins, kitchen, and stables open daily except closed Mon in Oct-April. Hours vary by sight: Reception rooms 9:00-17:00, Oct-April from 10:00 (may close for royal events); ruins and kitchen 10:00-17:00; stables and carriage museum 13:30-16:00, longer hours possible in July. See page 51.

▲▲**Thorvaldsen's Museum** Works of the Danish Neoclassical sculptor. **Hours:** Tue-Sun 10:00-17:00, closed Mon. See page 53.

⓫ **Royal Copenhagen store**—stacked with three floors of porcelain—and **Illums Bolighus**—a fine place to ogle modern Danish design (see "Shopping in Copenhagen," later). A block toward the canal—running parallel to the Strøget—starts Strædet, which is a "second Strøget" featuring cafés and antique shops.

North of Amagertorv, a broad pedestrian mall called **Købmagergade** leads past a fine modern bakery (Holm's) to Christian IV's Round Tower and the Latin Quarter (university district). The recommended Café Norden overlooks the fountain—a good place for a meal or coffee with a view. The second floor offers the best vantage point.

• *Looking downhill from the fountain, about halfway to an imposing palace in the distance, you'll see a great man on a horse. Walk here to*

▲**City Hall** Copenhagen's landmark, packed with Danish history and symbolism and topped with a tower. **Hours:** Mon-Fri 9:00-16:00, some Sat 9:30-13:00, closed Sun. See page 46.

▲**Ny Carlsberg Glyptotek** Scandinavia's top art gallery, featuring Egyptians, Greeks, Etruscans, French, and Danes. **Hours:** Tue-Sun 11:00-18:00, Thu until 22:00, closed Mon. See page 47.

▲**Danish Jewish Museum** Exhibit tracing the 400-year history of Danish Jews, in a unique building by American architect Daniel Libeskind. **Hours:** Tue-Sun 10:00-17:00; Sept-May Tue-Fri 13:00-16:00, Sat-Sun 12:00-17:00; closed Mon year-round. See page 56.

▲**Amalienborg Museum** Quick and intimate look at Denmark's royal family. **Hours:** May-Oct daily 10:00-16:00, mid-June-mid-Sept until 17:00; Nov-April Tue-Sun 11:00-16:00, closed Mon. See page 57.

▲**Rosenborg Gardens** Park surrounding Rosenborg Castle, filled with statues and statuesque Danes. See page 64.

▲**National Gallery of Denmark** Good Danish and Modernist collections. **Hours:** Tue-Sun 11:00-17:00, Wed until 20:00, closed Mon. See page 64.

▲**Our Savior's Church** Spiral-spired church with bright Baroque interior. **Hours:** Church—daily 11:00-15:30 but may close for special services; tower—May-Sept Mon-Sat 9:30-19:00, Sun from 10:30; shorter hours off-season, closed mid-Dec-Feb and in bad weather. See page 66.

view this statue of Copenhagen's founder, **⓬** ***Bishop Absalon,*** *shown in his Warrior Absalon get-up.*

From the bishop, you'll continue across a bridge toward the palace and the next statue—a king on a horse. As you cross the bridge, look right to see the City Hall tower, where this walk started. (A couple of the city's competing sightseeing boat tours depart from near here—see page 24.)

Christiansborg Palace and the Birthplace of Copenhagen

You're stepping onto the island of Slotsholmen ("Castle Island"), the easy-to-defend birthplace of Copenhagen in the 12th century. It's dominated by the royal palace complex. Christiansborg Palace (with its "three crowns" spire)—the imposing former residence of kings—is now the parliament building.

Ahead of you, the Neoclassical Lutheran church with the low dome is the ⓭ **Christiansborg Palace Chapel,** site of 350 years of royal weddings and funerals (free, only open Sun 10:00-17:00).

Walk to the next green copper equestrian statue. ⓮ **Frederik VII** was crowned in 1848, just months before Denmark got its constitution on June 5, 1849. (Constitution Day is celebrated with typical Danish understatement—stores are closed and workers get the day off.) Frederik, who then ruled as a constitutional monarch, stands in front of **Christiansborg Palace,** which Denmark's royal family now shares with its people's assembly (queen's wing on right, parliament on left; for information on visiting the palace, see page 51). This palace, the seat of Danish government today, is considered the birthplace of Copenhagen. It stands upon the ruins of Absalon's 12th-century castle (literally under your feet). The big stones between the statue and the street were put in for security after the 2011 terror attacks in Norway (in which 77 people were murdered, most of them teens and young adults). While Danes strive to keep government accessible, security measures like this are today's reality.

This is Denmark's power island, with the Folketing (Danish parliament), Supreme Court, Ministry of Finance (to the left), and ⓯ **Børsen**—the historic stock exchange (farther to the left, with the fanciful dragon-tail spire; not open to tourists). The eye-catching red-brick stock exchange was inspired by the Dutch Renaissance, like much of 17th-century Copenhagen. Built to promote the mercantile ambitions of Denmark in the 1600s, it was the "World Trade Center" of Scandinavia. The facade reads, "For the profitable use of buyer and seller." The dragon-tail spire with three crowns represents the Danish aspiration to rule a united Scandinavia—or at least be its commercial capital.

Notice Copenhagen's distinctive green copper spires all around you. Beyond the old stock exchange lies the island of **Christianshavn,** with its own distinct spire. It tops the Church of Our Savior and features an external spiral staircase winding to the top for an amazing view. While political power resided here on Slotsholmen, commercial power was in the merchant's district, Christianshavn (neighborhood and church described later, under "Sights in Copenhagen"). The Børsen symbolically connected Christianshavn with the rest of the city, in an age when trade was a very big deal.

• *Walk along the old stock exchange toward Christianshavn, but turn left at the crosswalk with the signal before you reach the end of the building. After crossing the street, go over the canal and turn right to walk along the harborfront promenade, enjoying views of Christianshavn across the water.*

⑯ Havnegade Promenade

The Havnegade promenade to Nyhavn is a delightful people zone with trampolines, harborview benches (a good place to stop, look

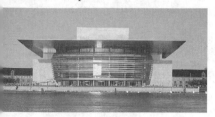

across the water, and ponder the trendy apartments and old-warehouses-turned-modern-office-blocks), and an ice-cream-licking ambience. Stroll several blocks from here toward the new ⑰ **Inderhavnsbroen sliding bridge** for pedestrians and bikes. This "Kissing Bridge" (it's called that because the two sliding, or retractable, sections "kiss" when they come together) is designed to link the town center with Christianshavn and to make the modern Opera House (ahead on the right, across the water) more accessible to downtown. Walk until you hit the Nyhavn canal.

Across the way, at the end of Nyhavn canal, stands the glassy Royal Danish Theatre's Playhouse. While this walk finishes on Kongens Nytorv, the square at the head of this canal, you could extend it by continuing north along the harbor from the playhouse.
• *For now, turn left and walk to the center of the bridge over the canal for a...*

⑱ View of Nyhavn

Established in the 1670s along with Kongens Nytorv, Nyhavn ("New Harbor") is a recently gentrified sailors' quarter. (Hong Kong is the last of the nasty bars from the rough old days.) With its trendy cafés, jazz clubs, and tattoo shops (pop into Tattoo Ole at #17—fun photos, very traditional), Nyhavn is a wonderful place to hang out. The canal is filled with glamorous old sailboats of all sizes. Historic sloops are welcome to moor here in Copenhagen's ever-changing boat museum. Hans Christian Andersen lived and wrote his first stories here (in the red double-gabled building at #20).

From the bridge, take a few steps left to the cheap **beer kiosk** (on Holbergsgade, open daily until late). At this minimarket, let friendly manager Nagib give you a little lesson in Danish beer,

and then buy a bottle or can. Choose from Carlsberg (standard lager, 4.6 percent alcohol), Carlsberg Elephant (strong, 7.2 percent), Tuborg Grøn (standard lager, 4.6 percent), Tuborg Gold (stronger, 5.8 percent), and Tuborg Classic (dark beer, 4.6 percent). The cost? About 15 DKK, depending on the alcohol level. Take your beer out to the canal and feel like a local.

A note about all the public beer-drinking here: There's no more beer consumption here than in the US; it's just out in public. Many young Danes can't afford to drink in a bar, so they "picnic drink" their beers in squares and along canals, at a quarter of the price for a bottle.

If you crave **ice cream** instead, cross the bridge, where you'll find a popular place with freshly made waffle cones facing the canal (Vaffelbageren).

Now wander the quay, enjoying the frat-party parade of tattoos (hotter weather reveals more tattoos). Celtic and Nordic mythological designs are in (as is bodybuilding, by the looks of things). The place thrives—with the cheap-beer drinkers dockside and the richer and older ones looking on from comfier cafés.

• *Make your way to the head of the canal, where you'll find a minuscule amber museum, above the House of Amber (see "Shopping in Copenhagen," page 74).*

⑲ Kongens Nytorv

The "King's New Square" is home to the National Theater, French embassy, and venerable Hotel d'Angleterre, where VIPs and pop stars stay. In the mid-1600s the city expanded, pushing its wall farther east. The equestrian statue in the middle of the square celebrates Christian V, who made this square the city's geographical and cultural center. In 1676, King Christian rode off to reconquer the southern tip of Sweden and reclaim Denmark's  dominance. He returned empty-handed and broke. Denmark became a second-rate power, but Copenhagen prospered. In the winter this square becomes a popular ice-skating rink.

Across the square on the left, small glass pyramids mark the Metro. The **Metro** that runs underground here features state-of-the-art technology (automated cars, no driver...sit in front to watch the tracks coming at you). As the cars come and go without drivers, compare this system to the public transit in your town.

Wander into ⑳ **Hviids Vinstue**, the town's oldest wine cellar (from 1723, just beyond the Metro station, at #19, under a bar) to check out its characteristic dark and woody interior and fascinating old Copenhagen photos. It's a colorful spot for an open-face sandwich and a beer (three sandwiches and a beer for 79 DKK at lunchtime). Their wintertime *gløgg* (hot spiced wine) is legendary. Across the street, towering above the Metro station, is Magasin du Nord, the grandest old department store in town.

• *You've reached the end of this walk. But if you'd like to extend it by heading out to Amalienborg Palace and* The Little Mermaid, *retrace your steps to the far side of Nyhavn canal.*

Nyhavn to Amalienborg

Stroll along the canal to the Royal Danish Theatre's Playhouse and follow the harborfront promenade left from there to a large plaza dotted with outdoor cafés and benches, and views across the harbor. You'll then follow a delightful promenade to the modern fountain of Amaliehaven Park, immediately across the harbor from Copenhagen's slick Opera House. The striking Opera House is bigger than it looks—of its 14 floors, five are below sea level. Completed in 2005 by Henning Larsen, it was a $400 million gift to the nation from an oil-shipping magnate.

• *A block inland (behind the fountain) is the orderly...*

❷ Amalienborg Palace and Square

Queen Margrethe II and her husband live in the mansion to your immediate left as you enter the square from the harborside. (If the flag's flying, she's home.) The mansion across the street (on the right as you enter) is where her son and heir to the throne, Crown Prince Frederik, lives with his wife, Australian businesswoman Mary Donaldson, and their four children. The royal guesthouse palace is on the far left. And the palace on the far right is the **Amalienborg Museum,** which offers an intimate look at royal living (described on page 57).

Though the guards change daily at noon, they do it with royal fanfare only when the queen is in residence (see page 57 for details). The royal guard often has a police escort when it marches through town on special occasions—leading locals to joke that theirs is "the only army in the world that needs police protection."

The equestrian statue of Frederik V is a reminder that this square was the centerpiece of a planned town he envisioned in 1750. It was named for him—Frederikstaden. During the 18th century, Denmark's population grew and the country thrived (as trade flourished and its neutrality kept it out of the costly wars impoverishing much of Europe). Frederikstaden, with its strong architectural harmony, was designed as a luxury neighborhood for the city's business elite. Nobility and other big shots moved in, but the king came here only after his other palace burned down in a 1794 fire.

Just inland, the striking Frederikskirke—better known as the

Marble Church—was designed to fit this ritzy new quarter. If it's open, step inside to bask in its vast, serene, Pantheon-esque atmosphere (free, Mon-Thu 10:00-17:00, Fri-Sun 12:00-17:00; dome climb—35 DKK, mid-June-Aug daily at 13:00; off-season Sat-Sun at 13:00).

• *From the square, Amaliegade leads two blocks north to...*

Kastellet Park

In this park, you'll find some worthwhile sightseeing. The 1908 **Gefion Fountain** illustrates the myth of the goddess who was

given one night to carve a hunk out of Sweden to make into Denmark's main island, Sjælland (or "Zealand" in English), which you're on. Gefion transformed her four sons into oxen to do the job, and the chunk she removed from Sweden is supposedly Vänern, Sweden's largest lake. If you look at a map showing Sweden and

Denmark, the island and the lake are, in fact, roughly the same shape. Next to the fountain is an Anglican church built of flint.

• *Climb up the stairs by the fountain and continue along the top of the rampart about five minutes to reach the harborfront site of the overrated, overfondled, and overphotographed symbol of Copenhagen, Den Lille Havfrue, or...*

② The Little Mermaid

The Little Mermaid statue was a gift to the city of Copenhagen in 1909 from brewing magnate Carl Jacobsen (whose art collection forms the basis of the Ny Carlsberg Glyptotek). Inspired by a ballet performance of Andersen's story, Jacobsen hired the young sculptor Edvard Eriksen to immortalize the mermaid as a statue. Eriksen used his wife Eline as the model. The statue sat unappreciated for 40 years until Danny Kaye sang "Wonderful Copenhagen" in the movie *Hans Christian Andersen,* and the tourist board decided to use the mermaid as a marketing symbol for the city. For the non-Disneyfied *Little Mermaid* story—and insights into Hans Christian Andersen—see the sidebar. For more on his life, see page 26.

• *This is the end of our extended wonderful, wonderful "Copenhagen City Walk." From here you can get back downtown on foot, by taxi, on bus #1A from Store Kongensgade on the other side of Kastellet Park, or bus #26 from farther north, along Folke Bernadottes Allé.*

The Little Mermaid and Hans Christian Andersen

"Far out in the ocean, where the water is as blue as a cornflower, as clear as crystal, and very, very deep..." there lived a young mermaid. So begins one of Hans Christian Andersen's best-known stories. The plot line starts much like the Disney movie, but it's spiced with poetic description and philosophical dialogue about the immortal soul.

The mermaid's story goes like this: One day, a young mermaid spies a passing ship and falls in love with a handsome human prince. The ship is wrecked in a storm, and she saves the prince's life. To be with the prince, the mermaid asks a sea witch to give her human legs. In exchange, she agrees to give up her voice and the chance of ever returning to the sea. And, the witch tells her, if the prince doesn't marry her, she will immediately die heartbroken and without an immortal soul. The mermaid agrees, and her fish tail becomes a pair of beautiful but painful legs. She woos the prince—who loves her in return—but he eventually marries another. Heartbroken, the mermaid prepares to die. She's given one last chance to save herself: She must kill the prince on his wedding night. She sneaks into the bedchamber with a knife...but can't bear to kill the man she loves. The mermaid throws herself into the sea to die. Suddenly, she's miraculously carried up by the mermaids of the air, who give her an immortal soul as a reward for her long-suffering love.

The tale of unrequited love mirrors Andersen's own sad love life. He had two major crushes—one of them for the famous opera singer Jenny Lind—but he was turned down both times, and he never married. He had plenty of interest in sex but likely died a virgin. He had close brotherly and motherly relations with women but stayed single, had time to travel and write, and maintained a childlike wonder about the world to his dying days.

Sights in Copenhagen

NEAR THE TRAIN STATION

Copenhagen's great train station, the Hovedbanegården, is a fascinating mesh of Scandinavian culture and transportation efficiency. From the station, delightful sights fan out into the old city. The following attractions are listed roughly in order from the train station to Slotsholmen Island.

▲▲▲Tivoli Gardens

The world's grand old amusement park—since 1843—is 20 acres, 110,000 lanterns, and countless ice-cream cones of fun. You pay one admission price and find yourself lost in a Hans Christian Andersen wonderland of rides, restaurants, games, marching bands, roulette wheels, and funny mirrors. A roller coaster screams through the middle of a tranquil Asian food court, and the Small World-inspired Den Flyvende Kuffert ride floats through Hans Christian Andersen fairy tales. It's a children's fantasyland midday, but it becomes more adult-oriented later on. With or without kids, this place is a true magic kingdom. Tivoli doesn't try to be Disney. It's wonderfully and happily Danish. (Many locals appreciate the lovingly  tended gardens.) I find it worth the admission just to see Danes—young and old—at play.

As you stroll the grounds, imagine the place in the mid-1800s, when it was new. Built on the site of the old town fortifications (today's lake was part of the old moat), Tivoli was an attempt to introduce provincial Danes to the world (for example, with the Asian Pavilion) and to bring people of all classes together.

Cost: 110-120 DKK, free for kids under 8. To go on rides, you must buy ride tickets (from booth at entrance or from machines in the park—machines take credit card only, 25 DKK/ticket, color-coded rides cost 1-4 tickets apiece); or you can buy a multiride pass for 230 DKK. If you'll be using at least eight tickets, buy the ride pass instead. To leave and come back later, you'll have to buy a  35-DKK re-entry ticket before you exit.

Hours: Late March-mid-Sept daily 11:00-23:00, Fri-Sat until 24:00. In winter, Tivoli opens daily 11:00-22:00 from mid-Oct to early Nov for Halloween, from mid-Nov to New Year's Day for a Christmas market with *gløgg* (hot spiced wine) and ice-skating on Tivoli Lake, and during most of Feb. Dress warmly for chilly evenings any time of year. There are lockers by each entrance.

Information: Tel. 33 15 10 01, www.tivoli.dk.

Getting There: Tivoli is across Bernstoffsgade from the train station. If you're catching a late train, this is *the* place to spend your last Copenhagen hours.

Entertainment at Tivoli: Upon arrival (through main entrance, on left in the service center), pick up a map and look for the events schedule. Take a moment to plan your entertainment for the evening. Events are generally spread between 15:00 and 23:00; the 19:30 concert in the concert hall can be as little as 75 DKK or more than 1,000 DKK, depending on the performer (box office tel. 33 15 10 01). If the Tivoli Symphony is playing, it's worth paying for. The ticket box office is outside, just to the left of the main entrance (daily 10:00-20:00; if you buy a concert ticket you get into Tivoli for free).

Free concerts, pantomime theater, ballet, acrobats, puppets, and other shows pop up all over the park, and a well-organized visitor can enjoy an exciting evening of entertainment without spending a single krone beyond the entry fee. Friday evenings feature a (usually free) rock or pop show at 22:00. People gather around the lake 45 minutes before closing time for the "Tivoli Illuminations." Fireworks blast a few nights each summer. The park is particularly romantic at dusk, when the lights go on.

Eating at Tivoli: Inside the park, expect to pay amusement-park prices for amusement-park-quality food. Still, a meal here is part of the fun. **$$ Søcafeen** serves traditional open-face sandwiches and main courses in a fun beer garden with lakeside ambience. They allow picnics if you buy a drink (and will rent you plates and silverware for 10 DKK/person). **$$$ Mazzoli's Caffé & Trattoria,** in a circular building near the lake, serves classic Italian fare and pizza. **$$$ Færgekroen Bryghus** offers a quiet, classy lakeside escape from the amusement-park intensity, with traditional dishes washed down by its own microbrew (open-face sandwiches, seafood, pub grub). They host live piano on Friday, as well as Saturday evenings from 20:00, often resulting in an impromptu sing-along with a bunch of very happy Danes. **$$$ Wagamama,** a modern pan-Asian slurpathon from the UK, serves healthy noodle dishes (at the far back side of the park, also possible to enter from outside). **$$$ Fru Nimb** offers a large selection of open-face sandwiches in a garden setting. The kid-pleasing **$$$ Piratiriet** lets you dine on a pirate ship. For cheaper fare, look for a *pølse* (sausage) stand. And if you're longing for something sweet, **Cakenhagen** serves classic Danish cakes and pastries that you can wash down with a cup of tea—or champagne.

For something more upscale, consider the complex of Nimb restaurants, in the big Taj Mahal-like pavilion near the entrance facing the train station. For dinner, **$$$$ Nimb Bar 'n' Grill** is a definite splurge, grilling up creative international meat and seafood dishes. **$$$$ Nimb Brasserie,** sharing the same lobby, serves rustic French classics.

And if these options aren't enough, check out the eateries in the glassy new Tivoli Food Hall (facing the train station) that promises "fast gourmet food."

▲City Hall (Rådhus)

This city landmark, between the train station/Tivoli and the Strøget, is free and open to the public (including a public WC). You can wander throughout the building and into the peaceful garden out back. It also offers private tours and trips up its 345-foot-tall tower.

Cost and Hours: Free to enter building, Mon-Fri 9:00-16:00; you can usually slip in Sat 9:30-13:00 when weddings are going on, or join the Sat tour; closed Sun. Guided English-language tours— 50 DKK, 45 minutes, gets you into more private, official rooms; Mon-Fri at 13:00, Sat at 10:00. Tower by escort only—30 DKK, 300 steps for the best aerial view of Copenhagen, Mon-Fri at 11:00 and 14:00, Sat at 12:00, closed Sun. Tel. 33 66 33 66.

Visiting City Hall: It's draped, inside and out, in Danish symbolism. The city's founder, Bishop Absalon, stands over the door. Absalon (c. 1128-1201)— bishop, soldier, and foreign-policy wonk—was King Valdemar I's right-hand man. In Copenhagen, he drove out pirates and built a fort to guard the harbor, turning a miserable fishing village into a humming Baltic seaport. The polar bears climbing on the rooftop symbolize the giant Danish protectorate of Greenland. Six night watchmen flank the city's gold-and-green seal under the Danish flag.

Step inside. The info desk (on the left as you enter) has racks of tourist information (city maps and other brochures). The building and its huge tower were inspired by the City Hall in Siena, Italy (with the necessary bad-weather addition of a glass roof). Enormous functions fill this grand hall (the iron grate in the center of the floor is an elevator for bringing up 1,200 chairs), while the marble busts of four illustrious local boys—fairy-tale writer Hans Christian Andersen, sculptor Bertel Thorvaldsen, physicist Niels Bohr, and the building's architect, Martin Nyrop—look on. Underneath the floor are national archives dating back to 1275, popular with Danes researching their family roots.

As you leave, pop into the amazing clock opposite the info desk. Jens Olsen's World Clock, built from 1943 to 1955, was the mother of all astronomical clocks in precision and function. And it came with something new: tracking the exact time across the world's time zones. One of its gears does a complete rotation only every 25,753 years.

▲Ny Carlsberg Glyptotek

Scandinavia's top art gallery is an impressive example of what beer money can do. Brewer Carl Jacobsen (son of J. C. Jacobsen, who

funded the Museum of National History at Frederiksborg Castle) was an avid collector and patron of the arts. (Carl also donated *The Little Mermaid* statue to the city.) His namesake museum has intoxicating artifacts from the ancient world, along with some fine art from our own times. The next time you sip a Carlsberg beer, drink a toast to Carl Jacobsen and his marvelous collection. *Skål!*

Cost and Hours: 95 DKK, free on Tue; open Tue-Sun 11:00-18:00, Thu until 22:00, closed Mon; behind Tivoli at Dantes Plads 7, tel. 33 41 81 41, www.glyptoteket.com. It has a classy $$$ cafeteria under palms, as well as a rooftop terrace with snacks, drinks, and city views.

Visiting the Museum: Pick up a floor plan as you enter to help navigate the confusing layout. For a chronological swing, start with Egypt (mummy coffins and sarcophagi, a 5,000-year-old hippo statue), Greece (red-and-black painted vases, statues), the Etruscan world (Greek-looking vases), and Rome (grittily realistic statues and portrait busts).

The sober realism of 19th-century Danish Golden Age painting reflects the introspection of a once-powerful nation reduced to second-class status—and ultimately embracing what made it unique. The "French Wing" (just inside the front door) has Rodin statues. A heady, if small, exhibit of 19th-century French paintings (in a modern building within the back courtyard) shows how Realism morphed into Impressionism and Post-Impressionism, and includes a couple of canvases apiece by Géricault, Delacroix, Monet, Manet, Millet, Courbet, Degas, Pissarro, Cézanne, Van Gogh, Picasso, Renoir, and Toulouse-Lautrec. Look for art by Gauguin—from before Tahiti (when he lived in Copenhagen with his Danish wife and their five children) and after Tahiti. There's also a fine collection of modern (post-Thorvaldsen) Danish sculpture.

Linger with marble gods under the palm leaves and glass dome of the very soothing winter garden. Designers, figuring Danes would be more interested in a lush garden than in classical art, used this wonderful space as leafy bait to cleverly introduce locals to a few Greek and Roman statues. (It works for tourists, too.) One of the original *Thinker* sculptures by Rodin (wondering how to scale the Tivoli fence?) is in the museum's backyard.

Museum of Copenhagen (Københavns Museum)
This museum offers an entertaining and creative telling of the story of Copenhagen, from its origins to contemporary culture.

Cost and Hours: May be closed when you visit, when open likely 40 DKK, daily 10:00-17:00, kitty-corner to the National Museum at Stormgade 18, tel. 33 21 07 72, www.copenhagen.dk.

▲▲▲National Museum
Focus on this museum's excellent and curiously enjoyable Danish collection, which traces this civilization from its ancient beginnings. Its prehistoric collection is the best of its kind in Scandinavia. Exhibits are laid out chronologically and are eloquently described in English.

Cost and Hours: 75 DKK, Tue-Sun 10:00-17:00, closed Mon, mandatory lockers, enter at Ny Vestergade 10, tel. 33 13 44 11, www.natmus.dk. The **$$** café overlooking the entry hall serves coffee, pastries, and lunch.

Visiting the Museum: Pick up the museum map as you enter, and head for the Danish history exhibit. It fills three floors, from the bottom up: prehistory, the Middle Ages and Renaissance, and modern times (1660-2000).

Danish Prehistory: Start before history did, in the Danish Prehistory exhibit (on the right side of the main entrance hall). Follow the room numbers in order, working counterclockwise around the courtyard and through the millennia.

In the Stone Age section, you'll see primitive tools and still-clothed skeletons of Scandinavia's reindeer hunters. The oak coffins were originally covered by burial mounds (called "barrows"). People put valuable items into the coffins with the dead, such as a

folding chair (which, back then, was a real status symbol). In the farming section, ogle the ceremonial axes and amber necklaces.

The Bronze Age brought the sword (several are on display). The "Chariot of the Sun"—a small statue of a horse pulling the sun across the

sky—likely had religious significance for early Scandinavians (whose descendants continue to celebrate the solstice with fervor). In the same room are those iconic horned helmets. Contrary to popular belief (and countless tourist shops), these helmets were not worn by the Vikings, but by their predecessors—for ceremonial purposes, centuries earlier. In the next room are huge cases filled with still-playable *lur* horns (see page 29).

Another room shows off a collection of well-translated rune stones proclaiming heroic deeds.

This leads to the Iron Age and an object that's neither Iron nor Danish: the 2,000-year-old Gundestrup Cauldron of art-textbook

fame. This 20-pound, soup-kitchen-size bowl made of silver was found in a Danish bog, but its symbolism suggests it was originally from either Thrace (in northeast Greece) or Celtic Ireland. On the sides, hunters slay bulls, and gods cavort with stags, horses, dogs, and dragons. It's both mysterious and fascinating.

Prehistoric Danes were fascinated by bogs. To make iron, you need ore—and Denmark's many bogs provided that critical material in abundance, leading people to believe that the gods dwelled there. These Danes appeased the gods by sacrificing valuable items (and even people) into bogs. Fortunately for modern archaeologists, bogs happen to be an ideal environment for preserving fragile objects. One bog alone—the Nydam bog—has yielded thousands of items, including three whole ships.

No longer bogged down in prehistory, the people of Scandinavia came into contact with Roman civilization. At about this time, the Viking culture rose; you'll see the remains of an old warship. The Vikings, so feared in most of Europe, are still thought of fondly here in their homeland. You'll notice the descriptions straining to defend them: Sure, they'd pillage, rape, and plunder. But they also founded thriving, wealthy, and cultured trade towns. Love the Vikings or hate them, it's impossible to deny their massive reach—Norse Vikings even carved runes into the walls of the Hagia Sophia church (in today's Istanbul).

Middle Ages and Renaissance: Next, go upstairs and follow signs to Room 101 to start this section. You'll walk through the

Middle Ages, where you'll find lots of bits and pieces of old churches, such as golden altars and *aquamaniles,* pitchers used for ritual handwashing. The Dagmar Cross is the prototype for a popular form of crucifix worn by many Danes (Room 102, small glass display case—with colorful enamel paintings). Another cross in this case (the Roskilde Cross, studded with gemstones) was found inside the wooden head of Christ displayed high on the opposite wall. There are also exhibits on tools and trade, weapons, drinking horns, and fine, wood-carved winged altarpieces. Carry on to find a fascinating room on the Norse settlers of Greenland, material on the Reformation, and an exhibit on everyday town life in the 16th and 17th centuries.

Modern Times: The next floor takes you through the last few centuries, with historic toys and a slice-of-Danish-life (1660-2000)

gallery where you'll see everything from rifles and old bras to early jukeboxes. You'll learn that the Danish Golden Age (which dominates most art museums in Denmark) captured the everyday pastoral beauty of the countryside, celebrated Denmark's smallness and peace-loving nature, and mixed in some Nordic mythology. With industrialization came the labor movement and trade unions. After delving into the World Wars, Baby Boomers, creation of the postwar welfare state, and the

"Depressed Decade" of the 1980s (when Denmark suffered high unemployment), the collection is capped off by a stall that, until recently, was used for selling marijuana in the squatters' community of Christiania.

The Rest of the Museum: If you're eager for more, there's plenty left to see. The National Museum also has exhibits on the history of this building (the Prince's Palace), a large ethnology collection, antiquities, coins and medallions, temporary exhibits, and a good children's museum. The floor plan will lead you to what you want to see.

▲National Museum's Victorian Apartment

The National Museum inherited an incredible Victorian apartment just around the corner. The wealthy Christensen family managed to keep its plush living quarters a 19th-century time capsule until the granddaughters passed away in 1963. Since then, it's been part of the National Museum, with all but two of its rooms looking just as they did in the late Victorian days.

Cost and Hours: 50 DKK, required one-hour tours leave from the National Museum reception desk (in English, June-Sept Sat only at 14:00; in Danish Sat-Sun at 11:00, 12:00, and 13:00 year-round).

ON SLOTSHOLMEN ISLAND

This island, where Copenhagen began in the 12th century, is a short walk from the train station and Tivoli, just across the bridge from the National Museum. It's dominated by Christiansborg Palace and several other royal and governmental buildings. Note that my "Copenhagen City Walk" (earlier) cuts right through Slotsholmen and covers other landmarks on the island (see page 37).

▲▲Christiansborg Palace

A complex of government buildings stands on the ruins of Copenhagen's original 12th-century fortress: the parliament, Supreme Court, prime minister's office, royal reception rooms, royal library, several museums, and royal stables. Although the current palace dates only from 1928 and the royal family moved out 200 years ago, this building—the sixth to stand here in 800 years—is rich with tradition.

Four palace sights (the reception rooms, old castle ruins, stables, and kitchen) are open to the public, giving us commoners a glimpse of the royal life.

COPENHAGEN

Cost and Hours: Reception rooms-90 DKK, castle ruins, stables, and kitchen-50 DKK each; a combo-ticket for all four-150 DKK. All sights are open daily (except in Oct-April, when they're closed on Mon) but have different hours: reception rooms open 9:00-17:00, Oct-April from 10:00 (may close for royal events); ruins and kitchen open 10:00-17:00; stables and carriage museum open 13:30-16:00—longer hours possible in July.

Information: Tel. 33 92 64 92, www.christiansborg.dk.

Visiting the Palace: From the equestrian statue in front, go through the wooden door; the entrance to the ruins is in the corridor on the right, and the door to the reception rooms is out in the next courtyard, also on the right.

Royal Reception Rooms: While these don't rank among Europe's best palace rooms, they're worth a look. This is still the place where Queen Margrethe II impresses visiting dignitaries. The information-packed, hour-long English tours of the rooms are excellent (included in ticket, daily at 15:00). At other times, you'll wander the rooms on your own in a one-way route, reading the sparse English descriptions. As you slip-slide on protect-the-floor slippers through 22 rooms, you'll gain a good feel for Danish history, royalty, and politics. Here are a few highlights:

After the Queen's Library you'll soon enter the grand Great Hall, lined with boldly colorful (almost gaudy) tapestries. The palace highlight is this dazzling set of modern tapestries—Danish-designed but Gobelin-made in Paris. This gift, given to the queen on her 60th birthday in 2000, celebrates 1,000 years of Danish history, from the Viking age to our chaotic times...and into the future. Borrow the laminated descriptions for blow-by-blow explanations of the whole epic saga. The Velvet Room is where royals privately greet VIP guests before big functions.

In the corner room on the left, don't miss the family portrait of King Christian IX, which illustrates why he's called the "father-in-law of Europe"—his children eventually became, or married into, royalty in Denmark, Russia, Greece, Britain, France, Germany, and Norway.

In the Throne Room you'll see the balcony where new monarchs are proclaimed (most recently in 1972). And at the end, in the Hall of Giants (where you take off your booties among heroic figures supporting the building), you'll see a striking painting of Queen Margrethe II from 2010 on her 70th birthday. The three playful lions, made of Norwegian silver, once guarded the throne and symbolize absolute power—long gone since 1849, when Denmark embraced the notion of a constitutional monarch.

Castle Ruins: An exhibit in the scant remains of the first fortress built by Bishop Absalon, the 12th-century founder of Copenhagen, lies under the palace. A long passage connects to another set of ruins, from the 14th-century Copenhagen Castle. There's precious little to see, but it is, um, old and well-described. A video covers more recent palace history.

Royal Stables and Carriages Museum: This facility is still home to the horses that pull the queen's carriage on festive days, as well as a collection of historic carriages. While they're down from 250 horses to about a dozen, the royal stables are part of a strong tradition and, as the little video shows, will live on.

Royal Kitchen: Unless you're smitten with old ladles and shiny copper pots and pans, I'd skip this exhibit.

▲▲Thorvaldsen's Museum

This museum, which has some of the best swoon-worthy art you'll see anywhere, tells the story and shows the monumental work of

the great Danish Neoclassical sculptor Bertel Thorvaldsen (see sidebar). Considered Canova's equal among Neoclassical sculptors, Thorvaldsen spent 40 years in Rome. He was lured home to Copenhagen with the promise to showcase his work in a fine museum, which opened in the revolutionary year of 1848 as Denmark's first public art gallery. Of the 500 or so sculptures Thorvaldsen completed in his life—including 90 major statues—this museum has most of them, in one form or another (the plaster model used to make the original or a copy done in marble or bronze).

Cost and Hours: 50 DKK, free on Wed, Tue-Sun 10:00-17:00, closed Mon, includes excellent English audioguide on request, located in Neoclassical building with colorful walls next to Christiansborg Palace.

Information: Tel. 33 32 15 32, www.thorvaldsensmuseum.dk.

Visiting the Museum: The ground floor showcases his statues. After buying your ticket, go straight in and ask to borrow a free audioguide at the desk. This provides a wonderful statue-by-statue narration of the museum's key works.

Just before the audioguide desk, turn left into the Great Hall, which was the original entryway of the museum. It's filled with replicas

Bertel Thorvaldsen (1770-1844)

Bertel Thorvaldsen was born, raised, educated, and buried in Copenhagen, but his most productive years were spent in Rome. There he soaked up the prevailing style of the time: Neoclassical. He studied ancient Greek and Roman statues, copying their balance, grace, and impassive beauty. The simple-but-noble style suited the patriotism of the era, and Thorvaldsen got rich off it. Public squares throughout Europe are dotted with his works, celebrating local rulers, patriots, and historical figures looking like Greek heroes or Roman conquerors.

In 1819, at the height of his fame and power, Thorvaldsen returned to Copenhagen. He was asked to decorate the most important parts of the recently bombed, newly rebuilt Cathedral of Our Lady: the main altar and nave. His *Risen Christ* on the altar (along with the 12 apostles lining the nave) became his most famous and reproduced work—without even realizing it, most people imagine the caring features of Thorvaldsen's Christ when picturing what Jesus looked like.

The prolific Thorvaldsen depicted a range of subjects. His grand statues of historical figures (Copernicus in Warsaw, Maximilian I in Munich) were intended for public squares. Portrait busts of his contemporaries were usually done in the style of Roman emperors. Thorvaldsen carved the Lion Monument, depicting a weeping lion, into a cliff in Luzern, Switzerland. He did religious statues, like the *Risen Christ*. Thorvaldsen's most accessible works are from Greek mythology—*The Three Graces,* naked *Jason with the Golden Fleece,* or Ganymede crouching down to feed the eagle Jupiter.

Though many of his statues are of gleaming white marble, Thorvaldsen was not a chiseler of stone. Like Rodin and Canova, Thorvaldsen left the grunt work to others. He fashioned a life-size model in plaster, which could then be reproduced in marble or bronze by his assistants. Multiple copies were often made, even in his lifetime.

Thorvaldsen epitomized the Neoclassical style. His statues assume perfectly balanced poses—maybe even a bit stiff, say critics. They don't flail their arms dramatically or emote passionately. As you look into their faces, they seem lost in thought, as though contemplating deep spiritual truths.

In Copenhagen, catch Thorvaldsen's *Risen Christ* at the Cathedral of Our Lady, his portrait bust at City Hall, and the full range of his long career at the Thorvaldsen's Museum.

of some of Thorvaldsen's biggest and grandest statues—national heroes who still stand in the prominent squares of their major cities (Munich, Warsaw, the Vatican, and others). Two great equestrian statues stare each other down from across the hall; while they both take the classic, self-assured pose of looking one way while pointing another (think Babe Ruth calling his home run), one of them (Jozef Poniatowski) is modeled after the ancient Roman general Marcus Aurelius, while the other (Bavaria's Maximilian I) wears modern garb.

Then take a spin through the smaller rooms that ring the central courtyard. Each of these is dominated by one big work—mostly classical subjects drawn from mythology. At the far end of the building stand the plaster models for the iconic *Risen Christ* and the 12 Apostles (the final marble versions stand in the Cathedral of Our Lady—see page 32). Peek into the central courtyard to see the  planter-box tomb of Thorvaldsen himself (who died in 1844). Continue into the next row of rooms: In the far corner room look for Thorvaldsen's (very flattering) self-portrait, leaning buffly against a partially finished sculpture.

Downstairs you'll find a collection of plaster casts (mostly ancient Roman statues that inspired Thorvaldsen) and a video about his career.

Upstairs, get into the mind of the artist by perusing his personal possessions and the private collection of paintings from which he drew inspiration.

Royal Library

Copenhagen's "Black Diamond" (Den Sorte Diamant) library is a striking, supermodern building made of shiny black granite, leaning over the harbor at the edge of the palace complex. From the inviting lounge chairs, you can ponder this stretch of harborfront, which serves as a showcase for architects. Inside, wander through the old and new sections, catch the fine view from the "G" level, read a magazine, and enjoy a classy—and pricey—lunch.

Cost and Hours: Free, special exhibits generally 50 DKK; Mon-Fri 8:00-21:00, Sat 9:00-19:00; July-Aug Mon-Sat 8:00-19:00, reading room hours vary, closed Sun year-round; tel. 33 47 47 47, www.kb.dk.

▲Danish Jewish Museum (Dansk Jødisk Museum)

In a striking building by American architect Daniel Libeskind, this museum offers a very small but well-exhibited display of 400 years of the life and impact of Jews in Denmark.

Cost and Hours: 60 DKK; Tue-Sun 10:00-17:00; Sept-May Tue-Fri 13:00-16:00, Sat-Sun 12:00-17:00; closed Mon year-round; behind "Black Diamond" library at Proviantpassagen 6—enter from the courtyard behind the red-brick, ivy-covered building.

Information: Tel. 33 11 22 18, www.jewmus.dk.

Visiting the Museum: Frankly, the architecture overshadows the humble exhibits. Libeskind—who created the equally conceptual Jewish Museum in Berlin, and whose design is the basis for the redevelopment of the World Trade Center site in New York City—has literally written Jewish culture into this building. The floor plan, a seemingly random squiggle, is actually in the shape of the Hebrew characters for *Mitzvah*, which loosely translated means "act of kindness."

Be sure to watch the two introductory films about the Jews' migration to Denmark, and about the architect Libeskind (12-minute loop total, English subtitles, plays continuously). As you tour the collection, the uneven floors and asymmetrical walls give you the feeling that what lies around the corner is completely unknown... much like the life and history of Danish Jews. Another interpretation might be that the uneven floors give you the sense of motion, like waves on the sea—a reminder that despite Nazi occupation in 1943, nearly 7,000 Danish Jews were ferried across the waves by fishermen to safety in neutral Sweden.

NEAR THE STRØGET
Round Tower

Built in 1642 by Christian IV, the tower connects a church, library, and observatory (the oldest functioning observatory in Europe) with a ramp that spirals up to a fine view of Copenhagen (though the view from atop Our Savior's Church is far better—see page 66).

Cost and Hours: 25 DKK, nothing to see inside but the ramp and the view; tower—daily 10:00-20:00, Oct-April Thu-Mon 10:00-18:00, Tue-Wed until 21:00; observatory—summer Sun 13:00-16:00, mid-Oct-mid-March Tue-Wed 18:00-21:00; just off the Strøget on Købmagergade.

AMALIENBORG PALACE AND NEARBY

For more information on this palace and nearby attractions, including the famous *Little Mermaid* statue, see the end of my "Copenhagen City Walk" (page 42).

▲Amalienborg Museum (Amalienborgmuseet)

While Queen Margrethe II and her husband live quite privately in one of the four mansions that make up the palace complex, another mansion has been open to the public since 1994. It displays the private studies of four kings of the House of Glucksborg, who ruled from 1863-1972 (the immediate predecessors of today's queen). Your visit won't take long—you'll see six to eight rooms on each of two floors—but it affords an intimate and unique peek into Denmark's royal family. On the first floor you'll see the private study of each of the last four kings of Denmark. They feel particularly lived-in—with cluttered pipe collections and bookcases jammed with family pictures—because they were. It's easy to imagine these blue-blooded folks just hanging out here, even today. The earliest study, Frederik VIII's (c. 1869), feels much older and more "royal"—with Renaissance gilded walls, heavy drapes, and a polar bear rug. On the second floor, your visit includes the Gothic library designed for dowager Queen Caroline Amalie, the cheery gala hall (the palace's largest room) with statues by Bertel Thorvaldsen, and a hall gleaming with large gilt-bronze table decorations.

Cost and Hours: 95 DKK, 145-DKK combo-ticket includes Rosenborg Palace—available on the website or at Rosenborg only; May-Oct daily 10:00-16:00, mid-June-mid-Sept until 17:00; Nov-April Tue-Sun 11:00-16:00, closed Mon; with your back to the harbor, entrance is at the far end of the square on the right; tel. 33 15 32 86, www.dkks.dk.

Amalienborg Palace Changing of the Guard

This noontime event is boring in the summer, when the queen is not in residence—the guards just change places. (This goes on for quite a long time—no need to rush here at the stroke of noon, or to crowd in during the first few minutes; you'll have plenty of good photo ops.) If the queen's at home (indicated by a flag flying above her home), the changing of the guard is accompanied by a military band.

Museum of Danish Resistance (Frihedsmuseet)

This museum tells the story of Denmark's Nazi-resistance struggle (1940-1945). While relatively small, the museum rewards those who take the time to read the English explanations and understand the fascinating artifacts. The building was destroyed by fire in 2013. The collection was saved, but the museum may still be closed during your visit—check details at their website (located on Churchillparken between Amalienborg Palace and the *Little Mermaid* site; bus #1A or #15 from downtown/Tivoli/train station stops right in front, a 10-minute walk from Østerport S-tog station, or bus #26 from Langelinie cruise port or downtown; tel. 41 20 62 91, www.frihedsmuseet.dk).

ROSENBORG CASTLE AND NEARBY
▲▲▲Rosenborg Castle (Rosenborg Slot) and Treasury
This finely furnished Dutch Renaissance-style castle was built by King Christian IV in the early 1600s as a summer residence.

Rosenborg was his favorite residence and where he chose to die. Open to the public since 1838, it houses the Danish crown jewels and 500 years of royal knickknacks. While the old palace interior is a bit dark and not as immediately impressive as many of Europe's later Baroque masterpieces, it has a certain lived-in charm. It oozes the personality of the fascinating Christian IV and has one of the finest treasury collections in Europe. For more on Christian, read the sidebar.

Cost and Hours: 110 DKK, 145-DKK combo-ticket includes Amalienborg Museum; mid-June-mid-Sept daily 9:00-17:00; mid-April-mid-June and mid-Sept-Oct daily 10:00-16:00, except closed Mon in April; shorter hours and generally closed Mon rest of the year; mandatory lockers take 20-DKK coin, which will be returned; Metro or S-tog: Nørreport, then 5-minute walk on Østervoldgade and through park.

Information: Tel. 33 15 32 86, www.dkks.dk.

Tours: Richard Karpen leads fascinating one-hour tours in Hans Christian Andersen garb (100 DKK plus entry fee, mid-May-mid-Sept Mon and Thu at 12:00, meet outside castle ticket office—no reservations needed; see listing on page 23). Or take the following self-guided tour that I've woven together from the highlights of Richard's walk. You can also use the palace's free Wi-Fi to follow the "Konge Connect" step-by-step tour through the palace highlights (with audio/video/text explanations for your smartphone or tablet—bring earphones; instructional brochure at ticket desk).

◗ **Self-Guided Tour:** Buy your ticket, then head back out

King Christian IV:
A Lover and a Fighter

King Christian IV (1577-1648) inherited Denmark at the peak of its power, lived his life with the exuberance of the age, and went to his grave with the country in decline. His legacy is ob-

vious to every tourist—Rosenborg Castle, Frederiksborg Palace, the Round Tower, Christianshavn, and on and on. Look for his logo adorning many buildings: the letter "C" with a "4" inside it and a crown on top. Thanks to both his place in history and his passionate personality, Danes today regard Christian IV as one of their greatest monarchs.

During his 50-year reign, Christian IV reformed the government, rebuilt the army, established a trading post in India, and tried to expand Denmark's territory. He took Kalmar from Sweden and captured strategic points in northern Germany. The king was a large man who also lived large. A skilled horseman and avid hunter, he could drink his companions under the table. He spoke several languages and gained a reputation as outgoing and humorous. His lavish banquets were legendary, and his romantic affairs were numerous.

But Christian's appetite for war proved destructive. In 1626, Denmark again attacked northern Germany, but was beaten back. In late 1643, Sweden launched a sneak attack, and despite Christian's personal bravery (he lost an eye), the war went badly. By the end of his life, Christian was tired and bitter, and Denmark was drained.

The heroics of Christian and his sailors live on in the Danish national anthem, "King Christian Stood by the Lofty Mast."

COPENHAGEN

and look for the *castle* sign. You'll tour the ground floor room by room, then climb to the third floor for the big throne room. After a quick sweep of the middle floor, finish in the basement (enter from outside) for the jewels.

• *Begin the tour on the palace's ground floor (turn right as you enter), in the Winter Room.*

Ground Floor: Here in the wood-paneled **Winter Room,** all eyes were on King Christian IV. Today, your eyes should be on him, too. Take a close look at his bust by the fireplace (if it's not here, look for it out in the corridor by the ticket taker). Check this guy out—fashionable braid, hard drinker, hard lover, energetic statesman, and warrior king. Christian IV was dynamism in the flesh, wearing a toga: a true Renaissance guy. During his reign, Copenhagen doubled in size. You're surrounded by Dutch paintings (the Dutch had a huge influence on 17th-century Denmark). Note the smaller statue of the 19-year-old king, showing him jousting jauntily on his coronation day. In another case, the golden astronomical clock—with musical works and moving figures—did everything you can imagine. Flanking the fireplace (opposite where you entered), beneath the windows, look for the panels in the tile floor that could be removed to let the music performed by the band in the basement waft in. (Who wants the actual musicians in the dining room?) The audio holes were also used to call servants.

The **study** (or "writing closet," nearest where you entered) was small (and easy to heat). Kings did a lot of corresponding. We know

a lot about Christian because 3,000 of his handwritten letters survive. The painting on the right wall shows Christian at age eight. Three years later, his father died, and little Christian technically ascended the throne, though Denmark was actually ruled by a regency until Christian was 19. A portrait of his mother hangs above the boy, and opposite is a portrait of Christian in his prime—having just conquered Sweden—standing alongside the incredible coronation crown you'll see later.

Going back through the Winter Room, head for the door to Christian's **bedroom.** Before entering, notice the little peephole

in the door (used by the king to spy on those in this room—well-camouflaged by the painting, and more easily seen from the other side), and the big cabinet doors for Christian's clothes and accessories, flanking the bedroom door (notice the hinges and keyholes).
Heading into the bedroom, you'll see paintings showing the king as an old man...and as a dead man. (Christian died in this room.) In the case are the clothes he wore at his finest hour. During a naval battle against Sweden (1644), Christian stood directing the action when an explosion ripped across the deck, sending him sprawling and riddling him with shrapnel. Unfazed, the 67-year-old monarch bounced right back up and kept going, inspiring his men to carry on the fight. Christian's stubborn determination during this battle is commemorated in Denmark's national anthem. Shrapnel put out Christian's eye. No problem: The warrior king with a knack for

heroic publicity stunts had the shrapnel bits removed from his eye and forehead and made into earrings as a gift for his mistress. The earrings hang in the case with his blood-stained clothes (easy to miss, right side). Christian lived to be 70 and fathered 25 children (with two wives and three mistresses). Before moving on, you can peek into Christian's private bathroom—elegantly tiled with Delft porcelain.

Proceed into the **Dark Room.** Here you'll see wax casts of royal figures. This was the way famous and important people were portrayed back then. The chair is a forerunner of the whoopee cushion. When you sat on it, metal cuffs pinned your arms down, allowing the prankster to pour water down the back of the chair (see hole)—making you "wet your pants." When you stood up, the chair made embarrassing tooting sounds.

The **Marble Room** has a particularly impressive inlaid marble floor. Imagine the king meeting emissaries here in the center, with the emblems of Norway (right), Denmark (center), and Sweden (left) behind him.

The end room, called the **King's Chamber,** was used by Christian's first mistress. Notice the ceiling painting, with an orchestra looking down on you as they play.

The long **stone passage** leading to the staircase exhibits an intriguing painting (by the door to the King's Chamber) show-ing the crowds at the coronation of Christian's son, Frederik III. After Christian's death, a weakened Denmark was invaded, occupied, and humiliated by Sweden (Treaty of Roskilde, 1658). Copenhagen alone held out through the long winter of 1658-1659 (the Siege of Copenhagen), and Sweden eventually had to withdraw from the country. During the siege, Frederik III distinguished himself with his bravery. He seized upon the resulting surge of popularity as his chance to be anointed an absolute, divinely ordained monarch (1660). This painting marks that event—study it closely for slice-of-life details. Next, near the ticket taker, a sprawling family tree makes it perfectly clear that Christian IV comes from good stock. Notice the tree is labeled in German—the second language of the realm.

• *The queen had a hand-pulled elevator, but you'll need to hike up two flights of stairs to the throne room.*

Throne Room (Third Floor): The **Long Hall**—considered one of the best-preserved Baroque rooms in Europe—was great for banquets. The decor trumpets the accomplishments of Denmark's great kings. The four corners of the ceiling feature the four continents known at the time. (America—at the far-right end of the hall as you enter—was still considered pretty untamed; notice the decapitated head with the arrow sticking out of it.) In the center, of course, is the proud seal of the Danish Royal Family. The tapestries, designed for this room, are from the late 1600s. Effective propaganda, they show

the Danes defeating their Swedish rivals on land and at sea. The king's throne—still more propaganda for two centuries of "absolute" monarchs—was made of "unicorn horn" (actually narwhal tusk from Greenland). Believed to bring protection from evil and poison, the horn was the most precious material in its day. The queen's throne is of hammered silver. The 150-pound lions are 300 years old.

The small room to the left holds a delightful **royal porcelain** display with Chinese, French, German, and Danish examples of the "white gold." For five centuries, Europeans couldn't figure out how the Chinese made this stuff. The difficulty in just getting it back to Europe in one piece made it precious. The Danish pieces, called "Flora Danica" (on the left as you enter), are from a huge royal set showing off the herbs and vegetables of the realm.

• *Heading back down, pause at the middle floor, which is worth a look.*

Middle Floor: Circling counterclockwise, you'll see more fine clocks, fancy furniture, and royal portraits. The queen enjoyed her royal lathe (with candleholders for lighting and pedals to spin it hidden away below; in the Christian VI Room). The small mirror room (up the stairs from the main hall) was where the king played Hugh Hefner—using mirrors on the floor to see what was under those hoop skirts. In hidden cupboards, he had a fold-out bed and a handy escape staircase.

• *Back outside, turn right and find the stairs leading down to the...*

Royal Danish Treasury (Castle Basement): The palace was a royal residence for a century and has been the royal vault right up until today. As you enter, first head to the right, into the **wine cellar,** with thousand-liter barrels and some fine treasury items. The first room has a vast army of tiny golden soldiers, and a wall lined with fancy rifles. Heading into the next room, you'll see fine items of amber (petrified tree resin, 30-50 million years old) and ivory. Study the large box made of amber (in a freestanding case, just to the right as you enter)—the tiny figures show a healthy interest in sex.

Now head back past the ticket taker and into the main part of the treasury, where you can browse through exquisite royal knickknacks.

The diamond- and pearl-studded **saddles** were Christian

IV's—the first for his coronation, the second for his son's wedding. When his kingdom was nearly bankrupt, Christian had these constructed lavishly—complete with solid-gold spurs—to impress visiting dignitaries and bolster Denmark's credit rating.

The next case displays **tankards.** Danes were always big drinkers, and to drink in the top style, a king had narwhal steins (#4030). Note the fancy Greenland Inuit (Eskimo) on the lid (#4023). The case is filled with exquisitely carved ivory. On the other side of that case, what's with the mooning snuffbox (#4063)? Also, check out the amorous whistle (#4064).

Drop by the case on the wall in the back-left of the room: The 17th century was the age of **brooches.** Many of these are made of freshwater pearls. Find the fancy combination toothpick and ear spoon (#4140). Look for #4146: A queen was caught having an affair after 22 years of royal marriage. Her king gave her a special present: a golden ring—showing the hand of his promiscuous queen shaking hands with a penis.

Step downstairs, away from all this silliness. Passing through the serious vault door, you come face-to-face with a big, jeweled **sword.** The tall, two-handed, 16th-century coronation sword was drawn by the new king, who cut crosses in the air in four directions, symbolically promising to defend the realm from all attacks. The cases surrounding the sword contain everyday items used by the king (all solid gold, of course). What looks like a trophy case of gold records is actually a collection of dinner plates with amber centers (#5032).

Go down the steps. In the center case is Christian IV's **coronation crown** (from 1596, seven pounds of gold and precious stones, #5124), which some consider to be the finest Renaissance crown in Europe. Its six tallest gables radiate symbolism. Find the symbols of justice (sword and scales), fortitude (a woman on a lion with a sword), and charity (a nursing woman— meaning the king will love God and his people as a mother loves her child). The pelican,  which according to medieval legend pecks its own flesh to feed its young, symbolizes God sacrificing his son, just as the king would make great sacrifices for his people. Climb the footstool to look inside—it's as exquisite as the outside. The shields of various Danish provinces remind the king that he's surrounded by his realms.

Circling the cases along the wall (right to left), notice the fine enameled lady's goblet with traits of a good woman spelled out in

Latin (#5128) and above that, an exquisite prayer book (with handwritten favorite prayers, #5134). In the fifth window, the big solid-gold baptismal basin (#5262) hangs above tiny oval silver boxes that contained the royal children's umbilical cords (handy for protection later in life, #5272); two cases over are royal writing sets with wax, seals, pens, and ink (#5320).

Go down a few more steps into the lowest level of the treasury and last room. The two **crowns** in the center cases are more modern (from 1670), lighter, and more practical—just gold and diamonds without all the symbolism. The king's crown is only four pounds, the queen's a mere two.

The cases along the walls show off the **crown jewels.** These were made in 1840 of diamonds, emeralds, rubies, and pearls from earlier royal jewelry. The saber (#5540) shows emblems of the realm's 19 provinces. The sumptuous pendant features a 19-carat diamond cut (like its neighbors) in the 58-facet "brilliant" style for maximum reflection (far-left case, #5560). Imagine these on the dance floor. The painting shows the anointing of King Christian V at the Frederiksborg Castle Chapel in 1671. The crown jewels are still worn by the queen on special occasions several times a year.

▲Rosenborg Gardens

Rosenborg Castle is surrounded by the royal pleasure gardens and, on sunny days, a minefield of sunbathing Danish beauties and picnickers. While "ethnic Danes" grab the shade, the rest of the Danes worship the sun. When the royal family is in residence, there's a daily changing-of-the-guard miniparade from the Royal Guard's barracks adjoining Rosenborg Castle (at 11:30) to Amalienborg Palace (at 12:00). The Queen's Rose Garden (across the moat from the palace) is a royal place for a picnic. The fine statue of Hans Christian Andersen in the park—erected while he was still alive (and approved by him)—is meant to symbolize how his stories had a message even for adults (gardens open daily 7:00-dusk).

▲National Gallery of Denmark (Statens Museum for Kunst)

This museum fills a stately building with Danish and European paintings from the 14th century through today. It's particularly worthwhile for the chance to be immersed in great art by the Danes, and to see its good collection of French Modernists, all well-described in English.

Cost and Hours: 110 DKK, Tue-Sun 11:00-17:00, Wed until 20:00, closed Mon, Sølvgade 48, tel. 33 74 84 94, www.smk.dk.

Visiting the Museum: The ground floor holds special exhibits; the second floor has collections of Danish and Nordic artists from 1750 to 1900, and European art from 1300 to 1800; and the Danish and International Art after 1900 is spread between the second and third floors. Museum upgrades may force the temporary closure of some exhibition rooms.

Head first to the Danish and Nordic artists section, and pick up the excellent floor plan that suggests a twisting route through the collection. Take the time to read the descriptions in each room, which put the paintings into historical context. In addition to Romantic works by well-known, non-Danish artists (such as the Norwegian J. C. Dahl and the German Caspar David Friedrich), this is a chance to learn about some

very talented Danish painters not well-known outside their native land. Make a point to meet the "Skagen Painters," including Anna Ancher, Michael Ancher, Peder Severin Krøyer, and others (find them in the section called "The Modern Breakthrough I-II"). This group, with echoes of the French Impressionists, gathered in the fishing village of Skagen on the northern tip of Denmark, surrounded by the sea and strong light, and painted heroic folk-fishermen themes in the late 1800s. Also worth seeking out are the canvases of Laurits Andersen Ring, who portrayed traditional peasant scenes with modern style; and Jens Ferdinand Willumsen, who pioneered "Vitalism" (celebrating man in nature). Other exhibits are cleverly organized by theme, such as gender or the body.

In the 20th-century section, the collection of early French Modernism is particularly impressive (with works by Matisse, Picasso, Braque, and more). This is complemented with works by Danish artists, who, inspired by the French avant-garde, introduced new, radical forms and colors to Scandinavian art.

CHRISTIANSHAVN

Across the harbor from the old town, Christianshavn—the former merchant's district—is one of the most delightful neighborhoods in town to explore. It offers pleasant canalside walks and trendy restaurants, along with two things to see: Our Savior's Church (with its fanciful tower) and Christiania, a colorful alternative-living community. Before visiting, make sure to read the background on Christianshavn, which helps explain what you'll see (see sidebar).

Your first look at the island will likely be its main square. Christianshavns Torv has a Metro stop, an early Copenhagen phone kiosk (from 1896), a fine bakery across the street (Lagkage-huset), and three statues celebrating Greenland. A Danish protectorate since 1721, Greenland, with 56,000 people, is represented by two members in the Danish parliament. The square has long been a hangout for Greenlanders, who appreciate the cheap beer and long hours of the big supermarket fronting the square.

▲Our Savior's Church (Vor Frelsers Kirke)

Following a recent restoration, the church gleams inside and out. Its bright Baroque interior (1696) is shaped like a giant cube. The magnificent pipe organ is supported by elephants (a royal symbol of the prestigious Order of the Elephant). Looking up to the ceiling, notice elephants also sculpted into the stucco of the dome, and a little one hanging from the main chandelier. Best of all, you can climb the unique spiral spire (with an outdoor staircase winding up to its top—398 stairs in all) for great views of the city and of the Christiania commune below.

Cost and Hours: Church interior-free, open daily 11:00-15:30 but may close for special services; church tower-40 DKK Mon-Thu, 45 DKK Fri-Sun; May-Sept Mon-Sat 9:30-19:00, Sun from 10:30; shorter hours off-season, closed mid-Dec-Feb and in bad weather; bus #2A, #19, or Metro: Christianshavn, Sankt Annægade 29, tel. 41 66 63 57, www.vorfrelserskirke.dk.

❿ Spin-Tour from the Top of Our Savior's Church: Climb up until you run out of stairs. As you wind back down, look for these landmarks:

The modern windmills are a reminder that Denmark generates 36 percent of its power from wind. Below the windmills is a great aerial view of the Christiania commune. Beyond the windmills, across Øresund (the strait that separates Denmark and Sweden), stands a shuttered Swedish nuclear power plant. The lone skyscraper in the distance—the first and tallest skyscraper in Scandinavia—is in Malmö, Sweden. The Øresund Bridge made Malmö an easy 35-minute bus or train ride from Copenhagen (it's become a bedroom community, with much cheaper apartments making the commute worthwhile).

Farther to the right, the big red-roof zone is Amager Island. Five hundred years as the city's dumping grounds earned Amager the nickname "Crap Island." Circling on, you come to the towering

Christianshavn: Then and Now

Christianshavn—Copenhagen's planned port—was vital to Danish power in the 17th and 18th centuries. Denmark had always been second to Sweden when it came to possession of natural resources, so the Danes tried to make up for it by acquiring resource-rich overseas colonies. They built Christianshavn (with Amsterdam's engineering help) to run the resulting trade business—giving this neighborhood a "little Amsterdam" vibe today.

Since Denmark's economy was so dependent on trade, the port town was the natural target of enemies. When the Danes didn't support Britain against Napoleon in 1807, the Brits bombarded Christianshavn. In this "blackest year in Danish history," Christianshavn burned down. That's why today there's hardly a building here that dates from before that time.

Christianshavn remained Copenhagen's commercial center until the 1920s, when a modern harbor was built. Suddenly, Christianshavn's economy collapsed and it became a slum. Cheap prices attracted artsy types, giving it a bohemian flavor. In 1971, squatters set up shop in an old military camp in Christianshavn and created their own community called Christiania, which still survives today (see below).

Over the past few decades, Christianshavn has had a resurgence, and these days, prices are driven up by wealthy locals (who pay about 60 percent of their income in taxes) spending too much for apartments, renting them cheaply to their kids, and writing off the loss. Demand for property is huge. Today the neighborhood is inhabited mostly by rich students and young professionals, living in some of the priciest real estate in town.

Radisson Blu Royal Hotel. The area beyond it is slated to become a forest of skyscrapers—the center of Europe's biomedical industry.

Downtown Copenhagen is decorated with several striking towers and spires. The tower capped by the golden ball is a ride in Tivoli Gardens. Next is City Hall's pointy brick tower. The biggest building, with the three-crown tower, is Christiansborg Palace. The Børsen (old stock exchange) is just beyond, with its unique dragon-tail tower. Behind that is Nyhavn. Just across from that and the Royal Danish Theatre's Playhouse is the dramatic Opera House (with the flat roof and big, grassy front yard).

▲▲▲Christiania

In 1971, the original 700 Christianians established squatters' rights in an abandoned military barracks just a 10-minute walk from the Danish parliament building. Two generations later, this "free city" still stands—an ultra-human mishmash of idealists, hippies, potheads, nonmaterialists, and happy children (900 people, 200 cats,

200 dogs, 2 parrots, and 17 horses). There are even a handful of Willie Nelson-type seniors among the 180 remaining here from the original takeover. And an amazing thing has happened: The place has become the second-most-visited sight among tourists in Copenhagen, behind Tivoli Gardens. Move over, *Little Mermaid*.

"Pusher Street" (named for the sale of soft drugs here) is Christiania's main drag. Get beyond this touristy side of Christiania, and you'll find a fascinating, ramshackle world of moats and earthen ramparts, alternative housing, cozy tea houses, carpenter shops, hippie villas, children's playgrounds, peaceful lanes, and people who believe that "to be normal is to be in a straitjacket." A local slogan claims, *"Kun døde fisk flyder med strømmen"* ("Only dead fish swim with the current").

Hours and Tours: Christiania is open all the time but quiet (and some restaurants closed) on Mondays, which is its rest day (though "resting" from what, I'm not sure). Guided tours leave from the main entrance (50 DKK, July-Aug daily at 13:00 and 15:00; Sat-Sun only the rest of the year, just show up, 1.5 hours, in English and Danish, info tel. 32 95 65 07, www.rundvisergruppen.dk). You're welcome to snap photos, except on Pusher Street (but ask residents before you photograph them).

The Community: Christiania is broken into 14 administrative neighborhoods on a former military base. Most of the land, once owned by Denmark's Ministry of Defense, has been purchased by the Christiania community; the rest of it is leased from the state (see the sidebar for details). Locals build their homes but don't own them—individuals can't buy or sell property. When someone moves out, the community decides who will be invited in to replace that person. A third of the adult population works on the outside, a third works on the inside, and a third doesn't work much at all.

There are nine rules: no cars, no hard drugs, no guns, no explosives, and so on. The Christiania flag is red and yellow because when the original hippies took over, they found a lot of red and yellow paint onsite. The three yellow dots in the flag are from the three "i"s in "Christiania" (or, some claim, the "o"s in "Love, Love, Love").

The community pays the city about $1 million a year for utili-

① Carl Madsens Plads
② Green Hall
③ Nemoland
④ Månefiskeren Café
⑤ Morgenstedet Vegetarian Café
⑥ Spiseloppen Restaurant
⑦ Tour Departure Point

ties and has about $1 million a year more to run its local affairs. A few "luxury hippies" have oil heat, but most use wood or gas. The ground here was poisoned by its days as a military base, so nothing is grown in Christiania. There's little industry within the commune (Christiania Cykler, which builds fine bikes, is an exception—www.pedersen-bike.dk). A phone chain provides a system of communal security (they have had bad experiences calling the police). Each September 26, the day the first squatters took over the barracks in 1971, Christiania has a big birthday bash.

Tourists are entirely welcome here, because they've become a major part of the economy. Visitors react in very different ways to the place. Some see dogs, dirt, and dazed people. Others see a haven of peace, freedom, and no taboos. It's true that this free city isn't always pretty. But watching parents here raise their children with Christiania values makes me a believer in this social experiment. My take: Giving alternative-type people a place to be alternative is a kind of alternative beauty that deserves a place.

Christiania Documentary: For a fascinating, one-hour insight into Christiania, watch the 2011 documentary *Christiania: 40 Years of Occupation*. This film, produced by Seattle production company Bus No. 8, does a wonderful job of chronicling the his-

COPENHAGEN

The Fight for Christiania

Ever since several hundred squatters took over an unused military camp in 1971, Christiania has been a political hot potato. No one in the Danish establishment wanted it. And no one had the nerve to mash it.

Part of Christiania's history has been ongoing government attempts to shut the place down. At first, city officials looked the other way because back then, no one cared about the land. But skyrocketing Christianshavn land values brought pressure to open Christiania to market forces. By the 1980s, the neighborhood had become gentrified, and both the city and developers were eyeing the land Christiania's hippies were squatting on. And when Denmark's conservative government took over in 2001, they vowed to "normalize" Christiania (with pressure from the US), with police regularly conducting raids on pot sellers.

Things were looking grim for the Christianians until 2012, when the Danish government offered to sell most of the land to the residents at below the market rate, and offered guaranteed loans. In exchange, the Christianians had to promise to upgrade and maintain water, sewage, and electrical services, and preserve rights of way and "rural" areas. Accepting the offer, Christianians formed a foundation—Freetown Christiania—to purchase and control the property. The parts of Christiania that were not sold are leased to the residents and are still owned by the state.

For many Christianians, it's an ironic, capitalistic twist that they now own property, albeit collectively. They even sell symbolic Christiania "shares" to help pay for the land. And, every adult over age 18 now owes a monthly rent that goes toward paying off the loans and to support services. But on the flip side, this is the greatest degree of security Christiania has ever experienced in its four-plus decades of existence. Even so, mistrust of the establishment is by no means dead, and there are still those who wonder what the government might be up to next.

tory of Europe's oldest still-existing squatters' community. Today, this community is closing in on the 50-year mark and is still going strong—but it hasn't been easy. See www.busno8.com for details.

Visiting Christiania: The main entrance is down Prinsessegade, behind the Our Savior's Church spiral tower. Passing under the gate, take Pusher Street directly into the community. The first square—a kind of market square (souvenirs and

marijuana-related stuff)—is named Carl Madsens Plads, honor-
ing the lawyer who took the squatters' case to the Danish supreme
court in 1976 and won. Beyond that is Nemoland (a food circus, on
the right). A huge warehouse called the Green Hall (Den Grønne
Hal) is a recycling center and hardware store (where people get
most of their building materials) that does triple duty as a night-
time concert hall and as a craft center for kids. If you go up the
stairs between Nemoland and the Green Hall, you'll climb up to
the ramparts that overlook the canal. As you wander, be careful
to distinguish between real Christianians and Christiania's motley
guests—drunks (mostly from other countries) who hang out here
in the summer for the freedom. Part of the original charter guaranteed that the community would stay open to the public.

On the left beyond the Green Hall, a lane leads to the Månefiskeren café, and beyond that, to the Morgenstedet vegetarian
restaurant (the best place for a simple, friendly meal; see "Eating
in Christiania," next page). Beyond these recommended restaurants, you'll find yourself lost in the totally untouristy, truly local

residential parts of Christiania,
where kids play in the street
and the old folks sit out on
the front stoop—just like any
other neighborhood. Just as St.
Mark's Square isn't the "real
Venice," the hippie-druggie
scene on Pusher Street isn't the
"real Christiania"—you can't
say you've experienced Christiania until you've strolled these back
streets.

A walk or bike ride through Christiania is a great way to see
how this community lives. When you leave, look up—the sign
above the gate says, "You are entering the EU."

Smoking Marijuana: Pusher Street was once lined with stalls
selling marijuana, joints, and hash. Residents intentionally destroyed the stalls in 2004 to reduce the risk of Christiania being
disbanded by the government. (One stall was spared and is on display at the National Museum.) Today, the stalls are back, and you'll

likely hear whispered offers of "hash"
during your visit. During my last visit
there was a small, pungent stretch of
Pusher Street, dubbed the "Green
Light District," where pot was being
openly sold (signs acknowledged
that this activity was still illegal,
and announced three rules here:
1. Have fun; 2. No photos; and 3. No

running—"because it makes people nervous"). However, purchasing and smoking may buy you more time in Denmark than you'd planned—possession of marijuana remains illegal.

About hard drugs: For the first few years, junkies were tolerated. But that led to violence and polluted the mellow ambience residents envisioned. In 1979, the junkies were expelled—an epic confrontation in the community's folk history now—and since then the symbol of a fist breaking a syringe is as prevalent as the leafy marijuana icon. Hard drugs are emphatically forbidden in Christiania.

Eating in Christiania: The people of Christiania appreciate good food and count on tourism as a big part of their economy. Consequently, there are plenty of decent eateries. Most of the restaurants are open from lunchtime until late and are closed on Monday (the community's weekly holiday). **Pusher Street** has a few grungy but tasty falafel stands, as well as a popular burger bar. **$ Nemoland** is the hangout zone—a fun collection of stands peddling Thai food, burgers, *shawarma,* and other fast hippie food with great, tented outdoor seating. Its stay-a-while atmosphere comes with backgammon, foosball, bakery goods, and fine views from the ramparts. **$$ Månefiskeren** ("Moonfisher Bar") looks like a modern-day Brueghel painting, with billiards, chess, snacks, and drinks. **$$ Morgenstedet** ("Morning Place") is a good, cheap vegetarian café with a mellow, woody interior and a rustic patio outside (left after Pusher Street). **$$$$ Spiseloppen** is *the* classy, good-enough-for-Republicans restaurant in the community (described on page 90). While there are lots of public concerts at the open-air Nemoland stage, for a music club experience, consider **Musik Loppen** (which has live music almost nightly, under the Spiseloppen restaurant).

GREATER COPENHAGEN
Harbor Baths
Swimming in the middle of a large city is unthinkable in most of the world, yet the enterprising Danes have made it happen. On a warm summer day there's no better way to see Copenhageners at play than to visit one of the city's Harbor Baths. The two

most centrally located baths are Havnebadet Fisketorvet, next to the Fisketorvet Mall behind Kødbyen, and Islands Brygge, just south of the Langebro bridge and Christianshavn.

The baths are open to all to enjoy a refreshing saltwater dip. How refreshing? Water temperatures peak at 65 degrees in August, which should be no problem for those with Viking blood. Though the baths are located in former industrial areas, the water is monitored, and the quality is as good as what you'll find at the pristine beaches around Copenhagen. On the rare occasions it dips below acceptable levels, the baths are closed.

Cost and Hours: Free, open long hours June-Sept (lifeguards on duty 11:00-19:00).

Information: Havnebadet Fisketorvet, tel. 30 89 04 70; Islands Brygge, tel. 30 89 04 69.

Getting There: Havnebadet Fisketorvet—from Kødbyen, head east on Dybbølsbro, across the train tracks to the Fisketorvet Mall. Skirt the mall to the left, following the wide promenade toward the water and you'll soon see the baths on the left. Islands Brygge—from Fisketorvet Mall, cross the Inner Harbor on the Bryggebroen pedestrian and bicycle bridge. On the other side, follow the waterside promenade north to the baths (best on a bike). Or, if coming from the main train station area, head east over Langebro bridge, then head a short distance south—you can't miss the baths. From Christianshavn, follow the ramparts west to where they meet the Inner Harbor. Pass under Langebro bridge, and you'll see the baths.

Visiting the Baths: The Havnebadet Fisketorvet is actually a huge, semisubmerged barge containing three pools: one for children, another for diving (from one-, two-, and three-meter-high boards), and an Olympic-size swimming pool. Here you'll be hemmed in on three sides by glassy modern office buildings and the Fisketorvet Mall.

The much busier Islands Brygge facility consists of five pools (two suitable for kids) and a prow-shaped diving platform offering three- and five-meter leaps into the water. The shore is one big cobbled promenade backed by a grassy area that's great for sunbathing, barbecues, and people-watching.

Carlsberg Brewery

Denmark's beloved source of legal intoxicants is Carlsberg. About 1.5 miles west of Rådhuspladsen (City Hall Square), Carlsberg welcomes you to its visitors center for a self-guided tour, a free beer, and a small gift. Mostly, it's a ruse to ply you with a beer and get you into their substantial gift shop. For a more in-depth visit, take the guided tour or do the beer tasting, though both cost extra.

Cost and Hours: 100 DKK, daily 10:00-20:00, Oct-April until 17:00; half-hour guided tour—50 DKK, in English at 13:00, 14:00, and 15:00; beer tasting—75 DKK, at 12:00, 14:00, and 16:00; catch the local train to Carlsberg Station or bus #26 (get off at the Kammasvej stop and walk five minutes), or take a free shuttle from near the Vesterbrogade TI (where the hop-on, hop-off buses stop); enter at Gamle Carlsbergvej 11 around corner from brewery entrance, tel. 33 27 12 82, www.visitcarlsberg.dk.

Nearby: The manicured gardens of the sprawling Frederiksberg Park (Frederiksberg Have) and adjacent Southern Field (Søndermarken) make a lovely setting for a picnic.

Open-Air Folk Museum (Frilandsmuseet)

This park, located north of Copenhagen in the suburb of Lyngby, is part of the National Museum. It's filled with traditional Danish architecture and folk culture, farm animals, and gardens. Bring a picnic or dine at the on-site restaurant.

Cost and Hours: 65 DKK; May-mid-Oct Tue-Sun 10:00-16:00, July-mid-Aug until 17:00, closed Mon and off-season; S-tog: Sorgenfri and 10-minute walk to Kongevejen 100 in Lyngby (see the Near Copenhagen map in the following chapter); tel. 41 20 64 55, http://natmus.dk.

Bakken

Danes gather at Copenhagen's *other* great amusement park, Bakken, situated in the Dyrehaven forest about a 10-minute drive north of the city.

Cost and Hours: Free entry, 269 DKK for all-ride pass; late June-mid-Aug daily 12:00-24:00, shorter hours April-late June and mid-Aug-mid-Sept, closed mid-Sept-March; S-tog: Klampenborg, then walk 10 minutes through the woods (see the Near Copenhagen map in the following chapter); tel. 39 63 73 00, www.bakken.dk.

Dragør

If you don't have time to get to the idyllic island of Ærø (see the Central Denmark chapter), consider the eight-mile trip south of Copenhagen to the fishing village of Dragør, near the airport (bus #350S from Nørreport). For information, see www.visit-dragoer.dk.

Shopping in Copenhagen

Shops are generally open Monday through Friday from 10:00 to 19:00 and Saturday from 9:00 to 16:00 (closed Sun). While big department stores dominate the scene, many locals favor the characteristic, small artisan shops and boutiques.

Uniquely Danish souvenirs to look for include intricate paper cuttings with idyllic motifs of swans, flowers, or Christmas themes; mobiles with everything from bicycles to Viking ships (look for the quality Flensted brand); and the colorful artwork of Danish artist Bo Bendixen (posters, postcards, T-shirts, and more). Jewelry lovers look for amber, known as the "gold of the North." Globs of this petrified sap wash up on the shores of all the Baltic countries.

If you buy anything substantial (minimum 300 DKK, about $50) from a shop displaying the **Danish Tax-Free Shopping** emblem, you can get a refund of the Value-Added Tax, roughly 20 to 25 percent of the purchase price (VAT is "MOMS" in Danish). If you have your purchase mailed, the tax can be deducted from your bill.

WHERE TO SHOP
Consider the following stores, markets, and neighborhoods:

For a street's worth of shops selling **"Scantiques,"** wander down Ravnsborggade from Nørrebrogade.

Copenhagen's colorful **flea markets** are small but feisty and surprisingly cheap (May-Nov Sat 8:00-14:00 at Israels Plads; May-Sept Fri and Sat 8:00-17:00 along Gammel Strand and on Kongens Nytorv). For other street markets, ask at the TI.

The city's top **department stores** (Illum at Østergade 52, and Magasin du Nord at Kongens Nytorv 13) offer a good, if expensive, look at today's Denmark. Both are on the Strøget and have fine cafeterias on their top floors. The department stores and the Politiken Bookstore on Rådhuspladsen have a good selection of maps and English travel guides.

The section of the Strøget called **Amagertorv** is a highlight for shoppers. The **Royal Copenhagen** store here sells porcelain on three floors (Mon-Fri 10:00-19:00, Sat 10:00-18:00, Sun 11:00-16:00). The first floor up features figurines and collectibles. The second floor has a second-quality department for discounts, proving that "even the best painter can miss a stroke." Next door, **Illums Bolighus** shows off three floors of modern Danish design (Mon-Sat 10:00-19:00, Fri until 20:00, Sun 11:00-18:00).

House of Amber has a shop and a tiny two-room museum with about 50 examples of prehistoric insects trapped in the amber (remember *Jurassic Park*?) under magnifying glasses. You'll also see remarkable items made of amber, from necklaces and chests to Viking ships and chess sets (25 DKK, daily May-Sept 9:00-19:30, Oct-April 10:00-17:30, at the top of Nyhavn at Kongens Nytorv 2). If you're visiting Rosenborg Castle, you'll see the ultimate examples of amber craftsmanship in its treasury.

Nightlife in Copenhagen

For the latest event and live music listings, check at the TI and pick up *The Copenhagen Post* (comes out weekly, read online or pick up free copy at TI and some hotels, also sold at newsstands, www. cphpost.dk).

Nightlife Neighborhoods: The **Meatpacking District,** which I've listed for its restaurants (see page 93), is also one of the city's up-and-coming destinations for bars and nightlife. On warm evenings, **Nyhavn** canal becomes a virtual nightclub, with packs of young people hanging out along the water, sipping beers. **Christiania** always seems to have something musical going on after dark. **Tivoli** has evening entertainment daily from mid-April through late September (see page 44).

Music Venues: Copenhagen Jazz House is a good bet for live jazz (two stages, closed Mon, Niels Hemmingsensgade 10, tel. 33 15 47 00, schedule at www.jazzhouse.dk). For blues, try the **Mojo Blues Bar** (nightly 20:00-late, music starts at 21:30, Løn-gangsstræde 21c, tel. 33 11 64 53, schedule in Danish at www. mojo.dk). For locations, see the Copenhagen Restaurants map later in this chapter.

Jazz Cruises: Canal Tours Copenhagen offers 1.5-hour jazz cruises along the canals of Copenhagen. You can bring a picnic dinner and drinks on board and enjoy a lively night on the water surrounded by Danes (150 DKK and up, June-mid-Sept Thu and Sun at 19:00, no tours mid-Sept-May, departs from Canal Tours Copenhagen dock at Nyhavn, tel. 32 96 30 00). Call to reserve on July and August evenings; otherwise try arriving 20 to 30 minutes in advance, www.stromma.dk.

Sleeping in Copenhagen

I've listed a few big business-class hotels, the best budget hotels in the center, and a few backpacker dorm options.

Big Copenhagen hotels have an exasperating pricing policy. Their high rack rates are charged only about 20 or 30 days a year (unless you book in advance and don't know better). As hotels are swamped at certain times, they like to keep their gouging options open. Therefore, you'll need to check their website for deals or be bold enough to simply show up and use the TI's booking service to find yourself a room on their push list (ask at their desk, 100-DKK fee). The TI swears that, except for maybe 10 days a year, you can land yourself a deeply discounted room in a three- or four-star business-class hotel in the center. That means a 1,500-DKK double with American-style comfort for about 1,000 DKK, including a big buffet breakfast.

Sleep Code

Hotels are classified based on the average price of a typical en suite double room with breakfast in high season.

$$$$	**Splurge:**	Most rooms over 1,100 DKK
$$$	**Pricier:**	900-1,100 DKK
$$	**Moderate:**	700-900 DKK
$	**Budget:**	500-700 DKK
¢	**Backpacker:**	Under 500 DKK
RS%	**Rick Steves discount**	

Unless otherwise noted, credit cards are accepted, hotel staff speak basic English, and free Wi-Fi is available. Comparison-shop by checking prices at several hotels (on each hotel's own website, on a booking site, or by email). For the best deal, *always book directly with the hotel.* Ask for a discount if paying in cash; if the listing includes **RS%,** request a Rick Steves discount.

HOTELS IN CENTRAL COPENHAGEN

All of these hotels are big and modern, with elevators and non-smoking rooms. Beware: Many hotels have rip-off phone rates even for local calls.

Near Nørreport

$$$$ Ibsens Hotel is a stylish 118-room hotel with helpful staff, located in a charming neighborhood away from the main train station commotion and a short walk from the old center (consider splurging on a larger room—smaller rooms can be very tight, great bikes-150 DKK/24 hours, pay parking, Vendersgade 23, S-tog and Metro: Nørreport—to find Vendersgade after surfacing from the Metro, head for the five-story brown building with the green copper dome, tel. 33 13 19 13, www.ibsenshotel.dk, hotel@ibsenshotel.dk).

$$$ Hotel Jørgensen is a friendly little 30-room hotel in a great location just off Nørreport, kitty-corner from the bustling Torvehallerne KBH food market. With fresh and tidy rooms and a welcoming lounge, it's a fine option, though the halls are a narrow, tangled maze (Rømersgade 11, tel. 33 13 81 86, www.hoteljoergensen.dk, hoteljoergensen@mail.dk). They also rent **¢** dorm beds.

Near Nyhavn

$$$$ 71 Nyhavn has 130 rustic but very classy rooms in a pair of beautifully restored, early-19th-century brick warehouses located at the far end of the colorful Nyhavn canal. With a professional, polite staff, lots of old brick and heavy timbers, and plenty of style, it's

Copenhagen Hotels

1 Ibsens Hotel
2 Hotel Jørgensen
3 71 Nyhavn
4 Hotel Bethel Sømandshjem
5 Axel Hotel
6 66 Guldsmeden
7 Star Hotel

8 Hotel Nebo
9 Wake Up Copenhagen
10 Cabinn (4)
11 Danhostel Copenhagen City
12 Copenhagen Downtown
13 To Danhostel Copenhagen Amager

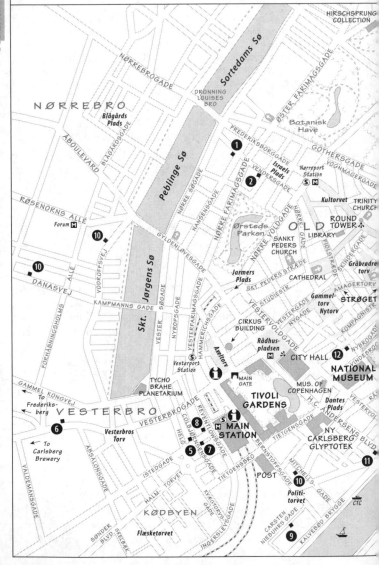

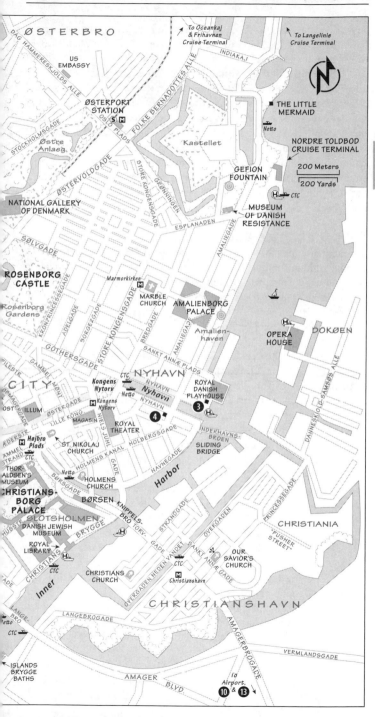

COPENHAGEN

ØSTERBRO

To Oceankaj & Frihavnen Cruise Terminal

To Langelinie Cruise Terminal

INDIAKAJ

US EMBASSY

DAG HAMMERSKJOLDS ALLE

THE LITTLE MERMAID

Netto

FOLKE BERNADOTTES ALLE

ØSTERPORT STATION S M

OSLO PLADS

Kastellet

NORDRE TOLDBOD CRUISE TERMINAL

200 Meters

200 Yards

STOCKHOLMSGADE

Østre Anlaeg

ØSTERVOLDGADE

STORE KONGENSGADE

GRØNNINGEN

GEFION FOUNTAIN

CTC

NATIONAL GALLERY OF DENMARK

ESPLANADEN

MUSEUM OF DANISH RESISTANCE

SØLVGADE

AMALIEGADE

ROSENBORG CASTLE

Marmorkirken

MARBLE CHURCH

AMALIENBORG PALACE

OPERA HOUSE

DOKØEN

Rosenborg Gardens

KRONPRINSESSEGADE

ADELGADE

BORGERGADE

STORE KONGENSGADE

DRONNINGENS

AMALIEGADE

Amalienhaven

GOTHERSGADE

PEDER SKRAMS GADE

SANKT ANNÆ PLADS

DANNESKIOLD-SAMSØES ALLE

PILESTR

GAMMEL MONT

NYHAVN

CITY

Kongens Nytorv

NYHAVN

Netto

Nyhavn

NYHAVN

ROYAL DANISH PLAYHOUSE

3

ORMAGERGADE

OST

ILLUM

ØSTERGADE

Kongens Nytorv

NIELS JUHLS

4

H

ÆDERSTR

LILLE KONG

MAGASIN

ROYAL THEATER

INDERHAVNS-BROEN

AMMEL STRAND

Højbro Plads

CTC

M

ST. NIKOLAJ CHURCH

HOLMENS KANAL

HOLBERGSGADE

HAVNEGADE

SLIDING BRIDGE

THOR-ALDSEN'S MUSEUM

Netto

BORGGADE

HOLMENS CHURCH

Harbor

CHRISTIANS-BORG PALACE

BØRSEN

KNIPPELS-BRO

STRANDGADE

OVERGADEN

PRINSESSEGADE

CHRISTIANIA

SLOTSHOLMEN

DANISH JEWISH MUSEUM

H

"PUSHER STREET"

ROYAL LIBRARY

CHRISTIANS BRYGGE

CTC

CHRISTIANS CHURCH

OVERGADEN NEDEN VANDET

SANKT ANNÆ GADE

CTC

OUR SAVIOR'S CHURCH

Inner

Christianshavn

CHRISTIANSHAVN

LANGE-BRO

LANGEBROGADE

etto

CTC

AMAGERBROGADE

VERMLANDSGADE

ISLANDS BRYGGE BATHS

AMAGER BLVD

To Airport, &

10 13

a worthwhile splurge (some rates include breakfast, air-con, rental bikes-125 DKK/day, next to the Playhouse at Nyhavn 71, tel. 33 43 62 00, www.71nyhavnhotel.dk, 71nyhavnhotel@arp-hansen.dk).

$$$ Hotel Bethel Sømandshjem ("Seamen's Home"), run by a Lutheran association, is a calm and stately former seamen's hotel facing the boisterous Nyhavn canal and offering 29 cozy rooms at the most reasonable rack rates in town. While the decor is college-dorm-inspired, the hotel boasts a kind, welcoming staff and feels surprisingly comfortable once you settle in. Plus, the colorful Nyhavn neighborhood is a great place to "come home" to after a busy day of sightseeing. Book long in advance (Metro: Kongens Nytorv, facing bridge over the canal at Nyhavn 22, tel. 33 13 03 70, www.hotel-bethel.dk, info@hotel-bethel.dk).

Behind the Train Station

The area behind the train station mingles elegant old buildings, trendy nightspots, and pockets of modern sleaze. The main drag running away from the station, Istedgade, has long been Copenhagen's red-light district; but increasingly, this area is gentrified and feels safe (in spite of the few remaining harmless sex shops). These hotels are also extremely handy to the Meatpacking District restaurant zone.

$$$$ Axel Hotel and $$$$ 66 Guldsmeden, operated by the Guldsmeden ("Dragonfly") company, have more character than most—a restful spa-like ambience decorated with imported Balinese furniture, four-poster beds, and an emphasis on sustainability and organic materials. (Axel: breakfast extra, 189 rooms, request a quieter back room overlooking the pleasant garden, restful spa area with sauna and hot tub-295 DKK/person per stay, a block behind the train station at Colbjørnsensgade 14, tel. 33 31 32 66, booking@hotelguldsmeden.com; 66 Guldsmeden: slightly cheaper than Axel, 64 rooms, Vesterbrogade 66, tel. 33 22 15 00, carlton@hotelguldsmeden.com). Both hotels rent bikes for 150 DKK/day. They share a website: www.hotelguldsmeden.com.

$$$ Star Hotel rents 134 rooms with modern Scandinavian decor and is just a block from the station (breakfast extra, nice courtyard, bike rental-130 DKK/day, Colbjørnsensgade 13, tel. 33 22 11 00, www.copenhagenstar.dk, star@copenhagenstar.dk).

$$$ Hotel Nebo, a secure-feeling refuge with a friendly welcome and 84 comfy if a bit creaky rooms, is just a half-block from the station (cheaper rooms with shared bath, breakfast extra, bike rental-120 DKK/day, Istedgade 6, tel. 33 21 12 17, www.nebo.dk, nebo@nebo.dk).

$$ Wake Up Copenhagen offers 510 compact, slick, and stylish rooms (similar to but a notch more upscale-feeling than Cabinn, described next). The rates can range wildly, and their pricing

structure is like the airlines' in that the further ahead and less flexibly you book, the less you pay). Rooms that are higher up—with better views and quieter—are also more expensive. It's in a desolate no-man's-land behind the station, between the train tracks and the harbor—about a 15-minute walk from the station or Tivoli, but ideal for biking (breakfast extra, air-con, bike rental, Carsten Niebuhrs Gade 11, tel. 44 80 00 00, www.wakeupcopenhagen. com, wakeupcopenhagen@arp-hansen.dk).

A DANISH MOTEL 6

$ Cabinn is a radical innovation and a great value, with several locations in Copenhagen (as well as Odense, Aarhus, and elsewhere):

identical, mostly collapsible, tiny but comfy, cruise-ship-type staterooms, all bright, molded, and shiny, with TV, coffeepot, shower, and toilet. Each room has a single bed that expands into a twin-bedded room with one or two fold-down bunks on the walls. It's tough to argue with this kind of efficiency (family rooms available, breakfast extra, easy pay parking, www.cabinn.com). The best of the bunch is **Cabinn City**, with 350 rooms and a great central location (a short walk south of the main train station and Tivoli at Mitchellsgade 14, tel. 33 46 16 16, city@cabinn.com). Two more, nearly identical Cabinns are a 15-minute walk northwest of the station: **Cabinn Copenhagen Express** (86 rooms, Danasvej 32, tel. 33 21 04 00, express@cabinn.com) and **Cabinn Scandinavia** (201 rooms, family rooms, Vodroffsvej 55, tel. 35 36 11 11, scandinavia@ cabinn.com). The largest is **Cabinn Metro,** near the Ørestad Metro station (710 rooms, family rooms, on the airport side of town at Arne Jakobsens Allé 2, tel. 32 46 57 00, metro@cabinn.com).

ROOMS AND APARTMENTS

At about 650 DKK or more per double, renting a room in a private home can be a great value. It offers a peek into Danish domestic life, and the experience can be as private or as social as you wish. These accommodations usually don't include breakfast, but you'll have access to the kitchen. **$ Bed & Breakfast Denmark** has served as a clearinghouse for local B&Bs since 1992. Peter Eberth and his staff rent piles of good local rooms in central apartments and take a 20-30 percent cut (the "deposit" you pay) but monitor quality. Their website lets you choose the type and location and gives you the necessary details when you pay (tel. 39 61 04 05, www.bbdk.dk).

Another great option is **AirBnB,** which offers scores of accommodations and options all over town, including rooms in private homes as well as apartments where you have privacy, can prepare your own meals, and come and go as you like (www.airbnb.com).

HOSTELS

¢ **Danhostel Copenhagen City,** an official HI hostel, is the hostel of the future. This huge harborside 16-story skyscraper is clean,

modern, nonsmoking, and a 10-minute walk from the train station and Tivoli. Some rooms on higher floors have panoramic views over the city (available on a first-come, first-served basis). This is your best bet for a clean, basic, and inexpensive room with private baths in the city center (private rooms and family rooms available, breakfast extra, elevator, rental bikes, H. C. Andersens Boulevard 50, tel. 33 11 85 85, www.danhostelcopenhagencity.dk, copenhagencity@danhostel.dk).

¢ **Copenhagen Downtown** is beautifully located on a pleasant street right in the city center, a few steps from Slotsholmen Island and two blocks from the Strøget. Its 300 beds are a bit institutional, but it promises free dinner and comes with a guest kitchen and a colorful, fun hangout bar, which doubles as the reception (private rooms available, breakfast extra, no curfew, Vandkunsten 5, tel. 70 23 21 10, www.copenhagendowntown.com, info@copenhagendowntown.com).

¢ **Danhostel Copenhagen Amager,** an official HI hostel, is on the edge of town (private rooms available, breakfast extra, family rooms, no curfew, excellent facilities, Vejlands Allé 200, tel. 32 52 29 08, www.danhostelcopenhagen.dk, copenhagen@danhostel.dk). To get from downtown to the hostel, take the Metro (Metro: Bella Center, then 10-minute walk).

Eating in Copenhagen

CHEAP MEALS

For a quick lunch, try a *smørrebrød,* a *pølse,* or a picnic. Finish it off with a pastry.

Smørrebrød

Denmark's 300-year-old tradition of open-face sandwiches survives. Find a *smørrebrød* takeout shop and choose two or three that look good (about 35 DKK each). You'll get them wrapped and

---

Restaurant Price Code

I've assigned each eatery a price category, based on the average cost of a typical main course. Drinks, desserts, and splurge items (steak and seafood) can raise the price considerably.

$$$$	**Splurge:**	Most main courses over 150 DKK
$$$	**Pricier:**	100-150 DKK
$$	**Moderate:**	50-100 DKK
$	**Budget:**	Under 50 DKK

In Denmark, a *pølsevogn* or other takeout spot is **$**; a sit-down café is **$$**; a casual but more upscale restaurant is **$$$**; and a swanky splurge is **$$$$**.

ready for a park bench. Add a cold drink, and you have a fine, quick, and very Danish lunch. Tradition calls for three sandwich courses: herring first, then meat, and then cheese. Downtown, you'll find these handy local alternatives to Yankee fast-food chains. They range from splurges to quick stop-offs.

Between Copenhagen University and Rosenborg Castle

My three favorite *smørrebrød* places are particularly handy when connecting your sightseeing between the downtown Strøget core and Rosenborg Castle.

$$ Restaurant Schønnemann is the foodies' choice—it has been written up in international magazines and frequently wins awards for "Best Lunch in Copenhagen." It's a cozy cellar restaurant crammed with small tables—according to the history on the menu, people "gather here in intense togetherness." The sand on the floor evokes a bygone era when passing traders would leave their horses out on the square while they lunched here. You'll need to reserve to get a table, and you'll pay a premium for their *smørrebrød* (two lunch seatings Mon-Sat: 11:30-14:00 & 14:15-17:00, closed Sun, no dinner, Hauser Plads 16, tel. 33 12 07 85, www.restaurantschonnemann.dk).

$$ Café Halvvejen is a small mom-and-pop place serving traditional lunches and open-face sandwiches in a woody and smoke-stained café, lined with portraits of Danish royalty. You can eat inside or at an outside table in good weather (food served Mon-Sat 12:00-15:00, closed Sun, next to public library at Krystalgade 11, tel. 33 11 91 12). In the evening, it becomes a hip and smoky student hangout, though no food is served.

$ Slagteren ved Kultorvet, a few blocks northwest of the uni-

COPENHAGEN

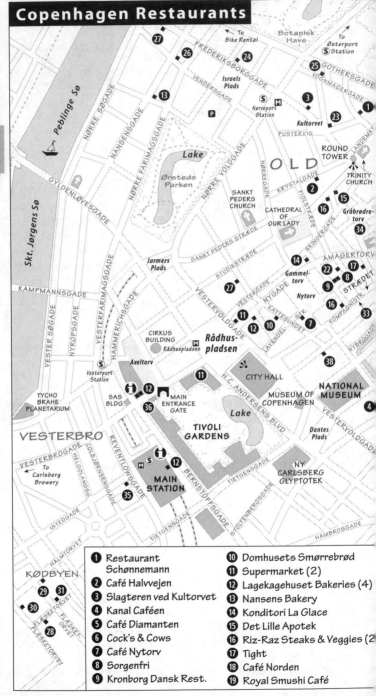

Copenhagen Restaurants

1. Restaurant Schønnemann
2. Café Halvvejen
3. Slagteren ved Kultorvet
4. Kanal Caféen
5. Café Diamanten
6. Cock's & Cows
7. Café Nytorv
8. Sorgenfri
9. Kronborg Dansk Rest.
10. Domhusets Smørrebrød
11. Supermarket (2)
12. Lagekagehuset Bakeries (4)
13. Nansens Bakery
14. Konditori La Glace
15. Det Lille Apotek
16. Riz-Raz Steaks & Veggies (2)
17. Tight
18. Café Norden
19. Royal Smushi Café

COPENHAGEN

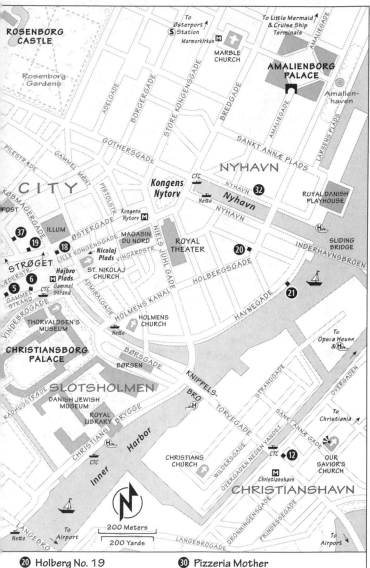

⓴ Holberg No. 19
㉑ Almanak
㉒ Københavner Caféen
㉓ The Ricemarket
㉔ TorvehallerneKBH
㉕ Brdr. Price Restaurant
㉖ Kalaset
㉗ Halifax Burgers (2)
㉘ Kødbyens Fiskebar
㉙ BioMio & Paté Paté

㉚ Pizzeria Mother
㉛ Nose2Tail Madbodega
㉜ Nyhavn Eateries
㉝ Kompagnistræde Eateries
㉞ Gråbrødretorv Eateries
㉟ Poonchai Thai Restaurant
㊱ Tivoli Food Hall
㊲ Copenhagen Jazz House
㊳ Mojo Blues Bar

versity, is a small butcher shop with bowler-hatted clerks selling good, inexpensive sandwiches to go for about 45 DKK. Choose from ham, beef, or pork (Mon-Fri 8:00-17:30, Sat until 15:00, closed Sun, sandwiches usually sell out by 13:00; just off Kultorvet square at Frederiksborggade 4, look for gold bull's head hanging outside).

Near Christiansborg Palace

These eateries are good choices when sightseeing on Slotsholmen.

$$ Kanal Caféen, on Frederiksholms Kanal across from Christiansborg Palace, serves lunch only and is a nice place for a traditional open-face sandwich. Inside, you'll rub elbows with locals in what feels like the cozy confines of a low-ceilinged old sailing ship; outside you can dine right above the canal and watch the tour boats go by (Mon-Fri 11:30-17:00, Sat until 15:00, closed Sun, Frederiksholms Kanal 18, tel. 33 11 57 70).

$$ Café Diamanten serves open-face sandwiches, warm dishes, and salads—and pours microbrews from the tap. Take a seat inside the comfy café or under the parasols out front, with a view across the square to Thorvaldsen's Museum (Mon-Fri 10:00-20:30, Sat-Sun until 19:00, Gammel Strand 50, tel. 33 93 55 45).

Burgers: $$$ Cock's & Cows is a trendy burger-and-cocktail bar with a happy, young vibe on an elegant street. Eat inside the brick-walled restaurant or in the courtyard out back (some burgers piled almost ridiculously high, daily 11:30-21:30, Gammel Strand 34, tel. 69 69 60 00).

Near Gammeltorv/Nytorv

$$ Café Nytorv has a nautical theme inside and pleasant outdoor seating on Nytorv. There's a great deal on a *smørrebrød* sampler for about 230 DKK—perfect for two people to share (if you smile, they'll serve it for dinner even though it's only on the lunch menu). This "Copenhagen City Plate" gives you a selection of the traditional sandwiches and extra bread on request (daily 9:00-22:00, Nytorv 15, tel. 33 11 77 06).

$$ Sorgenfri offers a local experience in a dark, woody spot just off the Strøget—give the herring open-face sandwich a try (Mon-Sat 11:00-20:45, Sun 12:00-18:00, Brolæggerstræde 8, tel. 33 11 58 80).

Or duck (literally) into **$$ Kronborg Dansk Restaurant,** across the street from Sorgenfri, for finer-quality *smørrebrød* in a wood-beamed nautical setting (meat and fish sandwiches plus herring specialties, Mon-Sat 11:00-17:00, closed Sun, Brolæggerstræde 12, tel. 33 13 07 08).

Another option is **$$ Domhusets Smørrebrød** (Mon-Fri 7:00-15:00, closed Sat-Sun, off the City Hall end of the Strøget at Kattesundet 18, tel. 33 15 98 98).

The *Pølse*

The famous Danish hot dog, sold in *pølsevogne* (sausage wagons) throughout the country, is another typically Danish institution

that has resisted the onslaught of our global, prepackaged, fast-food culture. Study the photo menu for variations. These are fast, cheap, tasty, and, like their American cousins, almost worthless nutritionally. Even so, what the locals call the "dead man's finger" is the dog Danish kids love to bite.

There's more to getting a *pølse* than simply ordering a "hot dog" (which in Copenhagen simply means a sausage with a bun on the side, generally the worst bread possible). The best is a *ristet* (or grilled) hot dog *med det hele* (with the works). Employ these other handy phrases: *rød* (red, the basic boiled weenie), *medister* (spicy, better quality), *knæk* (short, stubby, tastier than *rød*), *brød* (a bun, usually smaller than the sausage), *svøb* ("swaddled" in bacon), *Fransk* (French style, buried in a long skinny hole in the bun with sauce). *Sennep* is mustard and *ristet løg* are crispy, fried onions. Wash everything down with a *sodavand* (soda pop).

By hanging around a *pølsevogn,* you can study this institution. Denmark's "cold feet cafés" are a form of social care: People who have difficulty finding jobs are licensed to run these wiener-mobiles. As they gain seniority, they are promoted to work at more central locations. Danes like to gather here for munchies and *pølsesnak*—the local slang for empty chatter (literally, "sausage talk"). And traditionally, after getting drunk, guys stop here for a hot dog and chocolate milk on the way home—that's why the stands stay open until the wee hours.

Picnics

Throughout Copenhagen, small delis *(viktualiehandler)* sell fresh bread, tasty pastries, juice, milk, cheese, and yogurt (drinkable, in tall liter boxes). Two of the largest supermarket chains are **Irma** (in the glassy DI—Danish Industry—building on Vesterbrogade next to Tivoli) and **Super Brugsen. Netto** is a cut-rate outfit with the cheapest prices and a good bakery section (located on Rådhuspladsen at Vestergade). And, of course, there's the ever-present **7-Eleven** chain, with branches seemingly on every corner; while you'll pay a bit more here, there's a reason they're called "convenience" stores—and they also serve pastries and hot dogs.

Dine with the Danes

For a unique experience and a great opportunity to meet locals in their homes, consider having this organization arrange a dinner for you with a Danish family. You get a homey two-course meal with lots of conversation. Some effort is made to match your age, interests, and occupations. Book online at least two weeks in advance (450 DKK/person, www.facebook. com/DineWithTheDanes, dinewiththedanes@msn.com). Fill out an online questionnaire, and you'll soon be contacted via Facebook or by email.

Pastry

The golden pretzel sign hanging over the door or windows is the Danes' age-old symbol for a bakery. Danish pastries, called *wienerbrød* ("Vienna bread") in Denmark, are named for the Viennese bakers who brought the art of pastry-making to Denmark, where the Danes say they perfected it. Try these bakeries: **Lagkagehuset** (multiple locations around town; the handiest options include one right in the train station, another nearby inside the Vesterbrogade TI, one along the Strøget at Frederiksborggade 21, and another on Torvegade just across from the Metro station in Christianshavn) and **Nansens** (on corner of Nansensgade and Ahlefeldtsgade, near Ibsens Hotel). **Emmerys,** a trendy, gluten-free, Starbucks-like organic bakery and café, has more than 20 branches around Copenhagen, and sells good pastries and sandwiches. For a genteel bit of high-class 1870s Copenhagen, pay a lot for a coffee and a fresh Danish at **Konditori La Glace,** just off the Strøget at Skoubogade 3.

RESTAURANTS

I've listed restaurants in four areas: the downtown core, the funky Christianshavn neighborhood across the harbor, near Nørreport, and in the trendy Meatpacking District behind the main train station.

Downtown Core

$$$$ Det Lille Apotek ("The Little Pharmacy") is a candlelit place with seating spread among its four themed "parlours." It's been popular with locals for 200 years, and today it's a hit with tourists, serving open-face sandwiches at lunchtime and traditional dinners in the evening (nightly from 17:30, just off the Strøget, between Frue Church and Round Tower at Store Kannikestræde 15, tel. 33 12 56 06).

$$ Riz-Raz Steaks & Veggies has two locations in Copenhagen: around the corner from the canal boat rides at Kompagnistræde 20 (tel. 33 15 05 75) and across from Det Lille Apotek at Store Kannikestræde 19 (tel. 33 32 33 45). At both places, you'll find a combination of burgers and meat dishes as well as vegetarian, including an all-you-can-eat Middle Eastern/Mediterranean/vegetarian buffet lunch for 90 DKK (great falafel, daily 11:30-16:00) and a bigger dinner buffet for 100 DKK (16:00-24:00). Use lots of plates and return to the buffet as many times as you like.

$$$ **Tight** resembles a trendy gastropub, serving an eclectic international array of food and drink (Canadian, Aussie, French, and burgers, with Danish microbrews) in a split-level maze of hip rooms that mix old timbers and brick with bright colors (daily 17:00-22:00, just off the Strøget at Hyskenstræde 10, tel. 33 11 09 00).

$$$$ **Café Norden,** very Danish with modern "world cuisine," seasonal menus, good light meals, and fine pastries, is a big, venerable institution overlooking Amagertorv by the heron fountain. It's family-friendly, with good seats outside on the square, in the busy ground-floor interior, or with more space and better views upstairs (great people-watching from the window seats). Order at the bar—it's the same price upstairs or down (huge splittable portions, daily 9:00-24:00, Østergade 61, tel. 33 11 77 91).

$$$ **Royal Smushi Café** is a hit with dainty people who like the idea of small, gourmet, open-face sandwiches served on Royal Copenhagen porcelain. You can sit in their modern chandeliered interior or the quiet courtyard (daily 10:00-18:00, next to Royal Copenhagen porcelain store at Amagertorv 6, tel. 33 12 11 22).

$$ **Holberg No. 19,** a cozy Argentinian-run café with classic ambience, sits just a block off the tourist crush of the Nyhavn canal. With a loose and friendly vibe, it offers more personality and lower prices than the tourist traps along Nyhavn (no real kitchen but reasonably priced salads and sandwiches—some with an international twist, quiche, selection of wines and beers, order at the bar, Mon-Fri 8:00-22:00, Sat 10:00-20:00, Sun 10:00-18:00, Holberg 19, tel. 33 14 01 90).

$$$ **Almanak,** on the waterfront promenade near the entrance to Nyhavn, dishes artfully prepared (and tasty) open-face sandwiches and main courses in a cool and sleek restaurant and on its outdoor terrace facing the Inner Harbor. Look for the long green building on the promenade with a big sign on the roof that reads *The Standard* (Tue-Sun 12:00-22:00, closed Mon, Havnegade 44, tel. 72 14 88 08).

$$$ **Københavner Caféen,** cozy and old-fashioned, feels like a ship captain's dining room. The staff is enthusiastically traditional, serving local dishes and elegant open-face sandwiches for a good value. Lunch specials (80-100 DKK) are served until 17:00, when

the more expensive dinner menu kicks in (daily, kitchen closes at 22:00, at Badstuestræde 10, tel. 33 32 80 81).

$$$ The Ricemarket, an unpretentious Asian fusion bistro, is buried in a modern cellar between the Strøget and Rosenborg Castle. It's a casual, more affordable side-eatery of a popular local restaurant, and offers a flavorful break from Danish food (seven-dish family-style meal for 285 DKK, daily 12:00-22:00, Hausergade 38 near Kultorvet, tel. 35 35 75 30).

$$ Illum and **Magasin du Nord** department stores serve cheery, reasonable meals in their cafeterias. At Illum, eat outside at tables along the Strøget, or head to the elegant glass-domed top floor (Østergade 52). Magasin du Nord (Kongens Nytorv 13) also has a great grocery and deli in the basement.

Also try **Café Nytorv** at Nytorv 15 or **Sorgenfri** at Brolæggerstræde 8 (both are described under *"Smørrebrød,"* earlier).

Christianshavn

This neighborhood is so cool, it's worth combining an evening wander with dinner. It's a 10-minute walk across the bridge from the old center, or a 3-minute ride on the Metro. Choose one of my listings (for locations, see the Christianshavn map, next page), or simply wander the blocks between Christianshavns Torv, the main square, and the Christianshavn Canal—you'll find a number of lively neighborhood pubs and cafés.

$$$$ Ravelinen Restaurant, on a tiny island on the big road 100 yards south of Christianshavn, serves traditional Danish food to happy local crowds. Dine indoors or on the lovely lakeside terrace (which is tented and heated, so it's comfortable even on blustery evenings). This is like Tivoli without the kitsch and tourists. They offer a shareable "Cold Table" meal for 280 DKK at lunch only (mid-April-late Dec daily 11:30-21:00, closed off-season, Torvegade 79, tel. 32 96 20 45).

$ Lagkagehuset is everybody's favorite bakery in Christianshavn. With a big selection of pastries, sandwiches, excellent fresh-baked bread, and award-winning strawberry tarts, it's a great place for breakfast or picnic fixings (takeout coffee, daily 6:00-19:00, Torvegade 45). For other locations closer to the town center, see page 88.

Ethnic Strip on Christianshavn's Main Drag: Torvegade, which is within a few minutes' walk of the Christianshavn Metro station, is lined with appealing and inexpensive ethnic eateries, including Italian, cheap kebabs, Thai, Chinese, and more. **$$ Spicy Kitchen** serves cheap and good Indian food—tight and cozy, it's a hit with locals (daily 17:00-23:00, Torvegade 56).

In Christiania: $$$$ Spiseloppen ("The Flea Eats") is a wonderfully classy place in Christiania. It serves great 140-DKK

Christianshavn

To Nyhavn

To Opera House & ⊞

CHRISTIANS-BORG PALACE

Netto

HAVNEGADE

Canal

PRINSESSEGADE

REFSHALEVEJ

BØRSGADE

BØRSEN

KNIPPELS BRIDGE

STRANDGADE

TORVEGADE

OVERGADEN NEDEN VANDET

OVERGADEN OVEN VANDET

BÅDSMANDSSTR.

SLOTSHOLMEN

BRYGGE

ROYAL LIBRARY

CHRISTIANS- ⊞

⊞

Inner Harbor

CTC

To Train Station

CHRISTIANS CHURCH

WILDERSGADE

CTC

Christians-havn

Ⓜ Christianshavns Torv

SKT. ANNÆ GADE

● ❹

CHRISTIANIA

OUR SAVIOR'S CHURCH

CHRISTIANSHAVN

❷

❸

PRINSESSEGADE

AMAGERGADE

DRONNINGENSGADE

CHRISTIANSHAVNS VOLDGADE

Stadsgraven (former moat)

LANGEBROGADE

● ❶

PATH

AMAGER BLVD.

To Rådhuspladsen

MEDIEVAL RAMPARTS

400 Meters

400 Yards

To Airport

Ⓝ

❶ Ravelinen Restaurant
❷ Lagkagehuset Bakery
❸ Spicy Kitchen
❹ Spiseloppen Restaurant

COPENHAGEN

vegetarian meals and 185-250-DKK meaty ones by candlelight. It's gourmet anarchy—a good fit for Christiania, the free city/squatter town (Tue-Sun 17:00-22:00, kitchen closes at 21:00, closed Mon, reservations often necessary Fri-Sat; 3 blocks behind spiral spire of Our Savior's Church, on top floor of old brick warehouse, turn right just inside Christiania's main gate, enter the wildly empty warehouse, and climb the graffiti-riddled stairs; tel. 32 57 95 58, http://spiseloppen.dk). Other, less-expensive Christiania eateries are listed on page 90.

Near Nørreport

$$$ TorvehallerneKBH is in a pair of modern, glassy market halls right on Israel Plads. Survey both halls and the stalls on the square before settling in. In addition to produce, fish, and meat stalls, it has several inviting food counters where you can sit to eat a meal, or grab something to go. I can't think of a more enjoyable place in Copenhagen to browse for a meal than this upscale food court (pricey but fun, with quality food; Mon-Thu 10:00-19:00, Fri until 20:00, Sat until 18:00, Sun 11:00-17:00, some places closed Mon; Frederiksborggade 21).

$$-$$$ Brdr. Price Restaurant—an elegant, highly re-garded bistro serving creative Danish and international meals just across from Rosenborg Castle—is good for a dressy splurge in their

A Culinary Phe-noma-non

Foodies visiting Denmark probably already know that Copenhagen is home to one of the planet's top-rated restaurants. *Restaurant* magazine named Noma the "Best Restaurant in the World" for several years, making it *the* reservation to get in the foodie universe. Chef René Redzepi is a pioneer in the burgeoning "New Nordic" school of cooking, which combines modern nouvelle cuisine and molecular gastronomy techniques with locally sourced (and, in some cases, foraged) ingredients from Denmark and other Nordic lands. So, while they use sophisticated cooking methods, they replace the predictable French and Mediterranean ingredients with Nordic ones. The restaurant's name comes from the phrase *nordisk mad* (Nordic food). Noma closed for several years so it may have lost its official ranking—but it reopened with new energy. The seasonal menu focuses on seafood in winter; vegetables in early summer to early fall; and game and forest fare (like berries, mushrooms, nuts, and wild plants) from fall to January.

But Noma, northeast of the Opera House at Refshalevej 96, is not cheap. The menu runs 2,250 DKK; accompanying wines add 1,100 DKK to the bill (there is a student package for 1,000 DKK). A couple going for the whole shebang is looking at spending more than $1,000. And even if you're willing to take the plunge, you have to plan ahead—around three months in advance. Check their website (www.noma.dk) for the latest procedure; you can also put your name on their waiting list.

If you can't commit that far out (or don't want to spend that much), many of the top restaurants in Copenhagen (including Kødbyens Fiskebar, listed on page 93) are run by former chefs from Noma—giving you at least a taste of culinary greatness.

downstairs restaurant, or for classy lighter meals in their upstairs bistro (daily 12:00-22:00, Rosenborggade 15, tel. 38 41 10 20, www.brdr-price.dk).

$$$ Kalaset, in a funky daylight basement with mismatched furniture, bubbles with a youthful energy and is a local favorite. The creative, internationally inspired menu is constantly evolving, and the decent portions are prepared "the way our grandmothers taught us" (daily specials, outdoor seating available, daily 10:00-late, Vendersgade 16, kitty-corner from the recommended Ibsens Hotel, tel. 33 33 00 35).

$$ Halifax, part of a small local chain, serves up "build-your-own" burgers, where you select a patty, a side dish, and a dipping sauce for your fries (Mon-Sat 11:30-22:00, Sun until 21:00, Frederiksborggade 35, tel. 33 32 77 11). They have another location just off the Strøget (at Larsbjørnsstræde 9).

Meatpacking District (Kødbyen)

Literally "Meat Town," Kødbyen is an old warehouse zone huddled up against the train tracks behind the main station. Danes raise about 25 million pigs a year (five per person), so there's long been lots of "meatpacking." Today, much of the meatpacking action is diners chowing down.

There are three color-coded sectors in the district—brown, gray, and white—and each one is a cluster of old industrial buildings. At the far end is the white zone (Den Hvide Kødby), which has been overtaken by some of the city's most trendy and enjoyable eateries, which mingle with the surviving offices and warehouses of the local meatpacking industry. All of the places I list here are within a few steps of each other (except for the Mother pizzeria, a block away).

The curb appeal of this area is zilch (it looks like, well, a meatpacking district), but inside, these restaurants are bursting with life, creativity, and flavor. While youthful and trendy, this scene is also very accessible. Most of these eateries are in buildings with old white tile; this, combined with the considerable popularity of this area, can make the dining rooms quite loud. These places can fill up, especially on weekend evenings, when it's smart to reserve ahead.

It's a short stroll from the station: If you go south on the bridge called Tietgens Bro, which crosses the tracks just south of the station, and carry on for about 10 minutes, you'll run right into the area. Those sleeping in the hotels behind the station just stroll five minutes south. Or you can ride the S-tog to the Dybbølsbro stop.

$$$$ Kødbyens Fiskebar ("Fish Bar") is one of the first and still the most acclaimed restaurant in the Meatpacking District. Focusing on small, thoughtfully composed plates of modern Nordic seafood, the Fiskebar has a stripped-down white interior with a big fish tank and a long cocktail bar surrounded by smaller tables. It's extremely popular (reservations are essential), and feels a bit too trendy for its own good. While the prices are high, so is the quality; diners are paying for a taste of the "New Nordic" style of cooking that's so in vogue here (in summer daily from 17:30, in winter generally closed Sat-Sun; Flæsketorvet 100, tel. 32 15 56 56, http://fiskebaren.dk).

$$$$ BioMio, in the old Bosch building, serves rustic Danish, vegan, and vegetarian dishes, plus meat and fish. It's 100 percent organic, and the young boss, Rune, actually serves diners (daily 12:00-22:00, Halmtorvet 19, tel. 33 31 20 00, http://biomio.dk).

$$$ Paté Paté, next door to BioMio, is a tight, rollicking bistro in a former pâté factory. While a wine bar at heart—with a good selection of wines by the glass—it has a fun and accessible menu of creative modern dishes and a cozy atmosphere rare in the Meatpacking District. Ideally diners choose about three dishes per person and share (Mon-Sat from 17:30, closed Sun, Slagterboderne 1, tel. 39 69 55 57, www.patepate.dk).

$$$ Pizzeria Mother is named for the way the sourdough for their crust must be "fed" and cared for to flourish. You can taste that care in the pizza, which has a delicious tangy crust. Out front are comfortable picnic benches, while the interior curls around the busy pizza oven with chefs working globs of dough that will soon be the basis for your pizza (daily 11:00-23:00, a block beyond the other restaurants listed here at Høkerboderne 9, tel. 22 27 58 98).

$$ Nose2Tail Madbodega (*mad* means "food") prides itself on locally sourced, sustainable cooking, using the entire animal for your meal (hence the name). You'll climb down some stairs into an unpretentious white-tiled cellar (Mon-Sat 18:00-24:00, closed Sun, Flæsketorvet 13A, tel. 33 93 50 45, http://nose2tail.dk).

Other Central Neighborhoods to Explore

To find a good restaurant, try simply window-shopping in one of these inviting districts.

Nyhavn's harbor canal is lined with a touristy strip of restaurants set alongside its classic sailboats. Here thriving crowds are served mediocre, overpriced food in a great setting. On any sunny day, if you want steak and fries (130 DKK) and a 65-DKK beer, this can be fun. On Friday and Saturday, the strip becomes the longest bar in the world.

Kompagnistræde is home to a changing cast of great little eateries. Running parallel to the Strøget, this street has fewer tourists and lower rent, and encourages places to compete creatively for the patronage of local diners.

Gråbrødretorv ("Grey Friars' Square") is perhaps the most popular square in the old center for a meal. It's like a food court, especially in good weather, with a variety of international dining options outside and in. The French-inspired steakhouse **$$$$ Bøf & Ost** is pricey but good, serving elegant beef and veal dishes—even pigeon—and a wide selection of French and Danish cheeses (daily 11:00-22:00). Across the square, **$$$ Huks Fluks** enjoys a sunny location, dishing up southern European small plates, main courses, and shareable portions, and specializes in ham (daily 11:00-22:00).

Istedgade and the surrounding streets behind the train station (just above the Meatpacking District) are home to an assortment of inexpensive ethnic restaurants. You will find numerous places serving kebabs, pizza, Chinese, and Thai (including tasty meals at **$$ Poonchai Thai Restaurant**—across the street from Hotel Nebo at Istedgade 1). The area can be a bit seedy, especially right behind the station, but walk a few blocks away to take your pick of inexpensive, ethnic eateries frequented by locals.

Copenhagen Connections

BY PUBLIC TRANSPORTATION

From Copenhagen by Train to: Hillerød/Frederiksborg Castle (6/hour, 40 minutes on S-tog), **Roskilde** (7/hour, 30 minutes), **Humlebæk/Louisiana Art Museum** (3/hour, 30 minutes), **Helsingør** (3/hour, 45 minutes), **Odense** (3/hour, 1.5 hours), **Ærøskøbing** (2/hour Mon-Sat, hourly on Sun, 2.5 hours to Svendborg with a transfer in Odense, then 1.25-hour ferry crossing to Ærøskøbing—see page 142 for info on ferry), **Billund/Legoland** (2/hour, 2-2.5 hours to Vejle, then bus to Billund—see page 169), allow 3.5 hours total), **Aarhus** (2/hour, 3 hours), **Malmö** (3-5/hour, 40 minutes), **Stockholm** (almost hourly, 5-6 hours on high-speed train, some with a transfer at Malmö or Lund, reservation required; overnight service available but requires a change in Hässleholm or Lund), **Växjö** (hourly, 2.5 hours), **Kalmar** (hourly, 3.5-4 hours, most direct, some transfer in Alvesta), **Oslo** (4/day, 8-9 hours, transfer at Göteborg; also overnight boat option, see next page), **Hamburg** (3/day direct, 5 hours, 2 more with transfer, reservation required in summer); from Hamburg, connections run to **Berlin** (2 more hours, railway also operates 2 direct Copenhagen-Berlin buses, 7.5 hours), **Amsterdam** (5.5 more hours, change at Osnabrück), and **Frankfurt/Rhine** (hourly, 3.5 more hours). Train info tel. 70 13 14 15 (for English, press 1 for general information and tickets, and 2 for international trains). DSB (or Danske Statsbaner) is Denmark's national railway, www.rejseplanen.dk.

By Bus: Taking the bus to **Stockholm** is cheaper but more time-consuming than taking the train (1/day, 9.5 hours, longer for overnight trips, www.swebus.se).

BY CRUISE SHIP

More than half a million people visit Copenhagen via cruise ship each year. For a wealth of online information for cruise-ship pas-

sengers, see www.cruisecopenhagen. com. For more in-depth cruising information, pick up my *Rick Steves Scandinavian & Northern European Cruise Ports* guidebook.

Most cruise ships use one of two terminals, both north of downtown—**Oceankaj**, the farther port;

and **Langelinie,** about a mile closer to downtown. Another, smaller cruise port, **Nordre Toldbod,** is just south of *The Little Mermaid* and within easy walking distance (25 minutes) of Nyhavn. **Frihavnen** ("Freeport"), about three miles north of downtown, is used only on rare occasions. There are no ATMs at the piers. There is a tiny TI at Oceankaj, but none at other cruise ports.

Getting Downtown: Many cruise lines run **shuttle buses** between the port and town; if they're available, consider a shuttle for the convenience and time saved.

Langelinie is about a 10- to 15-minute walk from a **train** station on Copenhagen's S-tog suburban rail line, where you can take a train headed downtown. From Langelinie, you can also **walk** or take a **hop-on, hop-off** bus into town. There's also a hop-on, hop-off bus connection at Oceankaj. Taking a **taxi** to downtown is easy but expensive from any port (about 275 DKK from Oceankaj, 175 DKK from Langelinie).

Public buses are possible but a hassle. From Oceankaj, bus #27 connects to bus #26 at the Østerport train station and into the city center. From Langelinie, bus #26 runs directly to various points in downtown Copenhagen. See "Getting Around Copenhagen" at the beginning of the chapter for more bus information.

BY OVERNIGHT BOAT TO OSLO

Luxurious DFDS Seaways cruise ships leave daily from Copenhagen at 16:30 and arrive in Oslo at 9:45 the next day (17-hour sailing). They also depart from Oslo at 16:30 for the return to Copenhagen, allowing you to spend about seven hours in Norway's capital if doing it as a day trip (see page 181 for more info).

Cruise Costs: Cabins vary dramatically in price depending on the day and season (most expensive on weekends and late June-mid-Aug; cheapest on weekdays and Oct-April). For example, a bed in a four-berth "Seaways" shoehorn economy cabin starts at 325 DKK/person one-way for four people traveling together (370 DKK/person with a window); a luxurious double "Commodore class" cabin higher on the ship starts at 850 DKK/person one-way (and includes a TV, minibar, and breakfast buffet).

Onboard Services: DFDS Seaways operates two ships on this route—the MS *Pearl Seaways* and the MS *Crown Seaways.* Both offer all the cruise-ship luxuries: big buffets for breakfast and dinner, gourmet restaurants, bars, a kids' playroom, pool, hot tub, sauna, casino, nightclubs, and tax-free shopping. All shops and restaurants accept credit cards as well as euros, dollars, and Danish, Swedish, and Norwegian currency.

Reservations: Reservations are smart in summer and on weekends. Advance bookings get the best prices. Book online or call DFDS Seaway's Danish office (Mon-Fri 9:00-16:30, closed

Sat-Sun, tel. 33 42 30 10, www.dfdsseaways.us) or visit the **DSB Rejsebureau** at the main train station.

Port Details: The **Copenhagen Ferry Terminal** (a.k.a. DFDS Terminalen) is a short walk north of *The Little Mermaid*. The terminal is open daily 9:00-17:00 (luggage lockers available). Boarding is from 15:15 to 16:15.

Getting Downtown: Shuttle buses marked either *Axel Torv* or *Nørreport* meet arriving ships from Oslo (22 DKK—buy on DFDS website in advance, tickets not sold on buses). The Axel Torv bus drops you at Axel Torv—near Tivoli, the main train station, recommended hotels, and the start of my "Copenhagen City Walk." Buses marked *Nørreport* drop you at Øster Voldgade 2C—next to Nørreport Station (near recommended hotels). From here you can ride the Metro one stop to Kongens Nytorv at Nyhavn (and more recommended hotels).

To reach the ferry terminal *from* the city, catch the shuttle bus marked *DFDS Terminal* near Nørreport Station at Øster Voldgade 2C (22 DKK—buy on DFDS website in advance, tickets not sold on buses, daily at 14:45, 15:15, and 15:45). Or take the S-tog from downtown in the direction of Hellerup or Hillerød to the Nordhavn Station. Exit the station, cross under the tracks, and hike toward the water; you'll see the ship on your right.

NEAR COPENHAGEN

Roskilde • Frederiksborg Castle • Louisiana Art Museum • Kronborg Castle

Copenhagen's the star, but there are several worthwhile sights nearby on its island (called Zealand), and the public transportation system makes side-tripping a joy. Visit Roskilde's great Viking ships and royal cathedral. Tour Frederiksborg, Denmark's most spectacular castle, and slide along the cutting edge at Louisiana Art Museum—a superb collection with a coastal setting as striking as its art. At Helsingør, do the dungeons of Kronborg Castle before heading on to Sweden.

PLANNING YOUR TIME

The area's essential sights are Roskilde's cathedral (with the tombs of Danish royalty) and its Viking ships, along with Frederiksborg Castle. Each destination takes a half-day, and each one is an easy commute from Copenhagen in different directions (30- or 40-minute train ride, then a 20-minute walk or short bus ride). If you're really fast and well-organized, you could visit both Roskilde and Frederiksborg with public transportation in a day (see "The Zealand Blitz," later).

If you're choosing between castles, Frederiksborg is the beautiful showpiece with the opulent interior, and Kronborg—darker and danker—is more typical of the way most castles really were. Both are dramatic from the outside, but Kronborg—overlooking the raging sea channel to Sweden—has a more scenic setting. Castle collectors can hit both in a day (see the two-castle day plan, later).

Drivers can visit these sights on the way into or out of Copenhagen. By train, do day trips from Copenhagen, then sleep while traveling to and from Copenhagen to Oslo (by boat, or by train

Near Copenhagen

Kattegat

To Oslo

To Göteborg, Oslo & Kalmar

To Stockholm, Växjö & Kalmar

E-6

E-4

Gilleleje

KRONBORG CASTLE

Esrum Sø

Helsingborg

Helsingør

6

205

Arresø

Hundested

SWEDEN

FREDENSBORG PALACE

LOUISIANA ART MUSEUM

Humlebæk

To Rørvig

FREDERIKSBORG CASTLE

Frederikssund

Hillerød

201

Rungsted

Øresund

Ise-fjord

152

E-47

BAKKEN

E-6

OPEN-AIR FOLK MUSEUM

Z E A L A N D

Ballerup

E-47

Klampenborg

See detail maps in this area

Copenhagen

Saltholm

Lund

Roskilde

Roskildefjord

21

Høje Tåstrup

TUNNEL

Malmö

23

Lejre

Øm

14

E-20

Amager

Kastrup

ØRESUND

BRIDGE

Limhamn

To Holbæk

E-47

D E N M A R K

Dragør

To Ystad

To Ringsted, Odense, Ærø, Aarhus & Germany

Køge Bugt

10 Kilometers

10 Miles

NEAR COPENHAGEN

via Malmö, Sweden) or Stockholm (by train via Malmö). Consider getting a Copenhagen Card (see page 16), which covers your transportation to all of the destinations in this chapter, as well as admission to Roskilde Cathedral, Frederiksborg Castle, Kronborg Castle, and Louisiana Art Museum (but not the Roskilde Viking Ship Museum). Each train ride is just long enough for a relaxed picnic.

The Zealand Blitz—Roskilde Cathedral, Viking Ship Museum, and Frederiksborg Castle in a Day: If you have limited time and are well-organized, you can see the highlights of Zealand in one exciting day. Here's the plan (all times are rough, train connections take about 30-40 minutes, trains depart about every 10 minutes): Leave Copenhagen by train at 8:00, arrive in Roskilde at 8:30, wander through the town and be at the cathedral when it opens at 9:00 (later on Sun and in off-season). At 10:00, after an hour in the cathedral, stroll down to the harborfront to tour the Viking Ship Museum. They can call a taxi for you to return to the station for a 13:00 train back to Copenhagen. Buy a picnic lunch at Roskilde's station and munch your lunch on the train. Catch a 14:00 train from Copenhagen to Hillerød; there you'll catch the bus to Frederiksborg Castle, arriving at 15:00. This gives you two hours to enjoy the castle before it closes at 17:00 (earlier in off-season). Browse through Hillerød before catching a train at 18:00 to return to Copenhagen. You'll be back at your hotel by 19:00.

A Two-Castle Day (plus Louisiana) by Public Transportation: You can see both Frederiksborg and Kronborg castles, plus Louisiana Art Museum, in one busy day. (This works best Tue-Fri, when Louisiana is open until 22:00.) Take the train from Copenhagen to Hillerød (leaving about 9:00), then hop on the awaiting bus to Frederiksborg Castle; you'll hear the 10:00 bells and be the first tourist inside. Linger in the sumptuous interior for a couple of hours, but get back to the station in time for a midday train (about 12:30 or 13:00) to Helsingør, a 15-minute walk from Kronborg Castle. Either munch your picnic lunch on the train, or—if it's a nice day—save it for the ramparts of Kronborg Castle. If you're castled out, skip the interior (saving the ticket price, and more time for Louisiana) and simply enjoy the Kronborg grounds and Øresund views before catching a train south toward Copenhagen. Hop off at Humlebæk for Louisiana.

GETTING AROUND

All of these sights except Roskilde are served by Copenhagen's excellent commuter-train (S-tog) system (covered by Eurail Pass; Copenhagen Card; and "24-hour ticket" and "7-day FlexCard"— both of which include greater Copenhagen; not covered by City Pass, which includes only zones 1-4—see page 20). All of the train connections (including the regional train line to Roskilde, which is covered by the Copenhagen Card) depart from the main train station; but be aware that most lines also stop at other Copenhagen stations, which may be closer to your hotel (for example, the Nørreport Station is near the recommended Ibsens and Jørgensen hotels). Check schedules carefully to avoid needlessly going to the main train station.

At the main train station, S-tog lines do not appear on the overhead schedule screens (which are for longer-distance destinations); simply report to tracks 9-10 to wait for your train (there's a schedule at the head of those tracks).

If renting a car, see "Route Tips for Drivers" at the end of the chapter for more information.

Roskilde

Denmark's roots, both Viking and royal, are on display in Roskilde (ROSS-killa), a pleasant town 18 miles west of Copenhagen. The town was the seat of the bishop and the residence of Danish royalty until 1450, when these shifted to Copenhagen. In its day, Roskilde was the second biggest city in the country. Today the town that introduced Christianity to Denmark in A.D. 980 is much smaller, except for the week of its famous rock/jazz/folk festival—northern Europe's largest—when 100,000 fans pack the place and it becomes one of Denmark's biggest cities again

(early July, www.roskilde-festival.dk). Wednesday and Saturday are flower/flea/produce market days (8:00-14:00).

GETTING THERE

Roskilde is an easy side-trip from Copenhagen by train (7/hour, 30 minutes). Trains headed to Ringsted, Nykøbing, or Lindholm may not stop in Roskilde (which is an intermediate stop you won't see listed on departure boards)—confirm in advance. Returning to Copenhagen, hop on any train in the direction of Østerport or København H.

Orientation to Roskilde

TOURIST INFORMATION

Roskilde's helpful TI is on the main square, next to the cathedral (Mon-Fri 10:00-16:00, Sat until 13:00, closed Sun; Stændertorvet 1, tel. 46 31 65 65, www.visitroskilde.com).

ARRIVAL IN ROSKILDE

There are no lockers at the train station (or nearby), but the TI—about a five-minute walk away—will take your bags for a few hours if you ask nicely. Free WCs are right next door to the TI.

From the train station, consider this circular route: First you'll head to the TI, then the cathedral, and finally down to the Viking Ship Museum on the harborfront. Exit straight out from the station, and walk down to the bottom of the square. Turn left (at the Super Brugsen supermarket) on the pedestrianized shopping street,

Algade (literally "the street for all"). After walking down this main drag about four blocks, you emerge into the main square, Stænder-torvet, with the TI and the cathedral. After visiting the cathedral, you'll head about 10 minutes downhill (through a pleasant park) to the Viking Ship Museum: Facing the cathedral facade, turn left and head down the tree-lined path through the park. When you emerge at the roundabout (avoiding the temptation to eat a "Viking Pizza"), continue straight through it to reach the museum.

If you want to go directly from the station to the Viking Ship Museum, you can ride a bus; see page 106.

Sights in Roskilde

▲▲Roskilde Cathedral

Roskilde's imposing 12th-century, twin-spired cathedral houses the tombs of nearly all of the Danish kings and queens (39 royals in all; pick up the included guidebook as you enter). If you're a fan of Danish royalty or of evolving architectural styles, it's thrilling; even if you're neither, Denmark's "Westminster Abbey" is still interesting. It's a stately, modern-looking old church with great marble work, paintings, wood carvings, and an engaged congregation that makes the place feel very alive (particularly here in largely unchurched Scandinavia). A big museum and welcome center are in the works.

Cost and Hours: 60 DKK, included with Copenhagen Card; April-Sept Mon-Sat 9:00-18:00, Sun 12:30-17:00; Oct-March Tue-Sat 10:00-16:00, Sun from 12:30, closed Mon; often closed for funerals and on Sat-Sun afternoons for baptisms and weddings; free organ concerts offered July-Aug Thu at 20:00; tel. 46 35 16 24, www. roskildedomkirke.dk.

❷ Self-Guided Tour: Begun in the 1170s by Bishop Absalom (and completed in 1280), Roskilde Cathedral was cleared of its side chapels and altars by the Reformation iconoclasts—leaving a blank slate for Danish royals to fill with their tombs. The highlight here is slowly strolling through a half-millennium's worth of royal chapels, representing a veritable textbook's worth of architectural styles.

• *Before entering, walk around the outside of the cathedral.*

Exterior, King's Door, and Tomb of Frederik IX: Notice the big bricks, which date from the 12th century, and how the cathe-

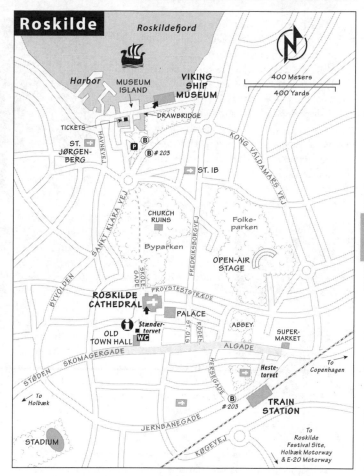

dral is built on the highest ground in town. Face the towering west facade. The main door—called the King's Door—was installed in 2010 and depicts scenes from the ministry of Jesus. This door is used by the congregation only to leave special services; the only people who may enter through this door are members of the royal family.

Find the freestanding brick chapel to the left. This holds the remains of Denmark's last king, Frederik IX (1899-1972), and his wife Ingrid (parents of the current queen, born in 1940). While all of the other monarchs are inside, Frederik—who was an avid sailor in his youth—requested to be buried here, with a view of the harbor.

• *Now go around the right side, buy a ticket, and go inside. First, head to the middle of the nave to look at...*

The King's Door, from Inside: The glittering-gold, highly stylized relief shows the scene after the Resurrection when Jesus breaks bread in the company of some apostles—who until this point had not recognized him (their mouths hang agape at their realization).

Glockenspiel: In the rear of the church, high on the wall, you can see the little glockenspiel that makes a racket at the top of every hour as George kills the dragon and the centuries-old billows wail.

• *Now we'll take a clockwise spin through the interior to see the significant royal burial chapels.*

While this tour is not chronological, neither are the tombs. Continue through the left aisle and into the big chapel housing some of the cathedral's most recent additions (from the late 19th through early 20th centuries).

Glücksburger Chapel: In the corner, the Glücksburger Chapel, with a plain light dome, holds the tomb of Christian IX, nicknamed the "father-in-law of Europe" for how he married his many children into royal families across the Continent. He died in 1906. The three mourning women were sculpted by Edvard Eriksen, who also produced Copenhagen's famed *Little Mermaid* statue (notice the middle woman).

St. Birgitta's Chapel: The next chapel, dedicated to St. Birgitta, will eventually ("Not soon," hope the Danes) have a new tenant: It has been restored to house the tomb of the current queen, Margrethe II, and her husband Henrik. She teamed up with an artist to design her own tomb (there's a model on display). Her body will reside in the stepped area at the bottom, upon which stand three columns representing the far-flung Danish holdings: one made of basalt from the Faroe Islands, another of marble from Greenland, and the third of stone from Denmark proper. Topping the columns are elephants (symbols of Danish royalty) and a semitransparent glass tomb, symbolizing the unpredictability of life and how death, like a seed, is a new beginning.

St. Andrew's Chapel: The next chapel, a modern addition to the church, is dedicated to St. Andrew and has a glittering mosaic over the altar. But pre-Reformation frescoes (1511) peek through the Protestant whitewash. Standing in front of this chapel, look across the nave to see the gorgeous 16th-century Baroque organ.

Christian IV Chapel: The next, larger chapel (up the stairs behind the small wooden organ) dates from the era of Christian IV, the larger-than-life 17th-century king who created modern Denmark. Christian also left his mark on Roskilde Cathedral, building the altarpiece, pulpit, distinctive twin towers...and this chapel. Walk around the stately yet humble tombs, marvel at the painting, and consider the huge personality of the greatest king in Danish history. In here you'll see a fine statue of the king, by Bertel Thorvaldsen; a large 3-D painting with Christian IV wearing his trademark eye patch, after losing his eye in battle; and his rather austere tomb (black with silver trim, surrounded by several others). Great he was...until his many wars impoverished his once-mighty country.

• *Head into the nave and climb up the stairs into the choir area.*

The Nave, Choir, and High Altar: Take in the gorgeous gilded altarpiece and finely carved stalls. The three-winged altarpiece, carved in 1560 in Antwerp, shows scenes from Christ's last week. The fine carvings above the chairs in the choir feature scenes from the Old Testament on one side and the New Testament on the other.

Tomb of Margrethe I: Behind the altar is the ornately decorated tomb of Margrethe I, the Danish queen who added Nor-

way to her holdings by marrying Norwegian King Håkon VI in 1363. Legend holds that buried in a nearby brick pilaster are the supposed remains of Harold (read the Latin: *Haraldus*) Bluetooth, who ruled more than a millennium ago (r. 958-985 or 986), made Roskilde the capital of his realm, and converted his subjects to Christianity.

• *Now explore the apse (the area behind the altar).*

Apse: Go down the stairs, walk over the well-worn tombs of 500-year-old aristocrats who had the money to buy prime tomb space, and go through the little door. Circle around the apse, noticing more fine tombs behind Margrethe's.

• *Hooking back around toward the front, dip into the many more chapels you'll pass, including...*

Frederik V's Chapel: The grand, textbook Neoclassical tomb of Frederik V has white pillars, gold trim, and mourning maidens—representing Norway and Denmark—in ancient Greek gowns. You'll also pass a room housing elaborate, canopied Baroque tombs. Imagine: Each king or queen commissioned a tomb that suited his or her time—so different, yet all so grand.

Christian I's Chapel: The next chapel, with the tomb of

Christian I, has a stone column marking the heights of visiting monarchs such as Prince Charles. The *P* is for the giant Russian czar Peter the Great—clearly the tallest.

• *Leaving the cathedral, turn right and walk downhill for 10 minutes along a peaceful tree-lined lane that will eventually take you to the harbor and the Viking Ship Museum.*

▲▲▲Viking Ship Museum (Vikingeskibsmuseet)

Vik literally means "shallow inlet," and "Vikings" were the people who lived along those inlets. Roskilde—and this award-winning

museum—are strategically located along one such inlet. (They call it a "fjord," but it's surrounded by much flatter terrain than the Norwegian fjords.) Centuries before Europe's Age of Exploration, Viking sailors navigated their sleek, sturdy ships as far away as the Mediterranean, the Black Sea, the Persian Gulf, and the

Americas. This museum displays five different Viking ships, which were discovered in the Roskilde fjord and painstakingly excavated, preserved, and pieced back together beginning in the 1960s. The ships aren't as intact or as evocative as those in Oslo, but this museum does a better job of explaining shipbuilding. The outdoor area (on "Museum Island") continues the experience, with a chance to see modern-day Vikings creating replica ships, chat with an old-time rope maker, and learn more about the excavation. The English descriptions are excellent—it's the kind of museum where you want to read everything.

Cost and Hours: 130 DKK, not covered by Copenhagen Card; daily May-mid-Oct 10:00-17:00, Nov-April until 16:00, tel. 46 30 02 00, www.vikingeskibsmuseet.dk.

Tours: Free 45-minute tours in English run mid-June-Aug daily at 12:00 and 15:00; May-mid-June and Sept Sat-Sun at 12:00; none off-season.

Boat Ride: The museum's workshop has re-created working replicas of all five of the ships on display here, plus others. For an extra 100 DKK, you can go for a fun hour-long sail around Roskilde's fjord in one of these replica Viking vessels (you'll row, set sail, and row again; frequent departures—up to 7/day—in summer, fewer off-season, ask about schedule when you arrive or call ahead).

Eating: Café Knarr serves salads, sandwiches, and "planks" of Viking tapas with ingredients the Vikings knew (decent prices, open daily 10:00-17:00).

Getting There: It's on the harbor at Vindeboder 12. From the train station, catch bus #203 toward Boserup (2/hour, 24 DKK,

7-minute ride). From the cathedral, it's a 10-minute downhill walk. The museum desk can call a taxi (120 DKK) when you want to go back to the station, or take the bus back.

Visiting the Museum: The museum has two parts: the Viking Ship Hall, with the remains of the five ships; and, across the draw-bridge, Museum Island with workshops, replica ships, a café, and more exhibits. There are ticket offices at each location; it's best to start with the Viking Ship Hall.

As you enter the **Viking Ship Hall,** check the board for the day's activities and demonstrations (including shipbuilding, weav-

ing, blacksmithing, and minting). Consider buying the 24-DKK guidebook and request the 14-min-ute English movie shown in the lobby's cinema.

Your visit is a one-way walk. You'll first see the five ships, then go through the preservation exhibit, the kids' zone with a video about the modern voyage of the *Sea Stallion*, and finally the popular shop.

The core of the exhibit is the re-mains of five ships, which were de-liberately sunk a thousand years ago to block an easy channel into this harbor (leaving open only the most challenging approach—virtu-ally impossible for anyone but a local to navigate). The ships, which are named for the place where they were found (Skuldelev), repre-sent an impressively wide range of Viking shipbuilding technology. *Skuldelev 1* is a big, sail-powered ocean-going trade ship made in Norway, with a crew of six to eight men and room for lots of cargo; it's like the ship Leif Eriksson took to America 1,000 years ago. *Skuldelev 2* is a 100-foot-long, 60-oar longship made in the Viking city of Dublin; loaded with 65 or 70 bloodthirsty warriors, it struck fear into the hearts of foes. It's similar to the ones depicted in the Bayeux Tapestry in Normandy, France. *Skuldelev 3* is a modest coastal trader that stayed closer to home (wind-powered with oar backup, similar to #1 in design and also made in Norway). *Skul-delev 5* is a smaller longship—carrying about 30 warriors, it's the little sibling of #2. And *Skuldelev 6* is a small fishing vessel—a row/sail hybrid that was used for whaling and hunting seals. (There's no #4 because they originally thought #2 was two different ships...and the original names stuck.)

Exhibits in the surrounding rooms show the 25-year process of excavating and preserving the ships, explain a step-by-step at-tack and defense of the harbor, and give you a chance to climb aboard a couple of replica ships for a fun photo op. You'll also see displays describing the re-creation of the *Sea Stallion*, a replica of the big longship (#2) constructed by modern shipbuilders using ancient techniques. A crew of 65 rowed this ship to Dublin in 2007 and then back to Roskilde in the summer of 2008. You can watch a 20-minute film of their odyssey.

Leaving the hall, cross the drawbridge to **Museum Island.** Replicas of all five ships—and others—bob in the harbor; you can

actually climb on board the largest, the *Sea Stallion* (if in port). At the boatyard, watch modern craftsmen re-create millennium-old ships using the original methods and materials. Poke into the various workshops, with exhibits on tools and methods. The little square called *Tunet* ("Gathering Place") is ringed by traditional craft shops—basket maker, rope maker, blacksmith, wood carver—which are sometimes staffed by workers doing demonstrations. In the archaeological workshop, exhibits explain how they excavated and preserved the precious timbers of those five ships.

Frederiksborg Castle

Frederiksborg Castle, rated ▲▲, sits on an island in the middle of a lake in the cute town of Hillerød.
This grandest castle in Scandinavia is often called the "Danish Versailles." Built from 1602 to 1620, Frederiksborg was the castle of Denmark's King Christian IV. Much of it was reconstructed after an 1859 fire, with the normal Victorian over-the-top flair, by the brewer J. C. Jacobsen and his Carlsberg Foundation.

You'll still enjoy some of the magnificent spaces of the castle's heyday: the breathtaking grounds and courtyards, the sumptuous chapel, and the regalia-laden Great Hall. But most of the place was turned into a fine museum in 1878. Today it's the Museum of National History, taking you on a chronological walk through the story of Denmark from 1500 until now (the third/top floor covers modern times). The countless musty paintings are a fascinating scrapbook of Danish history—it's a veritable national portrait gallery, with images of great Danes from each historical period of the last half-millennium.

A fine path leads around the lake, with ever-changing views of the castle. The traffic-free center of Hillerød is also worth a wander.

Tourist Information: Hillerød's TI, with information on the entire North Zealand region, is in the freestanding white house next to the castle parking lot (to the left as you face the main castle gate; July-mid-Sept Mon-Sat 10:00-16:00, shorter hours in June, closed mid-Sept-May, Frederiksværksgade 2A, tel. 49 21 13 33, www.visitnordsjaelland.com). Because the TI is inside an art gallery, if the TI is "closed" while the gallery is open, you can still slip inside and pick up a town map and brochures.

GETTING THERE

By Train: From Copenhagen, take the S-tog to Hillerød (line E, 6/hour, 40 minutes, bikes go free on S-tog trains).

From the Hillerød station, you can enjoy a pleasant 20-minute walk to the castle, or catch **bus** #301 or #302 (free with S-tog ticket or Copenhagen Card, buses are to the right as you exit station, ride three stops to Frederiksborg Slot bus stop; as buses go in two directions from here, confirm direction with driver).

If **walking,** just follow the signs to the castle. Bear left down the busy road (Jernbanegade) until the first big intersection, where you'll turn right. After a couple of blocks, where the road curves to the left, keep going straight; from here, bear left and downhill to the pleasant square Torvet, with great views of the castle and a café pavilion. At this square, turn left and walk through the pedestrianized shopping zone directly to the castle gate.

Linking to Other Sights: If continuing directly to Helsingør (with Kronborg Castle), hop on the regional train (departs from track 16 at Hillerød station, Mon-Fri 2/hour, Sat-Sun 1/hour, 30 minutes). From Helsingør, it's a quick trip on the train to the town of Humlebæk (where you'll find Louisiana Art Museum).

By Car: Drivers will find easy parking at the castle (for driving directions, see "Route Tips for Drivers" at the end of this chapter).

ORIENTATION TO FREDERIKSBORG CASTLE

Cost and Hours: 75 DKK, included with Copenhagen Card; daily April-Oct 10:00-17:00, Nov-March 11:00-15:00.

Tours: Take advantage of the free, informative, one-hour iPod audioguide; ask for it when you buy your ticket—it's also available as a smartphone app. My self-guided tour zooms in on the highlights, but the audioguide is more extensive. There are also posted explanations and/or borrowable English descriptions in many rooms. Daily English-language, 30-minute highlights tours leave at 14:00 (included in admission).

Information: Tel. 48 26 04 39, www.dnm.dk.

Eating: You can picnic in the castle's moat park or enjoy the **$$-$$$ Spisestedet Leonora** at the moat's edge (*smør-rebrød*, sandwiches, salads, hot dishes, open daily 10:00-17:00, slow service). Or, better, walk into the town center near the bus stop.

● SELF-GUIDED TOUR

The castle's included audio tour is excellent, and you can almost follow it in real time for a one-hour blitz of the palace's highlights. Use my self-guided tour to supplement the audioguide.

The Castle Approach

From the entrance of the castle complex, it's an appropriately regal approach to the king's residence. You can almost hear the clopping of royal hooves as you walk over the moat and through the first island (which housed the stables and small businesses needed to support a royal residence). Then walk down the winding (and therefore easy-to-defend) lane to the second island, which was home to the domestic and foreign ministries. Finally, cross over the last moat to the main palace, where the king lived.

Fountain of Neptune Courtyard

Survey the castle exterior from the Fountain of Neptune. Christian IV imported Dutch architects to create this "Christian IV style," which you'll see all over Copenhagen. The brickwork and sandstone are products of the local clay and sandy soil. The building, with its horizontal lines, triangles, and squares, is generally in Renaissance style, but notice how this is interrupted by a few token Gothic elements on the church's facade. Some say this

homey touch was to let the villagers know the king was "one of them."

• *Step over the last moat, through the ornate gate, and into the castle grounds. Go in the door in the middle of the courtyard to buy your ticket, pick up your free audioguide, and put your bag in a locker (mandatory). Pick up a free floor plan; room numbers will help orient you on this tour. You'll enter the Knights' Parlor, also called The Rose, a long room decorated as it was during the palace's peak of power. Go up the stairs on the left side of this hall to the...*

Royal Chapel

Christian IV wanted to have the grandest royal chapel in Europe. For 200 years the coronation place of Danish kings, this chapel is still used for royal weddings (and is extremely popular for commoner weddings—book long in advance). The chapel is nearly all original, dating back to 1620. As you walk around the upper level, notice the graffiti scratched on the windowpanes by the diamond rings of royal kids visiting for the summer back in the 1600s. Most of the coats of arms show off noble lineage—with a few exceptions we'll get to soon. At the far end of the chapel, the wooden organ is from 1620, with its original hand-powered bellows. (Hymns play on the old carillon at the top of each hour.)

Scan the hundreds of coats of arms lining the walls. These belong to people who have received royal orders from the Danish crown (similar to Britain's knighthoods).

While most are obscure princesses and dukes, a few interesting (and more familiar) names show up just past the organ. In the first window bay after the organ, look for the distinctive red, blue, black, and green shield of South Africa—marking Nelson Mandela's coat of arms. (Notice he was awarded the highly prestigious Order of the Elephant, usually reserved for royalty.) Around the side of the same column (facing the chapel interior), find the coats of arms for Dwight D. Eisenhower (with the blue anvil and the motto "Peace through understanding"), Winston Churchill (who already came from a noble line), and Field Marshal Bernard "Monty" Montgomery. Around the far side of this column is the coat of arms for France's wartime leader, Charles de Gaulle.

Leaving the chapel, you step into the king's private oratory, with evocative Neo-Romantic paintings (restored after a fire) from the mid-19th century.

• *You'll emerge from the chapel into the museum collection. But before seeing that, pay a visit to the Audience Room: Go through the door in the left corner marked Audienssalen, and proceed through the little room to the long passageway (easy to miss).*

Audience Room

Here, where formal meetings took place, a grand painting shows the king as a Roman emperor firmly in command (with his two sons prominent for extra political stability). This family is flanked by Christian IV (on the left) and Frederik III (on the right). Christian's military victories line the walls, and the four great continents—Europe, North America, Asia, and Africa—circle the false cupola (notice it's just an attic). Look for the odd trapdoor in one corner with a plush chair on it. This was where they could majestically lower the king to the exit.

• *Now go back to the museum section, and proceed through the numbered rooms.*

Museum Collection

Spanning three floors and five centuries, this exhaustive collection juxtaposes portraits, paintings of historical events, furniture, and other objects from the same time period, all combining to paint a picture of a moment in Danish history. While fascinating, the collection is huge, so I've selected only the most interesting items to linger over.

First Floor: Proceed to **Room 26,** which is focused on the Reformation. The case in the middle of the room holds the first Bible translated into Danish (from 1550—access to the word of God was a big part of the Reformation). Over the door to the next room is the image of a monk, Hans Tausen, invited by the king to preach the new thinking of the Reformation...sort of the "Danish Martin Luther." Also note the effort noble families put into legitimizing themselves with family trees and family seals.

Pass through Rooms 27, 28, and 29, and into **Room 30**—with paintings telling the story of Christian IV (for more on this dy-

namic Renaissance king, who built this castle and so much more, see page 59). Directly across from the door you entered is a painting of the chancellor on his deathbed, handing over the keys to the kingdom to a still-wet-behind-the-ears young Christian IV—the beginning of a long and fruitful career. On the right wall is a painting of Christian's coronation (the bearded gentleman looking out the window in the upper-left corner is Carlsberg brewer and castle benefactor J. C. Jacobsen—who, some 300 years before his birth, was probably not actually in attendance). Room 31 covers the royal family of Charles IV, while the smaller, darkened corner Room 32 displays the various Danish orders; find the most prestigious, the Order of the Elephant.

• *Hook back through Room 30, go outside on the little passage, and climb up the stairs.*

Second Floor: Go to the corner **Room 39,** which has a fascinating golden globe designed to illustrate Polish astronomer Nicolaus Copernicus' bold new heliocentric theory (that the sun, not the earth, was the center of our world). Look past the constellations to see the tiny model of the solar system at the very center, with a brass ball for the sun and little figures holding up symbols for each of the planets. The mechanical gears could actually make this model move to make the illustration more vivid.

Continue into one of the castle's most jaw-dropping rooms, the **Great Hall** (Room 38). The walls are lined with tapestries and royal portraits (including some modern ones, near the door). The

remarkable wood-carved ceilings include panels illustrating various industries. The elevated platform on the left was a gallery where musicians could play without getting in the way of the revelry.

Head back out and walk back along the left side of the hall. You can go quickly through the rooms numbered in the 40s and 50s (though pause partway down the long hallway; on the left, find the optical-illusion portrait that shows King Frederik V when viewed from one angle, and his wife when viewed from another). At the far end of this section, **Room 57** has a portrait of Hans Christian Andersen. Notice that fashion styles have gotten much more modern...suits and ties instead of tights and powdered wigs. It's time to head into the modern world.

• *Find the modern spiral staircase nearby. Downstairs are late-19th-century exhibits—which are skippable. Instead, head up to the top floor.*

Third Floor: This staircase puts you right in the middle of the modern collection. From here, the museum's focus shifts, focusing more on the art and less on the history. Highlights include:

The Art Critics, showing four past-their-prime, once-rambunctious artists themselves, now happily entrenched in the art institution, leaning back to critique a younger artist's work.

A room focusing on Denmark's far-flung protectorate of Greenland, with a porcelain polar bear and portraits of explorers.

A room of distinctive Impressionist/Post-Impressionist paintings, with a Danish spin.

The *Ninth of April, 1940,* showing the (ultimately unsuccessful) Danish defense against Nazi invaders on that fateful date.

A room focusing on the royal family, with a life-size, photorealistic portrait of the beloved Queen Margrethe II. Facing her is her daughter-in-law, Mary Donaldson—who, in this portrait at least, bears a striking resemblance to another young European royal.

Peter Carlsen's *Denmark 2009*—a brilliant parody of Eugène Delacroix's famous painting *Liberty Leading the People* (a copy of the inspiration is on the facing wall).  Carlsen has replaced the stirring imagery of the original with some dubious markers of contemporary Danish life: football flags, beer gut, shopping bags, tabloids, bikini babes, even a Christiania flag. It's a delightfully offbeat (and oh-so-Danish) note to end our visit to this seriously impressive palace.

NEAR THE CASTLE: HILLERØD TOWN

While there's not much here, the pedestrianized commercial zone is pleasant enough. It's best visited from the castle. Slotsgade, the main street, leads away from the castle bus stop toward the train station and is lined with shops and cafés. An inviting Scandinavian sweater shop is right at the bus stop. And if you feel like a little (very little) cruise, a tiny ferry leaves from a pier next to the castle and stops at the castle garden across the lake (30 DKK, free with Copenhagen Card, 2/hour, 30 minutes).

Louisiana Art Museum

This is Scandinavia's most-raved-about modern-art museum. Located in the town of Humlebæk, beautifully situated on the coast 18 miles north of Copenhagen, Louisiana is a holistic place that masterfully mixes its art, architecture, and landscape.

Getting There: Take the train from Copenhagen toward Helsingør, and get off at Humlebæk (3/hour, 30 minutes). It's a pleasant 10-minute walk (partly through a forest) to the museum: Exit the station and immediately go left onto Hejreskor Allé, a residential street; when the road curves right, continue straight along the narrow footpath through the trees. After you exit the trail, the museum is just ahead and across the street (at Gammel Strandvej 13).

If you're arriving by train from **Helsingør,** take the pedestrian underpass beneath the tracks, then follow the directions above. Louisiana is also connected to Helsingør by bus #388 (runs hourly, stops right at museum as well as at Humlebæk).

If you're coming from **Frederiksborg Castle,** you have two options: You can catch the Lille Nord train from Hillerød to Helsingør, then change there to a regional train heading south to Humlebæk (1-2/hour, 30 minutes). Alternatively, you can take the S-tog toward Copenhagen and Køge, get off at Hellerup, then catch a regional train north toward Helsingør to reach Humlebæk (6/hour, 30 minutes).

Cost and Hours: 125 DKK, included with Copenhagen Card; Tue-Fri 11:00-22:00, Sat-Sun until 18:00, closed Mon; tel. 49 19 07 19, www.louisiana.dk.

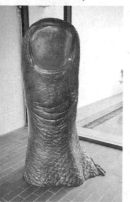

Cuisine Art: The **$$$** cafeteria, with indoor and outdoor seating, has reasonably priced sandwiches and welcomes picnickers who buy a drink.

Visiting the Museum: Wander from famous Chagalls and Picassos to more obscure art (everything is post-1945). Poets spend days here nourishing their creative souls with new angles, ideas, and perspectives. Even those who don't think they're art lovers can get sucked into a thought-provoking exhibit and lose track of time. There's no permanent exhibit; they constantly organize their substantial collection into ever-changing arrangements, augmented with borrowed and special exhibits (check www.louisiana.dk for the latest). An Andy Warhol *Marilyn Monroe* you see on one visit may not be there the next. (One favorite item, French sculptor César's *The Big Thumb*—which is simply a six-foot-tall bronze thumb—isn't going anywhere, since any time they move it, patrons complain.) There's no audioguide, but everything is labeled in English.

Outside, a delightful sculpture garden sprawls through the grounds, downhill toward the sea. The views over the Øresund, one of the busiest passages in the nautical world, are nearly as inspiring as the art. The museum's floor plan is a big loop, and the seaward side is underground—so as not to block the grand views. It's fun to explore the grounds, peppered with sculptures and made accessible by bridges and steps. There are sculptures by Alexander Calder, Jean Dubuffet, Joan Miró, and others.

Taken as a whole, the museum is a joy to explore. What you see from the inside draws you out, and what you see from the outside draws you in. The place can't be rushed. Linger and enjoy.

Kronborg Castle

Kronborg Castle is located in Helsingør, a pleasant, salty Danish seaside town that's often confused with its Swedish sister, Helsingborg, just two miles across the channel. Kronborg Castle (also called Elsinore, the Anglicized version of Helsingør) is a ▲▲ sight famous for its tenuous (but profitable) ties to Shakespeare. Most of the "Hamlet"  castle you'll see today—a darling of every big-bus tour and travelogue—was built long after the historical Hamlet died (more than a thousand years ago), and Shakespeare never saw the place. But this Renaissance castle existed when a troupe of English actors performed here in Shakespeare's time (Shakespeare may have known them). These days, various Shakespearean companies from around the world perform *Hamlet* in Kronborg's courtyard each August. Among the actors who've donned tights here in the title role are Laurence Olivier, Christopher Plummer, Kenneth Branagh, and Jude Law.

To see or not to see? The castle is most impressive from the outside. The free grounds between the walls and sea are great for picnics, with a close-up view of the strait between Denmark and

Sweden. If you're heading to Sweden, Kalmar Castle is a better medieval castle. And in Denmark, Frederiksborg (described earlier), which was built as an upgrade to this one, is far more opulent inside. But if Kronborg is handy to your itinerary—or you never met a castle you didn't like—it's worth a visit...even if just for a short romp across the ramparts (no ticket required). Many big-bus tours in the region stop both here and at Frederiksborg (you'll recognize some of the same fellow tourists at both places)—not a bad plan if you're a castle completist.

Tourist Information: The town of Helsingør has a TI (Mon-Fri 10:00-16:00, until 17:00 in summer, closed Sat-Sun except for short midday hours in summer; tel. 49 21 13 33, www.visithelsingor. dk), a medieval center, the ferry to Sweden, and lots of Swedes who come over for the lower-priced alcohol.

GETTING THERE

Helsingør is a 45-minute train ride from Copenhagen (3/hour). Exit the station out the front door: The TI is on the little square to your left, and the castle is dead ahead along the coast (about a 15-minute walk). Between the station and the castle, you'll pass through a harborfront zone with the town's cultural center and maritime museum (described later).

ORIENTATION TO KRONBORG CASTLE

Cost and Hours: 140 DKK June-Aug, 90 DKK Sept-May, 20 percent discount with Maritime Museum ticket, included with Copenhagen Card; open June-Sept daily 10:00-17:30, Oct-May daily 11:00-16:00 except closed Mon in Nov-March; tel. 33 95 42 00, www.kongeligeslotte.dk.

Tours: Free 30-minute **tours** in English are offered of the casements and of the royal apartments (1-2/day; call or check online for times). You can download a free **audioguide** to your mobile device. Dry English descriptions are posted throughout the castle.

VISITING THE CASTLE

Approaching the castle, pretend you're an old foe of the king, kept away by many layers of earthen ramparts and moats—just when you think you're actually at the castle, you find there's another gateway or waterway to pass. On the way in, you'll pass a small model of the complex to help get your bearings.

On a sunny day, you could have an enjoyable visit to Kronborg just walking around these grounds and playing "king of the castle," without buying a ticket. Many do.

Follow the signs into the ticket desk, buy your ticket, stick your bag in a locker (insert a 20-DKK coin, which will be returned), and head upstairs. You'll pop out at the beginning of the royal apartments.

Royal Apartments

Visitors are able to walk through one-and-a-half floors of the complex. The first few rooms are filled with high-tech exhibits, using touchscreens and projected videos to explain the history of the place. You'll learn how, in the 1420s, Danish King Eric of Pomerania built a fortress here to allow for the collection of "Sound Dues," levied on any passing ship hoping to enter the sound of Øresund. This proved hugely lucrative, eventually providing up to two-thirds of Denmark's entire income. By the time of Shakespeare, Kronborg was well-known both for its profitable ability to levy these dues, and for its famously lavish banquets—what better setting for a tale of a royal family unraveling?

Continuing into the apartments themselves, you'll find that the interior is a shadow of its former self; while the structure was rebuilt by Christian IV after a 1629 fire, its rooms were never returned to their former grandeur, making it feel like something of an empty shell. And yet, there are still some fine pieces of furniture and art to see. Frederik II ruled Denmark from the king's chamber in the 1570s; a model shows how it likely looked back in its heyday. After passing through two smaller rooms, you come to the queen's chamber; from there, stairs lead up to the queen's gallery, custom-built for Queen Sophie to be able to quickly walk directly from her chambers to the ballroom or chapel. Follow her footsteps into the ballroom, a vast hall of epic proportions decorated by a series of paintings commissioned by Christian IV (explained by the board near the entry). At the far end, a model (enlivened by seemingly holographic figures) illustrates how this incredible space must have looked in all its original finery. Beyond the ballroom, the "Little Hall" is decorated with a fine series of tapestries depicting Danish monarchs. Then wind through several more royal halls, chambers, and bedrooms on your way back down into the courtyard. Once there, go straight across and enter the chapel. The enclosed gallery at the upper-left was the private pew of the royal family.

Øresund Region

When the Øresund (UH-ra-soond) Bridge, which connects Denmark and Sweden, opened in July of 2000, it created a dynamic new metropolitan area. Almost overnight, the link forged an economic power with the 12th-largest gross domestic product in Europe. The Øresund region has surpassed Stockholm as the largest metro area in Scandinavia. Now 3.7 million Danes and Swedes—a highly trained and highly technical workforce—are within a quick commute of each other.

The bridge opens up new questions of borders. Historically, southern Sweden (the area across from Copenhagen, called Skåne) had Danish blood. It was Danish for a thousand years before Sweden took it in 1658. Notice how Copenhagen is the capital on the fringe of its realm—at one time it was in the center.

The 10-mile-long link, which has a motorway for cars (the toll is about 375 DKK) and a two-track train line, ties together the main islands of Denmark with Europe and Sweden. The $4 billion project consisted of a 2.5-mile-long tunnel, an artificial island called Peberholm, and a 5-mile-long bridge. With speedy connecting trains, Malmö in Sweden is now an easy half-day side-trip from Copenhagen (about 120 DKK each way, 3-5/hour, 35 minutes). The train drops you at the "Malmö C" (central) station right in the heart of Malmö, and all the important sights are within a short walk.

Citing security concerns and ongoing waves of immigration, Sweden has tightened controls at select border crossings. This means that anyone traveling from Denmark to Sweden on the Øresund Bridge needs to carry a passport, which will likely be checked by Swedish police.

Casements

You'll enter the underground part of the castle through a door on the main courtyard (diagonally across from the chapel). While not particularly tight, these passages are very dark (and a good place to use your mobile phone flashlight). This extensive network of dank cellars is a double-decker substructure that once teemed with activity. The upper level, which you'll see first, was used as servants' quarters, a stable, and a storehouse. The lower level was used to train and barrack soldiers during wartime (an efficient use of so much prime, fortified space). As you explore this creepy,

labyrinthine, nearly pitch-black zone (just follow the arrows), imagine the miserably claustrophobic conditions the soldiers lived in, waiting to see some action.

The most famous "resident" of the Kronborg casements was Holger Danske ("Ogier the Dane"), a mythical Viking hero revered by Danish children. The story goes that if the nation is ever in danger, this Danish superman will awaken and restore peace and security to the land (like King Arthur to the English, Barbarossa to the Germans, and Wenceslas to the Czechs). While this legend has been around for many centuries, Holger's connection to Kronborg was cemented by a Hans Christian Andersen tale, so now everybody just assumes he lives here. In one of the first rooms, you'll see a famous, giant statue of this sleeping Viking...just waiting for things to get *really* bad.

NEAR THE CASTLE: MARITIME MUSEUM OF DENMARK

Fans of nautical history and modern architecture should consider a visit to this museum, built within the old dry docks adjacent to the castle and designed by noted Danish firm BIG (Bjarke Ingels Group). Cutting-edge exhibits journey through Denmark's rich seafaring tradition, from the days of tall-masted sailing ships to the container-ship revolution, in which Danish shipping company Maersk is a world leader. Topics include life on board, wartime challenges, the globalization of trade, navigation, and maritime traditions (including tattoos!) in popular culture.

Cost and Hours: 110 DKK, included with Copenhagen Card, 25 percent discount with Kronborg Castle ticket; daily July-Aug 10:00-18:00, Sept 11:00-17:00, shorter hours off-season; café, tel. 49 21 06 85, www.mfs.dk.

Near Copenhagen Connections

ROUTE TIPS FOR DRIVERS

Copenhagen to Hillerød (45 minutes) to Helsingør (30 minutes): Just follow the town-name signs. Leave Copenhagen following signs for *E-47* and *Helsingør*. The freeway is great. *Hillerød* signs lead to the Frederiksborg Castle (not to be confused with the nearby Fredensborg Palace) in the pleasant town of Hillerød. Follow signs to *Hillerød C* (for "center"), then *slot* (for "castle"). Though the E-47 freeway is the fastest, the Strandvejen coastal road (152) is pleasant, passing some of Denmark's grandest mansions (including that of author Karen Blixen of *Out of Africa* fame).

Copenhagen to Sweden: The 10-mile Øresund Bridge conveniently links Denmark with Sweden (toll about 375 DKK), giving drivers and train travelers a direct route from Copenhagen to Malmö, Sweden (see sidebar, earlier). Swedish authorities have tightened border security, so be sure to carry your passport on any trip from Denmark to Sweden.

If you're heading to Sweden from Kronborg Castle—or if you're simply nostalgic for the pre-bridge days—the Helsingør-Helsingborg ferry putters across the Øresund Channel (follow signs to *Helsingborg, Sweden*—freeway leads to dock). Buy your ticket as you roll on board (about 360 DKK one-way for car, driver, and up to nine passengers). Reservations are free but not usually necessary, as ferries depart frequently (2-4/hour; tel. 33 15 15 15, or book online at www.scandlines.dk; also see www.hhferries.se). If you arrive early, you can probably drive onto any ferry. The 20-minute Helsingør-Helsingborg ferry ride gives you just enough time to enjoy the view of the Kronborg "Hamlet" castle, be impressed by the narrowness of this very strategic channel, and exchange any leftover Danish kroner into Swedish kronor (the ferry exchange desk's rate is decent).

In Helsingborg, follow signs for *E-4* and *Stockholm*. The road is good, traffic is light, and towns are all clearly signposted. At Ljungby, road 25 takes you to Växjö and Kalmar. Entering Växjö, skip the first Växjö exit and follow the freeway into *Centrum*, where it ends. It takes about four hours total to drive from Copenhagen to Kalmar.

CENTRAL DENMARK

Ærø • Odense

The sleepy isle of Ærø is the cuddle after the climax. It's the perfect time-passed world in which to wind down, enjoy the seagulls, and take a day off. Wander the unadulterated cobbled lanes of Denmark's best-preserved 18th-century town. Get Ærø-dynamic and pedal a rented bike into the essence of Denmark. Settle into a world of sailors, who, after the invention of steam-driven boat propellers, decided that building ships in bottles was more their style.

Between Ærø and Copenhagen, drop by bustling Odense, home of Hans Christian Andersen. Its Hans Christian Andersen House is excellent, and with more time, you can also enjoy its other museums (town history, trains, folk) and stroll the car-free streets of its downtown.

PLANNING YOUR TIME

Allow four hours to get from Copenhagen to Ærø (not counting a possible stopover in Odense). All trains stop in Roskilde (with its Viking Ship Museum—see previous chapter) and Odense (see the end of this chapter). On a quick trip, you can leave Copenhagen in the morning and do justice to both towns en route to Ærø. (With just one day, Odense and Roskilde together make a long but doable day trip from Copenhagen.)

While out of the way, Ærø is worth the journey. Once there, you'll want two nights

and a day to properly enjoy it (for details, see "Planning Your Time" for Ærøskøbing, later).

Ærø

This small (22 by 6 miles) island on the south edge of Denmark is as salty and sleepy as can be. A typical tombstone reads: "Here lies Christian Hansen at anchor with his wife. He'll not weigh until he stands before God." It's the kind of island where baskets of strawberries sit in front of houses—for sale on the honor system.

Ærø statistics: 7,000 residents, 500,000 visitors and 80,000 boaters annually, 350 deer, seven pastors, no crosswalks, and three police officers. The three big industries are farming (wheat and dairy), shipping, and tourism—in that order. Twenty percent of the Danish fleet still resides on Ærø, in the town of Marstal. But jobs are scarce, the population is slowly dropping, and family farms are consolidating into larger units.

Ærø, home to several windmills and one of the world's largest solar power plants, is going "green." They hope to become completely wind- and solar-powered. Currently, about half the island's heat and electricity is provided by renewable sources, and most of its produce is organically grown. New technology is expected to bring Ærø closer to its goal within the next few years.

GETTING AROUND ÆRØ

On a short visit, you won't need to leave Ærøskøbing, except for a countryside bike ride, if you like—everything is within walking or pedaling distance. But if you have more time or want to explore the rest of the island, you can take advantage of Ærø's **bus** network. Buses leave from a stop just above the ferry dock (leaving the ferry, walk up about a block and look right). Ærø's main bus line, Jesper Bus, is free (Mon-Fri hourly until about 19:00; Sat-Sun 3-4/day). There are two different branches—one going to Marstal at the east end of the island, and the other to Søby in the west (look for the town name on the front of the bus). The main reason to take the bus is to go to Marstal on a rainy day to visit its maritime museum.

Ærøskøbing

Ærøskøbing is Ærø's village in a bottle. It's small enough to be cute, but just big enough to feel real. The government, recognizing the value of this amazingly preserved little town, prohibits modern build- ing anywhere in the center. It's the only town in Denmark protected in this way. Drop into the 1680s, when Ærøskøbing was the wealthy home port of a hundred windjammers. The many Danes and Germans who come here for the tranquility—washing up the cobbled main drag in waves with

the landing of each boat—call it the fairy-tale town. The Danish word for "cozy," *hyggelig,* describes Ærøskøbing perfectly.

Ærøskøbing is simply a pleasant place to wander. Stubby little porthole-type houses, with their birth dates displayed in proud decorative rebar, lean on each other like drunk, sleeping sailors. Wander under flickering old-time lamps. Snoop around town. It's OK. Peek into living rooms (if people want privacy, they shut their drapes). Notice the many "snooping mirrors" on the houses— antique locals are following your every move. The harbor now ca- ters to holiday yachts, and on midnight low tides you can almost hear the crabs playing cards.

The town economy, once rich with the windjammer trade, hit the rocks in modern times. Kids 15 to 18 years old go to a boarding school in Svendborg; many don't return. About a third of Ærø's population is over age 60. And even though young couples on the island are having more babies, it's not enough to prevent a net population decline.

PLANNING YOUR TIME

You'll regret not setting aside a minimum of two nights for your Ærøskøbing visit. In a busy day you can "do" everything you like—except relax. If ever a place was right for recreating, this is it. I'd arrive in time for an evening stroll and dinner (and, when it's running, the Night Watchman's tour—see "Nightlife in Ærøskøbing," later). The next morning, do the island bike tour, returning by midafternoon. You can see the town's three museums in less than two hours (but note that they all close early—by 15:00 or 16:00), then browse the rest of your daylight away. Your second evening is filled with options: Stroll out to the summer huts for sunset, watch the classic sailing ships come in to moor for the evening (mostly Dutch and German boats crewed by vacationers), watch a movie in the pint-sized town cinema, go bowling with local teens, or check out live music in the pub.

Note that during the off-season (basically Sept-May), the town can be quite dead, but efforts are being made by local business owners to enliven the shorter days of fall and winter. Though several shops and restaurants close during the off-season, restaurant owners are trying to keep some dining establishments open on a rotating basis, so there should always be someplace to get a meal.

Orientation to Ærøskøbing

Ærøskøbing is tiny. Everything's just a few cobbles from the ferry landing.

TOURIST INFORMATION

The TI, which faces the ferry landing, has all the services you'd expect from a larger town's TI, including free Wi-Fi (late-June-mid-Aug Mon-Fri 9:00-18:00, Sat 10:00-18:00, Sun 10:00-15:00; off-season Mon-Fri 10:00-16:00, closed Sat-Sun; tel. 62 52 13 00, www.aeroe.dk).

HELPFUL HINTS

Money: The town's only ATM is at the blue building by the ferry dock, facing the TI.

Laundry: You'll find limited self-service laundry facilities at Ærøskøbing's marinas, on either side of the ferry dock.

Ferries: See "Ærøskøbing Connections" on page 142.

Bike Rental: Pilebækkens Cykler rents bikes year-round at the gas station at the top of town. Manager Janne hands out free

cykel maps so you can't get lost (seven-speed bikes-75 DKK/day, 150 DKK/2 days, 200 DKK/3 days; electric bikes also available—book a day ahead, deposit required; Mon-Fri 9:00-16:30, Sat until 13:00, closed Sun except July-Aug—when it's open 9:00-1:30; from Torvet Square, go through green door at Søndergade end of square, past garden to next road, in the gas station at Pilebækken 7; tel. 62 52 11 10). **Andelen Guesthouse** rents good, clean bikes too (100 DKK/day, Søndergade 28A, see "Sleeping in Ærøskøbing," later"). The campground also rents bikes. Most people on Ærø don't bother locking up their bikes—if your rental doesn't have a lock, don't fret.

Shopping: The town is speckled with cute little shops. Each July, local artisans show their creations in a warehouse facing the ferry landing.

Ærøskøbing Walk

This self-guided stroll, rated ▲▲▲, is ideal when the sun is low, the shadows long, and the colors rich. Start at the harbor.

Harbor: First, loiter around the harbor, where German and Dutch pleasure boaters come into port each evening. Because Ærø is only nine miles across the water from Germany, the island is popular with Germans who regularly return to this peaceful retreat on their grand old sailboats.

• *From the harbor and TI, walk up the main street a block and go left on...*

Smedegade: This is the poorest street in town, with the most architectural and higgledy-piggledy charm. Have a close look at the "street spies" on the houses—clever mirrors letting old women inside keep an eye on what's going on outside. The ship-in-a-bottle Bottle Peter Museum is on the right (described later, under "Sights in Ærøskøbing"). Notice the gutters—some protect only the doorway. Locals find the rounded modern drainpipes less charming than the old-school ones with hard angles. Appreciate the finely carved old

doors. Each is proudly unique—try to find two the same. Number 37 (on the left, after Arnfeldt Hotel), from the 18th century, is

CENTRAL DENMARK

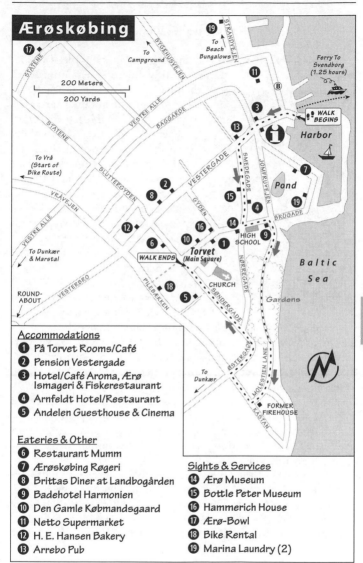

Ærøskøbing

Accommodations
1. På Torvet Rooms/Café
2. Pension Vestergade
3. Hotel/Café Aroma, Ærø Ismageri & Fiskerestaurant
4. Arnfeldt Hotel/Restaurant
5. Andelen Guesthouse & Cinema

Eateries & Other
6. Restaurant Mumm
7. Ærøskøbing Røgeri
8. Brittas Diner at Landbogården
9. Badehotel Harmonien
10. Den Gamle Købmandsgaard
11. Netto Supermarket
12. H. E. Hansen Bakery
13. Arrebo Pub

Sights & Services
14. Ærø Museum
15. Bottle Peter Museum
16. Hammerich House
17. Ærø-Bowl
18. Bike Rental
19. Marina Laundry (2)

Ærøskøbing's cutest house. Its tiny dormer is from some old ship's poop deck. The plants above the door have a traditional purpose—to keep this part of the house damp and slow to burn in case of fire.

Smedegade ends at the Folkehøjskole (folk high school). Inspired by the Danish philosopher Nikolaj Gruntvig—who wanted people to be able to say, "I am good at being me"—it offers people of any age the benefit of government-subsidized cultural education (music, art, theater, and so on).

• *Jog left, then turn right after the school, and stroll along the peaceful, harborside...*

Molestien Lane: This gravel path is lined with gardens, a quiet beach, and a row of small-is-beautiful houses—beginning with

humble and progressing to captain's class. These fine buildings are a reminder that through the centuries, independent-minded Ærøskøbing has been the last town in Germany, the first town in Denmark...and always into trade—legal and illegal. (The smuggling spirit survives in residents' blood even today. When someone returns from a trip, friends eagerly ask, "And what did you bring back?") Each garden is cleverly and lovingly designed. The harborfront path, nicknamed "Virgin's Lane," was where teens could court within view of their parents.

The dreamy-looking island immediately across the way is a nature preserve and a resting spot for birds making their long journey from the north to the Mediterranean. There's one lucky bull here (farmers raft over their heifers, who return as cows). Rainbows often end on this island—where plague victims were once buried. In the winter, when the water freezes (about once a decade), locals slip and slide over for a visit. The white building you can see at the end of the town's pier was the cooking house, where visiting sailors (who tried to avoid working with open flame on flammable ships) could do their baking.

At the end of the lane stands the former firehouse (with the tall brick tower, now a place for the high school garage band to practice). Twenty yards before the firehouse, a trail cuts left about 100 yards along the shore to a place the town provides for fishermen to launch and store their boats and tidy up their nets. A bench is strategically placed to enjoy the view.

• *Follow the rutted lane inland, back past the firehouse. Turn right and walk a block toward town. At the first intersection, take a right onto...*

Østergade: This was Ærøskøbing's east gate. In the days of German control, all island trade was legal only within the town. All who passed this point would pay various duties and taxes at a tollbooth that once stood here.

As you walk past the traditional houses, peer into living rooms. Catch snatches of Danish life. (After the bend, you can see right through the windows to the sea.) Ponder the beauty of a society with such a keen sense of civic responsibility that fishing permits entrust you "to catch only what you need." You're welcome to pick berries where you like...but "no more than what would fit in your hat."

The wood on these old houses prefers organic coverings to modern paint. Tar painted on beams as a preservative blisters in the sun. An old-fashioned paint of chalk, lime, and clay lets old houses breathe and feel more alive. (It gets darker with the rain and leaves a little color on your fingers.) Modern chemical paint has much less personality.

The first square (actually a triangle, at #55) was the old goose market. Ærøskøbing—born in the 13th century, burned in the 17th, and rebuilt in the 18th—claims (believably) to be the best-preserved town from that era in Denmark. The original plan, with 12 streets laid out by its founder, survives.

• *Leaving the square, stay left on...*

Søndergade: Look for wrought-iron girders on the walls, added to hold together bulging houses. (On the first corner, at #55,

notice the nuts that could be tightened like a corset to keep the house from sagging.) Ærøskøbing's oldest houses (check out the dates)—the only ones that survived a fire during a war with Sweden—are #36 and #32. At #32, the hatch upstairs was where masts and sails were stored for the winter. These houses also have some of the finest doors in town (and in Ærøskøbing, that's saying something). The red on #32's door is the original paint job—ox blood, which, when combined with the tannin in the wood, really lasts. The courtyard behind #18 was a parking lot in pre-car days. Farmers, in town for their shopping chores, would leave their horses here. Even today, the wide-open fields are just beyond.

• *Wander down to Ærøskøbing's main square.*

Torvet Square: Notice the two hand pumps, which still work. Until 1951, townspeople came here for their water. The linden tree is the town symbol. The rocks around it celebrate the reunion of a big chunk of southern Denmark (including this island), which was ruled by Germany from 1864 to 1920. See the town seal featuring a linden tree, over the door of the old City Hall (now the library, with Internet stations in former prison cells). Read the Danish on the wall: "With law shall man a country build."

• *Our walk is over. Continue straight (popping into recommended Restaurant Mumm, the best place in town, to make a reservation for dinner). You'll return to the main street (Vestergade) and—just when you need it—the town bakery (to the left). But, if you're ready to launch right into a bike ride, instead go through the green door to the right of City Hall to reach one of the town's bike-rental places (listed earlier, under "Helpful Hints").*

Sights in Ærøskøbing

MUSEUMS

Ærøskøbing's three tiny museums cluster within a few doors of each other just off Torvet Square. While quirky and fun (and with sketchy English handouts), these museums would be much more interesting and worthwhile if they translated their Danish descriptions for the rare person on this planet who doesn't speak *Dansk.* (Your gentle encouragement might help get results.) In July, they organize daily chatty tours.

Ærø Museum (Ærøskøbing Bymuseum)

This museum, which may be closed for renovation during your visit, fills two floors of an old house with the island's history, from sea-

faring to farming. Be on the lookout for household objects (such as pottery, kitchenware, and tools), paintings, a loom from 1683, an 18th-century peasant's living room with colorful furniture, and gear from a 100-year-old pharmacy. There's also a fun diorama showing an aerial view of Ærøskøbing in 1862—notice the big gardens behind nearly every house. (This museum carries on the tradition with its own garden out back—be sure to go out and explore it before you leave.)

Cost and Hours: 40 DKK; July-Aug Mon-Fri 10:00-16:00, Sat-Sun 11:00-15:00; mid-April-June and Sept-mid-Oct Mon-Sat 11:00-15:00, closed Sun; shorter hours and closed Sat-Sun off-season; Brogade 3, tel. 62 52 29 50, www.arremus.dk.

▲Bottle Peter Museum (Flaske-Peters Samling)

This fascinating house has 750 different bottled ships. Old Peter Jacobsen, who made his first bottle at 16 and his last at 85, created some 1,700 ships-in-bottles in his lifetime. He bragged that he drank the contents of each bottle...except those containing milk. This museum opened in 1943, when the mayor of Ærøskøbing offered Peter and his wife a humble home in exchange for the right to display his works. Bottle Peter died in 1960 (and is most likely buried in a glass bottle), leaving a lifetime of tedious little creations for visitors to squint and marvel at.

Cost and Hours: 40 DKK; July-Aug daily 10:00-16:00; May-June and Sept Mon-Sat 11:00-15:00, closed Sun; off-season call for viewing appointment; Smedegade 22, tel. 81 55 59 72.

Visiting the Museum: In two buildings facing each other across a cobbled courtyard, you'll see rack after rack of painstaking models in bottles and cigar boxes. Some are "right-handed" and some are "left-handed" (referring to the direction the bottle faced, and therefore which hand the model maker relied on to execute the fine details)—Bottle Peter could do it all.

In the entrance building, you'll see Peter's "American collection," which he sold to a Danish-American collector so he could have funds to retire. One of Peter's favorites was the "diver-bottle"—an extra-wide bottle with two separate ship models inside: One shipwreck on the "ocean floor" at the bottom of the bottle, and, above that, a second one floating on the "surface." A video shows the artist at work, and nearby you can see some of his tools.

The second building has some English panels about Peter's life (including his mischievous wit, which caused his friends great anxiety when he had an audience with the king) and the headstone he designed for his own grave: a cross embedded with seven ships-in-bottles, representing the seven seas he explored in his youth as a seaman.

Hammerich House (Hammerichs Hus)

These 12 funky rooms in three houses are filled with 200- to 300-year-old junk.

Cost and Hours: 40 DKK, late July-Aug Mon-Fri 12:00-15:00, otherwise ask for access at the Ærø Museum, closed off-season, Gyden 22.

ÆRØ ISLAND BIKE RIDE (OR CAR TOUR)

This 15-mile trip shows you the best of this windmill-covered island's charms. The highest point on the island is only 180 feet above sea level, but the wind can be strong and the hills seem long and surprisingly steep.

As a bike ride, it's good exercise, though it may be more exhausting than fun if you've done only light, recreational cycling

CENTRAL DENMARK

Ærø Island Bike Ride

To Svendborg

To Søby

Urehoved

100 KM
50 MI
DENMARK
Odense Copa.
Ærø
GER.

GÆSTGIVERI BREGNINGE

CHURCH
Bregninge

Borgnæs

BEACH BUNGALOWS

CAMPING

Drejø

Ommels-
hoved

DIKE

Synneshøj

Ærøskøbing
(start & end bike ride)

Vrå

SHORTCUTS BACK TO ÆRØSKØBING

Lilleø

VINDEBALLE KRO

Vindeballe

Stokkeby

Lille
Rise

Kragnæs

Tranderup

Olde

Vodrup
Klint
(Cliffs)

TINGSTEDET DOLMEN

Store
Rise

BREWERY

Dunkær

To Marstal
& Maritime
Museum

Baltic Sea

N

2 Kilometers

2 Miles

Vejnæs Nakke

at home. You'll pay more for seven gears instead of five, but it's worth it.

Rent your bike in town (see "Helpful Hints," earlier), and while my map and instructions work, a local cycle map is helpful (free loaner maps if you rent from Pilebækkens Cykler, or buy one at the TI). Bring along plenty of water, as there are few opportunities to fill up (your first good chance is at the WC at the Bregninge church; there are no real shops until downtown Bregninge).

• *Leave Ærøskøbing to the west on the road to Vrå (Vråvejen, signed* Bike Route #90). *From downtown, pedal up the main street (Vestergade) and turn right on Vråvejen; from the bike-rental place on Pilebækken, just turn right and pedal straight ahead—it turns into Vråvejen.*

Leaving Ærøskøbing: You'll see the first of many U-shaped farmhouses, typical of Denmark. The three sides block the wind and store cows, hay, and people. *Gård* (farm) shows up in many local surnames.

At Øsemarksvej, bike along the coast in the protection of the dike built in 1856 to make the once-salty swampland to your left farmable. While the weak soil is good for hay and little else, they get the most out of it. Each winter, certain grazing areas flood with seawater. (Some locals claim this makes their cows produce fatter milk and meat.) As you roll along the dike, the land on your left is about eight feet below sea level. The little white pump house—alone in the field—is busy each spring and summer.

• *At the T-junction, go right (over the dike) toward...*

Borgnæs: The traditional old "straw house" (50 yards down, on left) is a café and shop selling fresh farm products. Just past that, a few roadside tables sell farm goodies on the honor system. Borgnæs is a cluster of modern summer houses. In spite of huge demand, a weak economy, and an aging population, development like this is no longer allowed.

• *Keep to the right (passing lots of wheat fields); at the next T-junction, turn right, following signs for Ø.* Bregningemark *(don't turn off for* Vindeballe*). After a secluded beach, head inland (direction: Ø. Bregninge). Pass the island's only water mill, and climb uphill over the island's 2,700-inch-high summit toward Bregninge. The tallest point on Ærø is called Synneshøj (probably means "Seems High" and it sure does—if you're even a bit out of shape, you'll feel every one of those inches).*

Gammelgård: Take a right turn marked only by a *Bike Route #90* sign. The road deteriorates (turns to gravel—and can be slushy

if there's been heavy rain, so be careful). You'll wind scenically and sometimes steeply through "Ærø's Alps," past classic thatched-roofed "old farms" (hence the name of the lane—Gammelgård).

• *At the modern road, turn left (leaving Bike Route #90) and pedal to the big village church. Before turning left to roll through Bregninge, visit the church.*

Bregninge Church: The interior of the 12th-century Bregninge church is still painted as a Gothic church would have been.

Find the painter's self-portrait (behind the pulpit, right of front pew). Tradition says that if the painter wasn't happy with his pay, he'd paint a fool's head in the church (above third pew on left). Note how the fool's mouth—the hole for a rope tied to the bell—has been worn

wider and wider by centuries of ringing. (During services, the ringing bell would call those who were ill and too contagious to be allowed into the church to come for communion—distributed through the square hatches flanking the altar.)

The altarpiece—gold leaf on carved oak—is from 1528, six

years before the Reformation came to Denmark. The cranium carved into the bottom indicates it's a genuine masterpiece by Claus Berg (from Lübeck, Germany). This Crucifixion scene is such a commotion, it seems to cause Christ's robe to billow up. The soldiers who traditionally gambled for Christ's robe have traded their dice for knives. Even the three wise men (lower right; each perhaps a Danish king) made it to this Crucifixion. Notice the escaping souls of the two thieves—the one who converted on the cross being carried happily to heaven, and the other, with its grim-winged escort, heading straight to hell. The scene at lower left—a disciple with a bare-breasted, dark-skinned woman feeding her child— symbolizes the Great Commission: "Go ye to all the world." Since this is a Catholic altarpiece, a roll call of saints lines the wings. During the restoration, the identity of the two women on the lower right was unknown, so the lettering—even in Latin—is clearly gibberish. Take a moment to study the 16th-century art on the ceiling (for example, the crucified feet ascending, leaving only footprints on earth). In the narthex, a list of pastors goes back to 1505. The current pastor (Agnes) is the first woman on the list.

• *Now's the time for a bathroom break (public WC in the churchyard). If you need some food or drink, pop in to the* **$$$ Gæstgiveri Bregninge** *restaurant, to the right of the church as you face it (lunch and dinner, May-mid-Sept Wed-Thu 12:00-17:00, Fri-Sun until 21:00, closed Mon-Tue and in the off-season, guest rooms available, tel. 30 23 65 55, www.gaestgiveri.dk). Then roll downhill through...*

Bregninge: As you bike through what is supposedly Denmark's "second-longest village," you'll pass many more U-shaped *gårds*. Notice how the town is in a gully. Imagine pirates trolling along the coast, looking for church spires marking unfortified villages. Ærø's 16 villages are all invisible from the sea—their church spires carefully designed not to be viewable from sea level.

• *About a mile down the main road is Vindeballe. Just before the main part of the village (soon after you pass the official* Vindeballe *sign and the* din fart *sign—which tells you "your speed"), take the* Vodrup Klint *turnoff to the right.*

Vodrup Klint: A road leads downhill (with a well-signed jog to the right) to dead-end at a rugged bluff called Vodrup Klint (WC, picnic benches). If I were a pagan, I'd worship here for the sea, the wind, and the chilling view. Notice how the land steps in sloppy slabs down to the sea. When saturated with water, the slabs of clay that make up the land here get slick, and entire chunks can slide.

Hike down to the foamy beach (where you can pick up some flint, chalk, and wild thyme). While the wind at the top could drag a kite-flyer, the beach below can be ideal

for sunbathing. Because Ærø is warmer and drier than the rest of Denmark, this island is home to plants and animals found nowhere else in the country. This southern exposure is the warmest area. Germany is dead ahead.

• *Backtrack 200 yards and follow the signs to* Tranderup. *On the way, you'll pass a lovely pond famous for its bell frogs and happy little duck houses.*

Popping out in Tranderup, you can backtrack (left) about 300 yards to get to the traditional **$$$ Vindeballe Kro**—*a handy inn for a stop if you're hungry or thirsty (lunch served daily July-mid-Aug 12:00-14:00, dinners served daily year-round 18:00-21:00, tel. 62 52 16 13, www. vindeballekro.dk).*

If you're tired or if the weather is turning bad, you can shortcut from here back to **Ærøskøbing:** *Go down the lane across the street from the Vindeballe Kro, and you'll zip quickly downhill across the island to the dike just east of Borgnæs; turn right and retrace your steps back into town.*

But there's much more to see. To continue our pedal, head on into...

Tranderup: Still following signs for *Tranderup,* stay on Tranderupgade parallel to the big road through town. You'll pass a lovely farm and a potato stand. At the main road, turn right. At the Ærøskøbing turnoff (another chance to bail out and head home), side-trip 100 yards left to the big stone (commemorating the return of the island to Denmark from Germany in 1750) and a grand island panorama. Claus Clausen's rock (in the picnic area, next to WC) is a memorial to an extremely obscure pioneer who was born in Ærø, emigrated to America, and played a role in shaping the early history of Scandinavian Lutheranism in the US.

• *Return to the big road (continuing in direction: Marstal), pass through Olde, pedal past FAF (the local wheat farmers' co-op facility), and head toward Store Rise (STOH-reh REE-zuh), the next church spire in the distance. Think of medieval travelers using spires as navigational aids.*

Store Rise Prehistoric Tomb, Church, and Brewery: Thirty yards after the Stokkeby turnoff, follow the rough, tree-lined path on the right to the Langdysse (Long Dolmen) Tingstedet, just behind the church spire. This is a 6,000-year-old **dolmen,** an early Neolithic burial place. Though Ærø once had more than 200 of these prehistoric tombs, only 13 survive. The site is a raised mound the shape and length (about 100 feet) of a Viking ship, and archaeologists have found evidence that indicates a Viking ship may indeed have been burned and buried here.

Ting means assembly spot. Imagine a thousand years ago: Viking chiefs representing the island's various communities gathering here around their ancestors' tombs. For 6,000 years, this has been a holy spot. The stones were considered fertility stones. For centuries, locals in need of virility chipped off bits and took them home (the nicks in the rock nearest the information post are mine).

Tuck away your chip and carry on down the lane to the Store Rise **church.** Inside you'll find little ships hanging in the nave, a fine 12th-century altarpiece, a stick with offering bag and a ting-a-ling bell to wake those nodding off (right of altar), double seats (so worshippers can flip to face the pulpit during sermons), and Martin Luther in the stern keeping his Protestant hand on the rudder. The list in the church allows today's pastors to trace their pastoral lineage back to Doctor Luther himself. (The current pastor, Janet, is the first woman on the list.) The churchyard is circular—a reminder of how churchyards provided a last refuge for humble communities under attack. Can you find anyone buried in the graveyard whose name doesn't end in "-sen"?

Next follow the smell of hops (or the *Rise Bryggeri* signs) to Ærø's **brewery.** Located in a historic brewery 400 yards beyond the Store Rise church, it welcomes visitors with free samples of its various beers. The Ærø traditional brews are available in pilsner (including the popular walnut pilsner), light ale, dark ale, and a typical dark Irish-style stout. The Rise organic brews come in light ale, dark ale, and walnut (daily July-Aug 10:00-15:00; shorter hours Sept-mid-Oct, closed mid-Oct-June; tel. 62 52 11 32, www.risebryggeri.dk).

• *From here, climb back to the main road and continue (direction: Marstal) on your way back home to Ærøskøbing. The three 330-foot-high modern windmills on your right are communally owned and, as they are a nonpolluting source of energy, state-subsidized. At Dunkær (3 miles from Ærøskøbing), take the small road, signed* Lille Rise, *past the topless windmill. Except for the Lille Rise, it's all downhill from here, as you coast past great sea views back home to Ærøskøbing.*

Huts at the Sunset Beach: Still rolling? Bike past the campground along the Urehoved beach (*strand* in Danish) for a look at the coziest little beach houses you'll never see back in the "big is beautiful" US. This is Europe, where small is beautiful, and the

concept of sustainability is neither new nor subversive. (For
more details, see "Beach Bun-
galow Sunset Stroll," below.)

RAINY-DAY OPTIONS
Ærø is disappointing but not
unworkable in bad weather.
In addition to the museums listed earlier, you could check out the
evening options under "Nightlife in Ærøskøbing" (later), many of
which are good in bad weather. Or hop on the free bus to Marstal
to visit its maritime museum.

Marstal Maritime Museum (Marstal Søfartsmuseum)
To learn more about the island's seafaring history, visit this fine
museum in the dreary town of Marstal. You'll see plenty of model
ships, nautical paintings (including several scenes by acclaimed
painter Carl Rasmussen), an original ship's galley, a re-created
wheelhouse (with steering and navigation equipment), a collection
of exotic goods brought back from faraway lands, and a children's
area with a climbable mast. Designed by and for sailors, the museum presents a warts-and-all view of the hardships of the seafaring
life, rather than romanticizing it.

Cost and Hours: 60 DKK; June-Aug daily 9:00-17:00; mid-
April-May and Sept-Oct daily 10:00-16:00; shorter hours and
closed Sun off-season; Prinsensgade 1, tel. 62 53 23 31, www.
marmus.dk.

Getting There: Ride the free Jesper Bus from Ærøskøbing all
the way to the harbor in Marstal, where you'll find the museum. It's
about a 20-minute trip.

Nightlife in Ærøskøbing

These activities are best done in the evening, after a day of biking
around the island.

▲▲Beach Bungalow Sunset Stroll
At sunset, stroll to Ærøskøbing's sand beach. Facing the ferry
dock, go left, following the
harbor. Upon leaving the town,
you'll pass the Netto supermarket (convenient for pick-
ing up snacks, beer, or wine),
a minigolf course, and a children's playground. In the rosy
distance, past a wavy wheat
field, is Vestre Strandvejen—a

row of tiny, Monopoly-like huts facing the sunset. These beach escapes are privately owned on land rented from the town (no overnight use, WCs at each end). Each is different, but all are stained with merry memories of locals enjoying themselves Danish-style. Bring a beverage or picnic. It's perfectly acceptable—and very Danish—to borrow a porch for your sunset sit. From here, it's a fine walk out to the end of Urehoved (as this spit of land is called).

Town Walk with Night Watchman

On summer evenings in July and August, the night watchman leads visitors through town. It's a fine time to be outside, meeting other travelers (30 DKK, starts 21:00 at Torvet Square—just show up, English tours Wed and Sat).

Cinema

The cute little 30-seat Andelen Theater (in the Andelen Guesthouse—a former grain warehouse) plays movies in their original language (Danish subtitles, closed Mon and in July—when it hosts a jazz festival, new titles begin every Tue). It's run in a charming community-service kind of way. The management has installed heat, so tickets no longer come with a blanket (near Torvet Square at Søndergade 28A, tel. 62 52 17 11).

Bowling

Ærø-Bowl is a six-lane alley in a modern athletic club at the edge of town. In this old-fashioned town, where no modern construction is allowed in the higgledy-piggledy center, this hip facility is a magnet for young people. One local told me, "I've never seen anyone come out of there without a smile" (hot dogs, junk food, arcade games, kids on dates; Tue-Thu 16:00-22:00, later on Fri-Sat, shorter hours off-season, closed Sun-Mon, Statene 42A, tel. 62 52 23 06).

Pub

Arrebo Pub bills itself as "probably the best bar in town." Maybe that's because it's the *only* one in town. In any case, it attracts a young crowd and is the place to go for live music and beer, but there's no food (open daily from 13:00, at the bottom of Vestergade, near ferry dock).

Sleeping in Ærøskøbing

The accommodations scene here is boom or bust. Summer weekends and all of July are packed (book long in advance). It's absolutely dead in the winter. These places come with family-run personality, and each is an easy stroll from the ferry landing.

IN ÆRØSKØBING

$$$$ På Torvet ("On the Square") is a cheery hotel/café/wine shop that's bringing a lively new spirit to the town square. Owners Gunnar and Lili rent 11 modern, sparkling apartments, each with a private bathroom, and several with a kitchen (Torvet 7, tel. 62 52 40 50, www.paatorvet.dk, info@paatorvet.dk). The recommended café serves breakfast and lunch with seating inside and out on Torvet Square (see "Eating in Ærøskøbing," later). They also sell wine and specialty foods, and the grand piano in the dining area is ready for you to tickle its ivories.

$$$ Pension Vestergade is your best home away from home in Ærøskøbing. It's lovingly run by Susanna Greve and her daughters, Henrietta and Celia. Su-

sanna, who's fun to talk with and is always ready with a cup of tea, has a wealth of knowledge about the town's history and takes good care of her guests. Built in 1784 for a sea captain's daughter, this creaky, sagging, and venerable eight-room place—with each room named for its particular color scheme—is on the main street in the town center. Picnic in the back garden and get to know Tillie, the live-in dog. Reserve well in advance (RS%, payment via TransferWise app or cash, cuddly hot-water bottles, shared bathrooms, Vestergade 44, tel. 62 52 22 98, www.vestergade44.com, pensionvestergade44@post.tele.dk).

$$$ Hotel Aroma offers four bright, cheery, and modern rooms—two standard doubles and two large family rooms with kitchens—above the recommended Café Aroma (shared bathroom, laundry facilities, roof terrace, on Vestergade, just up the street from the ferry dock, open mid-April-Aug, closed in off-season, tel. 62 52 40 02, mobile 40 40 26 84, www.cafe-aroma.dk).

$$$ Arnfeldt Hotel, formerly Det Lille Hotel, was once a 19th-century captain's home. Now owned by an energetic husband-and-wife team, Morten and Katrine Arnfeldt, this cozy hotel offers six clean and tidy, freshly renovated rooms with shared baths (Smedegade 33, tel. 62 52 23 00, ma@arnfeldtgroup.com).

$$ Andelen Guesthouse, run by Englishman Adam, is brimming with a funky nautical charm. An old warehouse that's been converted into a hotel, it has five guest rooms that share two bathrooms and one two-level family room with private bath (no breakfast—but can be purchased nearby at På Torvet Café, free entry to downstairs movie theater, nice rental bikes-100 DKK/

day, pay laundry, Søndergade 28A, mobile 61 26 75 11, www.andelenguesthouse.com, info@andelenguesthouse.com).

OUTSIDE OF ÆRØSKØBING

$$ Vindeballe Kro, about three miles from Ærøskøbing, is a traditional inn in Vindeballe at the island's central crossroads. Maria and Steen rent 10 straightforward, well-kept rooms (free parking; for location, see the Ærø Island Bike Ride map; tel. 62 52 16 13, www.vindeballekro.dk, mail@vindeballekro.dk). They also have a restaurant (described earlier, under "Ærø Island Bike Ride").

¢ Ærø Campground is set on a fine beach a few minutes' walk out of town. This three-star campground offers a lodge with a fireplace, campsites, cabins, and bike rental (open April-mid-Oct; facing the water, follow waterfront to the left; tel. 62 52 18 54, www.aeroecamp.dk, info@aeroecamp.dk).

Eating in Ærøskøbing

Ærøskøbing has a handful of charming and hardworking little eateries. Business is so light that chefs and owners come and go constantly, making it tough to predict the best value for the coming year. As each place has a distinct flavor, I'd spend 20 minutes enjoying the warm evening light and do a strolling survey before making your choice. I've listed only the serious kitchens. Note that almost everything closes by 21:00—don't wait too late to eat (if you'll be taking a later ferry from Svendborg to Ærø, either eat before your boat trip or call ahead to reserve a place...otherwise you're out of luck). During the winter, some of my recommended restaurants take turns staying open, so you should be able to find a decent place to eat (the TI posts a list of restaurant opening days and times).

$$$$ Restaurant Mumm is where visiting yachters go for a good and classy meal. Portions are huge, and on balmy days their garden terrace out back is a hit. Call ahead to reserve or book online (daily specials, starters, main courses, daily 18:00-21:00, shorter hours and closed Sun-Tue in off-season, near Torvet Square at Søndergade 12, tel. 62 52 12 12, www.mumm.restaurant).

$$ På Torvet Café, right on Torvet Square, offers a tasty lunch menu, with hearty portions that are stylishly presented. Dine in the cozy café or out on the square (daily May-mid-Sept 12:00-15:30, shorter hours off-season, tel. 62 52 40 50).

$$ Café Aroma, a reasonably priced Danish café that feels like a rustic old diner, has a big front porch filled with tables and good entrées, sandwiches, and burgers. Ask about the daily special, which will save you money and is not listed on the menu. Order at the bar (mid-April-Aug Thu-Mon 11:00-20:00, closed Tue-Wed and in off-season, on Vestergade, just up from the ferry dock, tel. 62 52 40 02). They also run a delicious ice-cream shop; a high-quality, pricey fish restaurant next door (**Fiskerestaurant,** open July only); and produce gourmet handmade licorice just across the street.

$$ Ærøskøbing Røgeri serves wonderful smoked-fish meals on paper plates. With picnic tables facing the harbor, it's great for a light meal. Eat there or find a pleasant picnic site at the beach or at the park behind the fish house. A smoked-fish dinner with potato salad, bread, and a couple of cold Carlsbergs or Ærø brews are a well-earned reward after a long bike ride (daily April-mid-Oct 11:00-19:00, mid-June-mid-Aug 10:00-21:00, Havnen 15, tel. 62 52 40 07).

$$$$ Brittas Diner at Landbogården prides itself on serving "honest and special" dishes using local ingredients in its changing menu (meat, fish, international dishes, Tue-Sun 17:30-21:00, closed Mon, near the top of Vestergade at #54, tel. 23 92 41 30).

Hotel Restaurants: Two hotels in town have dining rooms with good but expensive food; I'd eat at the restaurants I've listed above, unless they're closed. But in a pinch, try these: **$$$ Badehotel Harmonien** serves Italian dishes and wood-fired pizza, and owns the best location in town, with views of the sea from its bright and lively perch (pizza made right in the dining room, Thu-Tue 17:30-22:00, closed Wed, tel. 42 50 00 05). **$$$$ Arnfeldt Hotel** offers gourmet meals using local ingredients. After stints in London and Copenhagen, chef Morten Arnfeldt is bringing upscale dining to Ærø, serving internationally inspired dishes in an inviting dining room and garden (four-course dinners, reservations required, Smedegade 33, tel. 62 52 23 00).

CENTRAL DENMARK

SNACKS, PICNICS, AND DESSERT

Here are some places for lighter fare.

Market for Local Specialties: At **Den Gamle Købmandsgaard** ("The Old Merchants' Court") on Torvet Square you'll find a remarkable selection of mostly locally sourced and produced foods, including meat, sausage, salami, bread, fruit, honey, jam, chocolate, beer, cigars, and whiskey—which is distilled on-site (ask about tours and tastings). Grab a seat in their café for lunch or cake (Mon-Sat 10:00-17:30, closed Sun, Torvet 5, tel. 20 24 30 07).

Grocery: The **Netto** supermarket has picnic fixings and drinks, including chilled beer and wine—handy for walks to the little huts on the beach at sunset (daily 7:00-22:00, kitty-corner from ferry dock).

Bakery: Ærøskøbing's old-school **H. E. Hansen** bakery sells fresh bread and delicious pastries, plus cheese, yogurt, and drinks

(Tue-Fri 7:00-17:00, Sat-Sun until 14:00, closed Mon, top of Vestergade).

Ice Cream: The ice-cream shop at Café Aroma, **Ærø Ismageri,** serves good, flavorful ice cream—try gooseberry beer (made from Ærø stout—way better than it sounds), or the local favorite, the "Ærø Special"—walnut ice cream with maple syrup (daily mid-April-Aug 9:00-23:00, closed Sept-mid-April, just up from the ferry dock).

Ærøskøbing Connections

ÆRØ-SVENDBORG FERRY

The ferry ride between **Svendborg,** with connections to Copenhagen, and **Ærøskøbing,** on the island of Ærø, is a relaxing 1.25-hour crossing. Just get on, and the crew will come to you for payment. American credit cards with a chip work (2.50-DKK surcharge), or you can pay cash (218 DKK round-trip per person, 476 DKK round-trip per car—not including driver/passengers, ferry not covered by or discounted with rail pass, significant off-season discounts). You can leave the island via any of the three different Ærø ferry routes.

The ferry always has room for walk-ons, but drivers should reserve a spot in advance, especially on weekends and in summer. During these busy times, reserve as far ahead as you can—ideally at least a week in advance. Car reservations by phone or email are free and easy—simply give your name and license-plate number. If you don't know your license number (i.e., you're reserving from home and haven't yet picked up your rental car), try asking nicely if they're willing to just take your name. They may want you to call them with the number when you pick up your car, but if that's not practical, you can usually just tell the attendant your name before you drive onto the boat. Ferries depart daily in summer (roughly 10/day in each direction). Call or look online for the schedule (office open Mon-Fri 8:00-15:30, Sat-Sun 9:00-15:00, tel. 62 52 40 00, www.aeroe-ferry.dk, info@aeroe-ferry.dk).

Drivers with reservations just drive on (be sure to get into the *med* reservations line). If you won't use your car in Ærø, park it in Svendborg (big, safe lot two blocks in from ferry landing, or at the far end of the harbor near the Bendix fish shop). On Ærø, parking is free.

Trains Connecting with Ærø-Svendborg Ferry

The train from **Odense** dead-ends at the Svendborg harbor (2/hour Mon-Sat, hourly on Sun, 45 minutes; don't get off at Svendborg Vest Station—wait until you get to the end of the line, called simply "Svendborg").

Arriving in Svendborg: It takes about 10 minutes to walk from the station to the dock (5 minutes if you walk briskly). Don't dawdle—the boat leaves stubbornly on time, even if trains are running late. I recommend taking a train from Odense that arrives about 30 minutes before your ferry departure to give yourself time to absorb delays and find your way. If you're cutting it close, be ready to hop off the train and walk swiftly.

To get from the Svendborg train station to the dock, turn left after exiting the train, following the sidewalk between the tracks and the station, then take a left (across the tracks) at the first street, Brogade. Head a block downhill to the harbor, make a right, and the ferry dock is ahead, across from Hotel Ærø. If you arrive early, you can head to the waiting room in the little blue building across the street from the hotel. There are several carry-out restaurants along Brogade, and a few hotels overlooking the ferry line have restaurants.

Departing from Svendborg: All Svendborg trains go to Odense (where you can connect to Copenhagen or Aarhus). A train tends to leave shortly after the ferry arrives (a tight connection—it's a good idea to buy your train ticket in advance instead of making a mad rush to use the one ticket machine at the station). To reach the train from the Svendborg ferry dock, pass Hotel Ærø and continue a block along the waiting lane for the ferry, turn left and go up Brogade one block, then take a right and follow the sidewalk between the tracks and the train station. Look for a train signed *Odense* waiting on the single track.

CENTRAL DENMARK

Odense

Founded in A.D. 988 and named after Odin (the Nordic Zeus), Odense is the main city of the big island of Funen (Fyn in Danish) and the birthplace of storyteller Hans Christian Andersen (whom the Danes call simply H. C., pronounced "hoe see"; for more on the author, see the Copenhagen chapter). Although the author was born here in poverty and left at the tender age of

14 to pursue a career in the theater scene of Copenhagen, H. C. is Odense's favorite son—you'll find his name and image all over town. He once said, "Perhaps Odense will one day become famous because of me." Today, Odense (OH-then-za) is one of Denmark's most popular tourist destinations.

Orientation to Odense

As Denmark's third-largest city, with 170,000 people, Odense is big and industrial. But its old center, tidy and neatly urbanized, re-

tains some pockets of the fairy-tale charm it had in the days of H. C. Everything is within easy walking distance, except for the open-air folk museum.

The train station sits at the north end of the town center. A few blocks south runs the main pedestrian shopping bou-

levard, Vestergade. Near the eastern end of this drag, and a couple of blocks up, is a tight tangle of atmospheric old lanes, where you'll find the Hans Christian Andersen Museum and Møntergården, Odense's urban history museum.

TOURIST INFORMATION

The TI is in the Town Hall (Rådhuset), the big brick palace overlooking the square at the east end of the Vestergade pedes-

trian street (July-Aug Mon-Fri 9:30-18:00, Sat 10:00-15:00, Sun 11:00-14:00; shorter hours and closed Sun off-season; tel. 63 75 75 20, www.visitodense.com). For all the information needed for a longer stop, pick up their excellent and free *Odense* guide. If you plan to visit multiple sights, consider the **Odense Pass,**

which covers the Hans Christian Andersen Museum, urban history museum, art museum, railway museum, and open-air folk museum. It saves you money if you visit at least three sights (169 DKK/24 hours, buy at TI).

ARRIVAL IN ODENSE

The train station is located in the Bånegard Center, a large shopping complex, which also holds the bus station, library, shops, eateries, and a movie theater. For a quick visit, check your luggage at the train station (pay lockers in corridor next to DSB Resjebureau

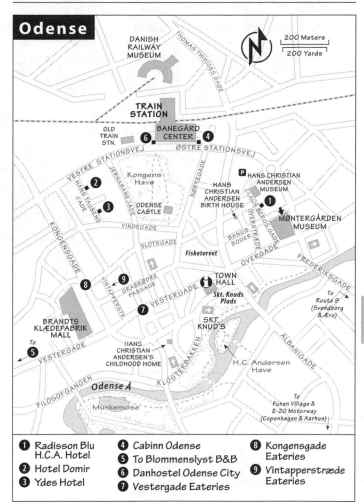

Odense

DANISH RAILWAY MUSEUM

THOMAS THIRGES GADE

200 Meters
200 Yards

TRAIN STATION

OLD TRAIN STN.

❻ BANEGÅRD CENTER ❹

VESTRE STATIONSVEJ

ØSTRE STATIONSVEJ

JERNBANEGADE

HANS TAUSENS GADE

Kongens Have

NØRREGADE

❷

❸

ODENSE CASTLE

VINDEGADE

SLOTSGADE

❿ P HANS CHRISTIAN ANDERSEN MUSEUM

HANS CHRISTIAN ANDERSEN BIRTH HOUSE

CLAUS BERGS GADE

❶

MØNTERGÅRDEN MUSEUM

BANGS BODER

OVERGADE

KONGENSGADE

Fisketorvet

FREDERIKSGADE

❽

❾

GRÅBRØDRE PASSAGE

VINTAPPERSTR.

VESTERGADE

❼

TOWN HALL

Skt. Knuds Plads

SKT. KNUD'S

To Route 9 (Svendborg & Ærø)

BRANDTS KLÆDEFABRIK MALL

❺

VESTERGADE

HANS CHRISTIAN ANDERSEN'S CHILDHOOD HOME

KLOSTERBAKKEN

H.C. Andersen Have

ALBANIGADE

FILOSOFGANGEN

Odense Å

Munkemose

To Funen Village & E-20 Motorway (Copenhagen & Aarhus)

❶ Radisson Blu H.C.A. Hotel
❷ Hotel Domir
❸ Ydes Hotel
❹ Cabinn Odense
❺ To Blommenslyst B&B
❻ Danhostel Odense City
❼ Vestergade Eateries
❽ Kongensgade Eateries
❾ Vintapperstræde Eateries

office), pick up a free town map inside the ticket office, jot down the time your train departs, and hit the town (follow signs to *Odense Centrum*).

To get to the **TI**, turn right out of the station, cross the busy road, then cut through the Kongens Have (King's Garden) park and head down Jernabanegade. When you come to Vestergade, take a left and follow this fine pedestrian street 100 yards to the TI.

Sights in Odense

Note that some of Odense's museums charge higher admission (about 15-20 DKK extra) during school holidays.

▲▲▲Hans Christian Andersen Museum

As a new Hans Christian Andersen Museum is under construction into 2020, the museum has moved some of its exhibits to a temporary venue a few blocks away. This space is smaller than the original but still offers "an insight into Andersen's life through a number of clues that link to the poet's art"—check the museum's website for the latest info. The home where Andersen was born, a part of the original museum, remains open to visitors. And another H. C. house, the writer's childhood home (with a small exhibit of its own), is a few blocks from here at Munkemøllestræde 3.

Cost and Hours: 110 DKK combo-ticket (125 DKK in summer) includes Andersen's birthplace, childhood home, and the Møntergården Museum with the Fyrtøjet ("Tinderbox") children's activity center; daily 10:00-16:00, July-late-Aug until 17:00, Claus Bergs Gade 11 (next to the recommended Radisson Blu H. C. A. Hotel), tel. 65 51 46 01, www.museum.odense.dk.

Fyrtøjet ("Tinderbox")

This fun hands-on center for children, based on works by Hans Christian Andersen, is in a temporary location (through 2020) as its original site at the Hans Christian Andersen Museum is being rebuilt. As a result, there may be changes to what's described here (check their website for updates). Normally, the centerpiece is Fairytale Land, with giant props and sets inspired by one of the author's tales. Kids can dress up in costumes and get their faces painted at the "magical wardrobe," act out a fairy tale, and do arts and crafts in the "atelier." Ask about performances (generally daily at 12:00 and 14:00; some are in Danish only, but others are done without dialogue).

Cost and Hours: 80 DKK for ages 3-69 (free to other ages), higher prices during holidays; July-mid-Aug daily 10:00-17:00; shorter hours and closed Mon-Thu off-season; at the Møntergården Museum in the Nyborgladen building, Møntestræde 1, tel. 66 14 44 11, www.museum.odense.dk.

▲Møntergården (Urban History Museum)

This well-presented museum fills several medieval buildings with exhibits on the history of Odense. You'll time-travel from prehistoric times (lots of arrow, spear, and ax heads) through to 1660, when the king stripped the town of its independent status. The main exhibit, "Life of the City," fills a stately 17th-century, red house (Falk Gøyes Gård) with a high-tech, well-presented exhibit about Odense in medieval and Renaissance times, covering historical events as well as glimpses of everyday life. Wedged along the side of this building is a surviving medieval lane; at the far end are four minuscule houses that the city used to house widows and orphaned students who couldn't afford to provide for themselves. It's fascinating to squeeze into these humble interiors and imagine that people lived in these almshouses through 1955 (open only in summer, but at other times you can ask at the ticket desk to have them unlocked). A new museum building with expanded exhibits may be open by the time you visit.

Cost and Hours: 50 DKK, Tue-Sun 10:00-16:00, closed Mon; Møntestræde 1, tel. 65 51 46 01, www.museum.odense.dk.

▲Danish Railway Museum (Danmarks Jernbanemuseum)

Conveniently (and appropriately) located directly behind the train station, this is an ideal place to kill time while waiting for a train—and is worth a look for anyone who enjoys seeing old locomotives and train cars. Here at Denmark's biggest (and only official) rail museum, the huge roundhouse is filled with classic trains, while up- stairs you'll walk past long

display cases of model trains and enjoy good views down onto the trains. The information is in English, picnicking is encouraged, and there are lots of children's activities.

Cost and Hours: 65 DKK, more during special exhibits, daily 10:00-16:00; Dannebrogsgade 24—just exit behind the sta- tion, near track 7/8, and cross the street; tel. 66 13 66 30, www. railmuseum.dk.

▲Funen Village/Den Fynske Landsby Open-Air Museum

The sleepy gathering of 26 old buildings located about two miles out of town preserves the 17th- to 19th-century culture of this region. During the summer, you'll meet people dressed in period costumes who recount what life was like in 19th-century Funen as they perform their daily chores. Dozens of farm animals also bring to life the sounds—and smells—of the era. Families can enjoy tales of Hans Christian Andersen performed on an outdoor stage (mid- July-mid-Aug). Explanations in the buildings are sparse, so buy the guidebook to help make your visit meaningful.

Cost and Hours: 85 DKK July-Aug, 60 DKK rest of the year; July-Aug daily 10:00-18:00 except closes at 17:00 last half of Aug; April-June and Sept-late Oct Tue-Sun 10:00-17:00, closed Mon; closed late Oct-March; bus #110 or #111 from Odense Station, or take train to Fruens Bøge Station and walk 15 minutes; tel. 65 51 46 01, www.museum.odense.dk.

Sleeping in Odense

Demand (and prices) are higher in Odense on weekdays and in winter; in summer and on weekends, you can often get a better deal.

$$$ Radisson Blu H. C. A. Hotel is big, comfortable, and impersonal, with 145 rooms near the Hans Christian Andersen sights. It's older but nicely updated, and offers great rates every day through the summer (elevator, Claus Bergs Gade 7, tel. 66 14 78 00, www.radissonblu.com/hotel-odense, hcandersen@radissonblu.com).

$$ Hotel Domir has 35 tidy, basic, stylish little rooms along its tiny halls. It's located on a quiet side street just a few minutes from the train station and features extra soundproofing (elevator, limited pay parking, Hans Tausensgade 19, tel. 66 12 14 27, www.domir.dk, booking@domir.dk). They also run **$ Ydes Hotel,** just down the street, with industrial and metallic simplicity (breakfast extra).

$ Cabinn Odense brings its no-frills minimalist economy to town, with 201 simple, comfy, and modern rooms (breakfast extra, elevator, pay parking for small cars only, next to the station at Østre Stationsvej 7, tel. 63 14 57 00, www.cabinn.com, odense@cabinn.com). For more about this chain, see page 81.

$ Blommenslyst B&B rents four rooms in two private guesthouses just outside Odense (breakfast extra, 10-minute drive from town center, Ravnebjerggyden 31, tel. 65 96 81 88, www.blommenslyst.dk, ingvartsen-speth@post.tele.dk, Marethe and Poul Erik Speth).

Hostel: ¢ Danhostel Odense City is a huge, efficient hostel towering above the train station (private rooms available, elevator, reception open 8:00-12:00 & 16:00-20:00 but self-service check-in kiosk at other times, Østre Stationsvej 31, tel. 63 11 04 25, http://odensedanhostel.dk, info@cityhostel.dk).

Eating in Odense

Odense's main pedestrian shopping streets, **Vestergade** and **Kongensgade,** offer the best atmosphere and most options for lunch and dinner.

Vintapperstræde is an alleyway full of restaurants just off Vestergade (look for the ornamental entryway). Choose from Danish, Mexican, Italian, and more. Study the menus posted outside each restaurant to decide, then grab a table inside or join the locals at an outdoor table.

Odense Connections

From Odense by Train to: Copenhagen (3/hour, 1.5 hours, some go directly to the airport), **Aarhus** (2/hour, 1.5 hours), **Billund/ Legoland** (2/hour, 50-minute train to Vejle, then transfer to bus— see page 169; allow 2 hours total), **Svendborg/Ærø ferry** (2/hour Mon-Sat, hourly Sun, 45 minutes, to Svendborg dock; Ærø ferry— roughly 10/day, 1.25 hours), **Roskilde** (2/hour, 70 minutes).

ROUTE TIPS FOR DRIVERS

Aarhus or Billund to Ærø: Figure about two hours to drive from Billund (or 2.5 hours from Aarhus) to Svendborg. The freeway takes you over a bridge to the island of Funen (or *Fyn* in Danish); from Odense, take the highway south to Svendborg.

Leave your car in Svendborg (at the convenient long-term parking lot two blocks from the ferry dock or at the far end of the harbor near the Bendix fish shop) and sail for Ærø (see page 142 for ferry details). Cars need reservations but walk-on passengers don't.

Ærø to Copenhagen via Odense: From Svendborg, drive north on Route 9, past Egeskov Castle, and on to Odense. To visit the open-air folk museum just outside Odense (Den Fynske Landsby), leave Route 9 just south of town at Højby, turning left toward Dalum and the Odense campground (on Odensevej). Look for *Den Fynske Landsby* signs (near the train tracks, south edge of town). If you're going directly to the Hans Christian Andersen Museum (in temporary quarters through 2020), follow the signs.

Continuing toward Copenhagen, you'll take the world's third-longest suspension bridge (Storebælt Bridge, 245-DKK toll, 12.5 miles long). Follow signs marked *København* (Copenhagen). If you're following my three-week itinerary by car: When you get to Ringsted, signs point you to Roskilde—aim toward the twin church spires and follow signs for *Vikingskibene* (Viking ships). Otherwise, if you're heading to Copenhagen or the airport, stay on the freeway, following signs to *København C* or to *Dragør/Kastrup Airport*.

JUTLAND

Aarhus • Legoland • Jelling

Jutland (Jylland—pronounced "YEW-lan"—in Danish) is the part of Denmark that juts up from Germany. It's a land of windswept sandy beaches, inviting lakes, Lego toys, moated manor houses, and fortified old towns. In Aarhus, the lively and student-filled capital of Jutland, you can ogle the artwork in one of Denmark's best art museums, experience centuries-old Danish town life in its open-air folk museum, and meet a boggy prehistoric man. After you wander the pedestrian street, settle in for a drink along the canalside people zone. This region is particularly family-friendly. Make a pilgrimage to the most famous land in all of Jutland: the pint-sized kids' paradise, Legoland. The nearby village of Jelling is worth a quick stop to see the ancient rune stones known as "Denmark's birth certificate."

PLANNING YOUR TIME

Aarhus makes a natural stop for drivers connecting Kristiansand, Norway and Hirtshals, Denmark by ferry. Trains also link Aarhus to Hirtshals, as well as to points south, such as Odense and Copenhagen. Allow one day and an overnight to enjoy this busy port town.

Families will likely want a whole day at Legoland (near the town of Billund), while historians might consider a brief detour to Jelling, just 10 minutes off the main Billund-Vejle road. Both are best by car but doable by public transportation.

Aarhus

Aarhus (OAR-hoos, sometimes spelled Århus), Denmark's sec-
ond-largest city, has a popu-
lation of 310,000 and calls itself the "World's Smallest Big
City." I'd argue it's more like
the world's biggest little town:
easy to handle and easy to like.
Aarhus is Jutland's capital and
cultural hub. Its Viking found-
ers settled here—where a river
hit the sea—in the eighth cen-
tury, calling their town Aros. Today, modern Aarhus bustles with
an important university, an inviting café-lined canal, a bursting-
with-life pedestrian boulevard (Strøget), a collection of top-notch
museums (modern art, open-air folk, and prehistory/ethnography),
and an adorable "Latin Quarter" filled with people living very, very
well. Aarhus, a pleasant three-hour train ride from Copenhagen,
is well worth a stop.

Orientation to Aarhus

Aarhus lines up along its tranquil canal—formerly a busy highway—called Åboulevarden, which runs through the middle of
town. The cathedral and lively Latin Quarter are directly north of
the canal, while the train station is about five blocks to the south
(along the main pedestrianized shopping street—the Strøget). The
main museums are scattered far and wide: The ARoS art museum
is at the western edge of downtown, the Den Gamle By open-air
folk museum is a bit farther to the northwest, and the Moesgård
Museum (prehistory and ethnography) is in the countryside far to
the south.

TOURIST INFORMATION

The Aarhus TI is in Dokk1, a library/cultural center at the Aarhus
Harbor (generally Mon-Thu 10:00-19:00, Fri until 17:00, Sat-Sun
until 16:00). There's also a branch near the bus station at Fredensgade 45 and one in the summer on the main square. All branches
share a telephone number and website (tel. 87 31 50 10, www.
visitaarhus.com).

ARRIVAL IN AARHUS

At Aarhus' user-friendly **train** station, all tracks feed into a con-
course, with ticket offices (*billetsalg;* open Mon-Fri 7:00-18:00, Sat-

JUTLAND

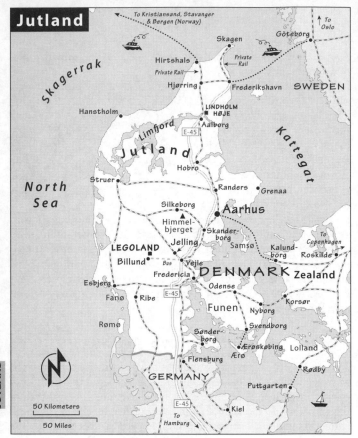

Jutland

To Kristiansand, Stavanger
& Bergen (Norway)

To Oslo

Skagerrak

Skagen

Göteborg

Hirtshals

Private Rail →

Private Rail

Hjørring

Frederikshavn

SWEDEN

Hanstholm

LINDHOLM HØJE

Aalborg

E-45

Limfjord

Jutland

Hobro

North Sea

Struer

Randers

Grenaa

Silkeborg

Aarhus

Himmelbjerget

Skanderborg

Kattegat

LEGOLAND

Jelling

Samsø

To Copenhagen

Billund

Bus

Vejle

Kalundborg

Roskilde

Fredericia

DENMARK

Zealand

Esbjerg

Odense

Fanø

Ribe

E-45

Funen

Korsør

Rømø

Nyborg

Sønderborg

Svendborg

Lolland

Flensburg

Ærøskøbing

Ærø

Rødby

GERMANY

Puttgarten

50 Kilometers

50 Miles

E-45

Kiel

To Hamburg

Sun 10:15-17:00) and a waiting room between tracks 2-3 and 4-5. A side entrance (marked *Bruun's Galleri*) takes you directly into a shopping mall; the other entrance (under the clock) leads into the blocky main terminal hall, with pay lockers, fast food, and ticket machines. Near the main doors, screens show departure times for upcoming city and regional buses.

To get into town, it's a pleasant 10-minute walk: Exit straight ahead, cross the street, and proceed up the wide, traffic-free shopping street known as the Strøget, which takes you directly to the canal, cathedral, and the start of my Aarhus Walk.

If arriving by **car** or **cruise ship,** see "Aarhus Connections," later.

GETTING AROUND AARHUS

The sights mentioned in my self-guided walk, along with the ARoS art museum, are all within a 15-minute **walk;** the Den Gamle By open-air folk museum is a few minutes farther, but still walkable. The Moesgård Museum and Tivoli Friheden amusement park are best reached by bus. While Aarhus has a new light-rail line, the route is of little use to tourists.

You can buy **bus** tickets from the coin-op machines on board the bus (a 20-DKK, 2-zone ticket covers any of my recommended sights, and is good for 2 hours). Bus drivers are friendly and speak English.

A few local buses leave from in front of the train station, but most depart around the corner, along Park Allé in front of the Town Hall. Bus #3A to the Den Gamle By open-air folk museum leaves from a stop across the street from the station. Other buses leave from in front of the Town Hall, about two blocks away: Cross the street in front of the station, turn left and walk to the first major corner, then turn right up Park Allé; the stops are in front of the blocky Town Hall (with the boxy tower, on the left). From here, bus #16 goes to the Tivoli Friheden amusement park; and bus #18 goes to the Moesgård Museum. To find your bus stop, look for the handy diagram at the start of the Strøget.

Taxis are easy to flag down but pricey (45-DKK drop fee).

HELPFUL HINTS

Sightseeing Pass: The **Aarhus Card** provides small discounts on major sights and free entry to some minor sights, and includes public transportation. This can be a money-saver for busy sightseers (299 DKK/24 hours, 499 DKK/48 hours, purchase at hotels, the Dokk1 TI, or at www.visitaarhus.com).

Festival: The 10-day **Aarhus Festival,** which takes place in late summer (Aug-Sept), fills the city's streets and venues with music, dance, food, kids' activities, and much more (www.aarhusfestuge.dk).

Laundry: An unstaffed, coin-op launderette *(mønt-vask)* is four short blocks south of the train station, on the square in front of St. Paul's Church (daily 7:00-21:00, bring lots of coins, M.P. Bruunsgade 64).

Aarhus Walk

This quick little self-guided walk acquaints you with the historic center, covering everything of sightseeing importance except the three big museums (modern art, prehistory, and open-air folk). You'll begin at the cathedral, check out the modest sights in its vicinity, wander the cute Latin Quarter, take a stroll down the "most beautiful street" in Aarhus, and end at the canal (for walking route, see the "Aarhus Center" map). After touring the impressive cathedral, the rest of the walk should take about an hour.

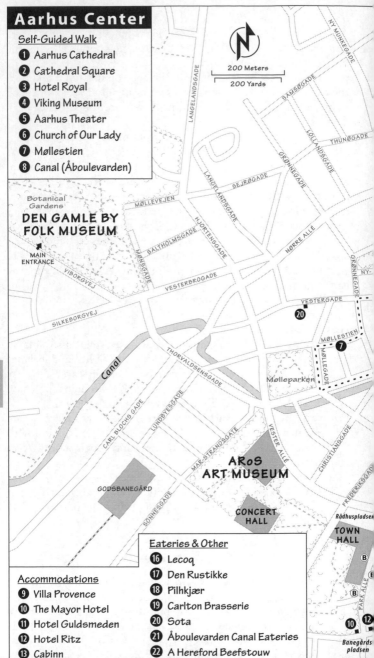

Aarhus Center

Self-Guided Walk
1. Aarhus Cathedral
2. Cathedral Square
3. Hotel Royal
4. Viking Museum
5. Aarhus Theater
6. Church of Our Lady
7. Møllestien
8. Canal (Åboulevarden)

200 Meters
200 Yards

JUTLAND

Botanical Gardens

DEN GAMLE BY FOLK MUSEUM

MAIN ENTRANCE

Canal

Mølleparken

AROS ART MUSEUM

GODSBANEGÅRD

CONCERT HALL

Rådhuspladsen

TOWN HALL

Banegårds pladsen

Accommodations
9. Villa Provence
10. The Mayor Hotel
11. Hotel Guldsmeden
12. Hotel Ritz
13. Cabinn
14. To Danhostel Aarhus
15. City Sleep-In

Eateries & Other
16. Lecoq
17. Den Rustikke
18. Pilhkjær
19. Carlton Brasserie
20. Sota
21. Åboulevarden Canal Eateries
22. A Hereford Beefstouw
23. Teater Bodega
24. To Launderette

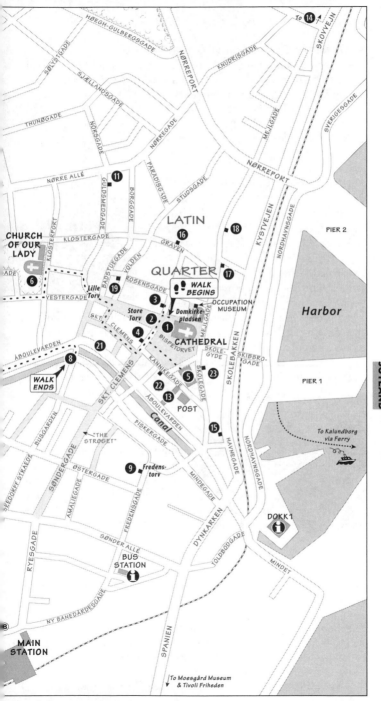

HØEGH-GULBERGSGADE
SØLYSTGADE
SJÆLLANDSGADE
THUNØGADE
NØRREGADE
NØRREPORT
KNUDRISGADE
MEJLGADE
SVERIGESGADE
NØRRE ALLÉ
GULDSMEDGADE
BORGGADE
PARADISGADE
STUDSGADE
NØRREPORT
KYSTVEJEN
NORDHAVNSGADE
SKOVVEJEN
To **14**

11

LATIN

CHURCH
OF OUR
LADY
KLOSTERGADE
KLOSTERGADE
KLOSTERPORT
ADE
6
VESTERGADE
Lille
Torv
RADSTUEGADE
VOLDEN
ROSENGADE
KØBENGADE
19

16
GRAVEN
18

QUARTER
17

WALK
BEGINS

Store
Torv
3
2
1
Domkirke-
pladsen
BISPETORVET
OCCUPATION
MUSEUM

PIER 2

Harbor

4
CATHEDRAL
SKOLE-
GYDE
SKIBBROGADE
SKOLEBAKKEN
SKT. CLEMENS
21
8
WALK
ENDS
ÅBOULEVARDEN
KANNIKEGADE
5
SKOLEGADE
23

PIER 1

"THE
STRØGET"
22
13
POST
ÅBOULEVARDEN
Canal
FISKERGADE
15
HAVNEGADE
NORDHAVNSGADE

To Kalundborg
via Ferry

SEEDORFF STRÆDE
BUSGÅRDEN
SØNDERGADE
ØSTERGADE
AMALIEGADE
9 Fredens-
torv
FREDENSGADE
MINDEGADE
DYNKARKEN

DOKK1
i

RYESGADE
SØNDER ALLÉ
**BUS
STATION**
i
TOLDBODGADE
MINDET

8

NY BANEGÅRDSGADE

**MAIN
STATION**
SPANIEN

To Moesgård Museum
& Tivoli Friheden

JUTLAND

• *Start by touring Aarhus Cathedral.*

▲▲Aarhus Cathedral (Domkirke)

While Scandinavia's biggest church (330 feet long and tall) is typically stark-white inside, it also comes with some vivid decorations dating from before the Reformation.

Cost and Hours: Free entry; Mon-Sat 9:30-16:00; Oct-April Mon-Sat 10:00-15:00; closed Sun except for services at 10:00 and 17:00; www.aarhus-domkirke.dk.

Visiting the Cathedral: The cathedral was finished in 1520 in all its Catholic glory. Imagine it with 55 side chapels, each dedicated to a different saint and wallpapered with colorful frescoes. Bad timing. Just 16 years later, in 1536, the Reformation hit this region and Protestants cleaned out the church—side altars gone, paintings whitewashed over—and added a pulpit in the middle of the nave so parishioners could hear the sermon. The front pews were even turned away from the altar to face the pulpit (a problem for weddings today).

Ironically, that Lutheran whitewash protected the fine 16th-century Catholic art. When it was peeled back in the 1920s, the

frescoes were found perfectly preserved. In 1998, the surrounding whitewash was redone, making the old original paintings, which have never been restored, pop. Noble tombs that once lined the floor (worn smooth by years of traffic) now decorate the walls. The fancy text-filled wall medallions are epitaphs, originally paired with tombs. Ships hang from the ceilings of many Danish churches (you'll find a fine example in the left transept)—in this nation of seafarers, there were invariably women praying for the safe return of their sailors.

Step into the enclosed choir area at the front of the church. The main altarpiece, dating from 1479, features the 12 apostles flanking St. Clement (the patron saint of Aarhus and sailors—his symbol is the anchor), St. Anne, and John the Baptist. On top, Jesus is crowning Mary in heaven.

Head down the stairs to the apse area behind the altar. Find the model of the altarpiece, which demonstrates how the polyptych (many-paneled altarpiece) you just saw can be flipped to different scenes throughout the church year.

Also in this area, look for the fresco in the aisle (right of altar, facing windows) that shows a three-part universe: heaven, earth (at Mass), and—under the thick black line—purgatory...an ugly land with angels and devils fighting over souls. The kid on the gallows illustrates how the medieval Church threatened even little children with ugly damnation. Notice the angels trying desperately to save the damned. Just a little more money to the Church and...I...think...we...can...pull...Grandpa...OUT.

An earlier Romanesque church—just as huge—once stood on this spot. As you exit, notice the tiny, pointy-topped window in the back-right. It survives with its circa-1320 fresco from that earlier church. Even back then—when the city had a population of 1,000—the church seated 1,200. Imagine the entire community (and their dogs) assembled here to pray and worship their way through the darkness and uncertainty of medieval life.

• *Then, standing at the cathedral door, survey the...*

Cathedral Square

The long, triangular square is roughly the shape of the original Viking town from A.D. 770. Aarhus is the Viking word for "mouth

of river." The river flows to your left to the beach, which—before modern land reclamation—was just behind the church. The green spire peeking over the buildings dead ahead is the Church of Our Lady (which we'll visit later on this walk). Fifty yards to the right, the nubile caryatids by local artist Hans Krull decorate the entry to the **Hotel Royal** and town casino. (Krull's wildly decorated bar is just beyond, down the stairs at the corner.) Also nearby (around the corner from the cathedral) is the fine **Occupation Museum 1940-1945,** about the Danish resistance during World War II (described later, under "Sights in Aarhus").

• *Fifty yards to the left of the church (as you face the square), in the basement of the Nordea Bank, is the tiny...*

Viking Museum

When excavating the site for the bank building in 1960, remains of Viking Aarhus were uncovered. Today you can ride an escalator down to the little bank-sponsored museum showing a surviving bit of the town's original boardwalk in situ (where it was found), Viking artifacts, and a murder victim (missing his head)—all well-described in English.

Cost and Hours: Free, open bank hours: Mon-Fri 10:15-16:00, Thu until 17:00, closed Sat-Sun.

• *Leaving the bank, walk straight ahead along the substantial length of the cathedral (brides have plenty of time to reconsider things during their procession) to the fancy building opposite.*

Aarhus Theater

This ornate facade, with its flowery stained glass, is Danish Art Nouveau from around 1900. Under the tiny balcony is the town

seal, featuring towers, the river, St. Clement with his anchor, and St. Paul with his sword. High above, on the roofline, crouches the devil. The local bishop made a stink when this "house of sin" was allowed to be built facing the cathedral. The theater builders had the last say, finishing their structure with this smart-aleck devil triumphing (this was a hit with the secular, modern locals).

• *Return to the square in front of the cathedral.*

Latin Quarter

The higgledy-piggledy old town encompasses the six or eight square blocks in front of the cathedral and to the right. Latin was never

spoken here—the area was named in the 1960s after the cute, boutique-ish, and similarly touristy zone in Paris. Though Aarhus' canal strip is a newer trendy spot, the Latin Quarter is still great for shopping, cafés, and strolling. Explore these streets: Volden (named for the rampart), Graven (moat), and Badstuegade ("Bath Street"). In the days when fires routinely decimated towns, bathhouses—with their open fires necessary to heat the water— were located outside the walls. Back in the 15th century, finer people bathed monthly, while everyday riff-raff took their "Christmas bath" once a year.

• *Back at the far end of Cathedral Square, side-trip away from the cathedral to the green spire of the...*

Church of Our Lady (Vor Frue Kirke)

The smart brick building you see today is in the Dutch Renaissance style from the early 16th century, but this local "Notre-Dame" is the

oldest church in town. After Christianity came to Viking Denmark in 965, a tiny wooden church was built here. Step down into the crypt of today's church (below the main altar). This evocative arcaded space (c. 1060) was originally an 11th-century stone rebuild of the first church (and only discovered in 1955). Four rune stones were also discovered on this site. Back upstairs, find the graphic crucifix, with its tangled thieves flanking Christ, which was carved and painted by a Lübeck artist in 1530. As at Aarhus Cathedral, the church's whitewashed walls are covered with fine epitaph medallions with family portraits. Step through the low door behind the rear pew (on the right with your back to the altar) into the peaceful cloister. With the Reformation, this became a hospital. Today, it's a retirement home for lucky seniors.

Cost and Hours: Free; Mon-Fri 10:00-16:00, Sat until 14:00; closed Sun, www.aarhusvorfrue.dk.

• *Walk west on Vestergade to the next street, Grønnegade. Turn left, then take the next right onto...*

Møllestien

Locals call this quiet little cobbled lane the "most beautiful street in Aarhus." The small, pastel cottages—draped in climbing roses

and hollyhock in summer—date from the 18th century. Notice the small mirrors on one of the windows. Known as "street spies," they allow people inside to inconspicuously watch what's going on outside.

• *At the end of the lane, head left toward the canal. The park on your right,* **Mølleparken,** *is a good spot for a picnic. The big, boxy building with the rainbow ring on top is the* **ARoS** *art museum (described later)—consider visiting it now, or backtrack here when the walk is over.*

When you reach the canal, turn left and walk about four blocks toward the cathedral spire until you get to the concrete pedestrian bridge.

Canal (Åboulevarden)

You're standing on the site of the original Viking bridge. The open sea was dead ahead. A protective harbor was behind you. When the town was attacked, the bridge on this spot was raised, ships were tucked safely away, and townsmen stood here to defend their fleet. Given the choice, they'd let the town burn and save their ships.

In the 1930s, the Aarhus River was covered over to make a new road—an event marked by much celebration. In the 1980s, locals reconsidered the change, deciding that the road cut a boring, people-mean swath through the center of their town. They removed the road, artfully canalized the river, and created a new people zone—the town's place to see and be seen. This strip of modern restaurants ensures the street stays as lively as possible even after the short summer.

• *Your walk is over. Retreating back up the canal takes you to the **ARoS** art museum, then to the **Den Gamle By** open-air folk museum. Following the canal ahead takes you past the best of the Aarhus canal zone. Crossing the canal bridge and going straight (with a one-block jog left) gets you to the Strøget pedestrian boulevard, which leads all the way to the train station (where you can catch a bus—either at the station or the Town Hall nearby—to Tivoli Friheden amusement park, the Den Gamle By open-air folk museum, or the Moesgård Museum). All of these sights are described in the next section.*

Sights in Aarhus

▲▲ARoS

The ARoS Aarhus Art Museum is a must-see sight, both for the building's architecture and for its knack for making cutting-edge art accessible and fun. Everything is described in English. Square and unassuming from the outside, the bright white interior—with its spiral staircase winding up the museum's eight floors—is surprising. The building has two sections, one for the exhibits and one for administration. The halves are divided by a vast atrium, which is free to enter if you just want to peek at the building itself (or to visit the gift shop or café). But to see any of the items described later, you'll have to buy a ticket. In addition to the permanent collections that I've described, the museum displays an impressive

range of temporary exhibits—be sure to find out what's on during your visit.

Cost and Hours: 130 DKK; Tue-Sun 10:00-17:00, Wed until 22:00; closed Mon, ARoS Allé 2, tel. 87 30 66 00, www.aros.dk.

Cuisine Art: The **$$** lunch café on the museum's ground floor serves light meals, while the **$$$** wine and food hall on the top floor features regional specialties from local producers.

Visiting the Museum: After entering at the fourth-floor lobby, buy your ticket, pick up a museum floor plan, and walk two

floors down the spiral staircase (to floor 2) to find one of the museum's prized pieces: the squatting sculpture called *Boy* (by Australian artist Ron Mueck)—15 feet high, yet astonishingly realistic, from the wrinkly skin on his elbows to the stitching on his shorts.

Next, head down to the lowest level. Here, amid black walls, artists from around the world (including Tony Oursler, Elmgreen & Dragset, and James Turrell) exhibit their immersive works of light

and sound in each of nine spaces *(De 9 Rum)*. In this unique space, you're plunged into the imagination of the artists.

Now ride the elevator all the way to the top floor (floor 8), then climb up the stairs (or ride a different elevator) to the rooftop.

Here you can enjoy the museum's icon: Olafur Eliasson's *Your Rainbow Panorama,* a 150-yard-long, 52-yard-diameter circular walkway enclosed in glass that gradually incorporates all the different colors of the spectrum. The piece provides 360-degree views over the city, while you're immersed in mind-bending, highly saturated hues. (It's "your" panorama because you are experiencing the colors.) It's a striking contrast to the mostly dark and claustrophobic works you've just seen in the nine spaces down below—yet, like those, it's all about playing with light. It's also practical—from a distance, it can be used by locals throughout the city as a giant compass (provided they know which color corresponds with which direction).

Back on floor 8, stroll through the manageable permanent collection of works from 1770 to 1930. Paintings dating from the **Danish Golden Age** (1800-1850) are evocative of the dewy-eyed Romanticism that swept Europe during that era: pastoral scenes of

JUTLAND

flat Danish countryside and seascapes, slices of peasant life, aristocratic portraits, "postcards" from travels to the Mediterranean world, and poignant scenes of departures and arrivals at Danish seaports. The **Danish Modernist** section, next, mostly feels derivative of big-name artists (you'll see the Danish answers to Picasso, Matisse, Modigliani, and others).

Continue down the spiral staircase, past various temporary exhibits. On floor 5, take a spin through the **classic art gallery,** featuring temporary art and multimedia installations. Like the rest of this museum, these high-concept, navel-gazing works are well-presented and very accessible.

▲▲Den Gamle By

"The Old Town" open-air folk museum has 75 half-timbered houses and craft shops. Unlike other Scandinavian open-air museums

that focus on rural folk life, Den Gamle By is designed to give you the best possible look at Danish urban life in centuries past. A fine botanical garden is next door.

Cost and Hours: Because peak-season days offer more activities, the cost depends on the time of year, from 75 DKK off-season to 135 DKK during busy times. Open daily 10:00-17:00, until 18:00 in July-mid-Aug; shorter hours off-season; after hours, the buildings are locked, but the peaceful park is open. Tel. 86 12 31 88, www.dengamleby.dk.

Getting There: Stroll 20 minutes up the canal from downtown, or catch a bus from near the train station: Bus #3A departs directly across the street from the station; otherwise use the transit route planner at www.rejseplanen.dk.

Eating: This is a perfect place to enjoy a picnic lunch (bring your own, or order a lunch packet at the reception desk by the ticket booth)—outdoor and indoor tables are scattered around the grounds. The only eatery in the park open year-round is the cheery indoor/outdoor **$$ Simonsens Have,** an inviting cafeteria serving affordable light meals. In peak season, you'll have many other options, including *pølse* and other snack stands, a bakery, a café next to the ticket kiosk, and another café in the 1970s neighborhood.

Visiting the Museum: At the ticket desk, pick up the free map of the grounds; also pick up the flier listing what's on (and plan your time around those options). Though each building is described with a plaque, and there are maps throughout the park, the guidebooklet (small fee) is a worthwhile investment and a nice souvenir. The grounds reward an adventurous spirit. They're designed

to be explored, so don't be too shy to open doors or poke into seemingly abandoned courtyards—you may find a chatty docent inside, telling their story, answering questions, or demonstrating an old-timey handicraft. Follow sounds and smells to discover a whole world beyond the main streets.

The main part of the exhibit focuses on the 18th and 19th centuries. You'll start by heading up Navnløs, then hanging a right at Vestergade (passing a row house and a flower garden with samples for sale) to the canal. Head straight over the bridge and hike up the cute street lined with market stalls, shops, and a bakery until you pop out on the main square, Torvet. The building on the left side of Torvet, the Mayor's House (from 1597), contains a museum upstairs featuring home interiors from 1600 to 1850, including many with gorgeously painted walls. At the top of Torvet is the Mintmaster's Mansion, the residence of a Copenhagen noble (from 1683). Enter around back to tour the boldly colorful, 18th-century Baroque rooms. Under the heavy

timbers of the attic is an exhibit about the history of this restored building.

Continuing out the far end of Torvet on Søndergade, you enter the 20th century. The streets and shops here evoke the year 1927, including a hardware store and (down Havbogade) a brewery where you can often buy samples (in the courtyard behind). At the end of Søndergade (on the left) is the Legetoj toy museum, with two floors of long hallways crammed with nostalgic playthings.

Walking into the next zone, you come to a street scene from 1974, with re-created apartments, a radio and TV repair shop, a hairdresser, a gynecology clinic, and a jazz bar where you can order a beer or pastry. In the Udstillinger building, you'll find the Danish Poster Museum (a delightful collection of retro posters) and the Gallery of Decorative Arts (porcelain, clocks, and silverware).

Occupation Museum 1940-1945

Nazi occupiers used Aarhus' police station as their Gestapo headquarters throughout World War II. It was the scene of tortures and executions. Today, it's a fine exhibit telling the story of the resis-

JUTLAND

tance and what it was like to live here under Nazi rule. You'll learn of heroic acts of sabotage, find out how guns were dropped out of British airplanes in the night, and see underground newspapers that kept occupied Danes connected and in the know. Sadly, much of the exhibit is without English descriptions (though free loaner English info sheets are available).

Cost and Hours: 30 DKK; June-Aug Tue-Sun 11:00-16:00, closed Mon; Sept-May Sat-Sun and Tue 11:00-16:00, closed Mon and Wed-Fri; facing the cathedral, it's around to the left, just off Cathedral Square at Mathilde Fibigers Have 2; tel. 86 18 42 77, www.besaettelsesmuseet.dk.

▲▲Moesgård Museum

This museum, dedicated to prehistory and ethnography, is housed in a state-of-the art venue, south of Aarhus in the suburb of Højbjerg. The building juts dramatically from a hill, with grass growing on a sloping roof that visitors can walk on.

Cost and Hours: 140 DKK; Tue-Sun 10:00-17:00, Wed until 21:00, closed Mon; café, tel. 87 16 10 16, www.moesmus.dk.

Getting There: The museum is located outside Aarhus at Moesgård Allé 15 in Højbjerg, in a lush, wooded park sprawling down to the sea. It's a pricey taxi trip or easy, cheap bus ride: Bus #18 leaves Aarhus from directly in front of the Town Hall on Park Allé (around the corner from the train station). On weekdays, the bus runs three to four times hourly during the museum's opening times (2/hour on Sat-Sun, ride 20 minutes to end of line, covered by bus ticket that includes zone 2, see www.midttrafik.dk for bus details). Once at the museum, carefully check what time the return bus departs (posted at the bus stop, or ask at the ticket desk).

Visiting the Museum: Divided into three main periods—the Bronze Age (1800 to 500 b.c.), Iron Age (500 b.c. to a.d. 800), and Viking Age (a.d. 700 to 1050), the prehistory section features lots of real artifacts (primitive tools and pottery, plenty of spearheads and arrowheads), all well-described in English, along with an impressive collection of rune stones.

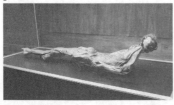

But the highlight is the well-preserved body of an Iron Age man. Believing that the gods dwelled in the bogs, prehistoric people threw offerings (such as spearheads) into the thick peat. The peat did a remarkable job of preserving these artifacts, many of which are now on display in the museum. The prehistoric people also sacrificed humans to the bog gods—resulting in the incredibly intact Graub-alle Man, the world's best-preserved "bog-corpse." Reclining in his stately glass tomb, the more than 2,000-year-old "bog man" looks like a fellow half his age. He still has his skin, nails, hair, and even the slit in his throat he got at the sacrificial banquet (back in 300 B.C.). Spend some time with this visitor from the past. The story of his discovery (in a Jutland peat bog in 1952) and conservation is also interesting.

The Grounds: The museum sits on the pleasant grounds of the Moesgård Manor; while the manor itself is closed to the public, its grounds are fun to explore. Behind the museum, a two-mile-long circular trail stretches down to a fine beach. This "Prehistoric Trackway" runs past a few model Viking buildings, including a 12th-century stave church.

Tivoli Friheden Amusement Park

The local Tivoli, about a mile south of the Aarhus train station, offers great fun for the family.

Cost and Hours: 90-120 DKK for entry only, 250-350 DKK includes rides; July-early Aug 11:30-20:00, longer hours in late July, weekends only and shorter hours off-season, closed Oct-April except for special events; bus #16 from Park Allé near Town Hall, tel. 86 14 73 00, www.friheden.dk.

Sleeping in Aarhus

Aarhus has a good variety of lodgings. My recommendations range from charming hotels with personality to backpacker-friendly hostel bunks.

$$$$ Villa Provence, named for owners Steen and Annette's favorite vacation destination, is a *petit* taste of France in the center of Aarhus, and makes a very cozy and convenient home base. Its 40 fun-yet-tasteful rooms, decorated with antique furniture and old French movie posters, surround a quiet courtyard. The pub across the street can get noisy on weekends, so ask for a room facing away from the street (pay parking, 10-minute walk from station, near Åboulevarden at the end of Fredensgade, Fredens Torv 12, tel. 86 18 24 00, www.villaprovence.dk, hotel@villaprovence.dk).

$$$$ The Mayor Hotel, affiliated with the Best Western chain, rents 162 sleek, well-furnished, business-class rooms 100 yards from the station (elevator, free fitness room, pay parking, Banegårdspladsen 14, tel. 87 32 01 00, www.themayor.dk, hotel@themayor.dk).

$$$ Hotel Guldsmeden ("Dragonfly") is a small, welcoming, and clean hotel with 27 rooms, fluffy comforters, a delightful stay-awhile garden, and a young, disarmingly friendly staff. A steep staircase takes you to the best rooms, while the cheaper rooms (five rooms sharing two bathrooms) are in a ground-floor annex behind the garden (RS%, 15-minute walk in Aarhus' quiet Latin Quarter at Guldsmedgade 40, tel. 86 13 45 50, www.guldsmedenhotels.com, aarhus@guldsmedenhotels.com).

$$$ Hotel Ritz, across the street from the station, offers 67 clean, bright rooms done in Art Deco style (elevator, Banegårdspladsen 12, tel. 86 13 44 44, www.hotelritz-aarhus.com, mail@hotelritz.dk).

$$ Cabinn, overlooking the atmospheric Åboulevarden canal, is extremely practical. Rooms are minimalist yet comfy, and service is no-nonsense (family rooms, breakfast extra, pay parking—reserve ahead, rooms overlook boisterous canal or quieter courtyard, at Kannikegade 14 but main entrance on the canal at Åboulevarden 38, tel. 86 75 70 00, www.cabinn.dk, aarhus@cabinn.dk). For more on this chain, see page 81.

¢ Danhostel Aarhus, an official HI hostel, is near the water two miles out of town (served by several buses from the train station—see website for details, Marienlundsvej 10, tel. 86 21 21 20, www.aarhusdanhostel.dk, info@aarhusdanhostel.dk).

¢ City Sleep-In, a creative independent hostel, has a shared kitchen, fun living and games room, laundry service, and lockers. It's on a busy road facing the harbor (with thin windows—expect some street noise), a 15-minute hike from the station. It's pretty grungy, but is the only centrally located hostel option in town (private rooms available, elevator, no curfew; reception open daily 8:00-11:00 & 16:00-22:00, Fri-Sat until 23:00; Havnegade 20, tel. 86 19 20 55, www.citysleep-in.dk, sleep-in@citysleep-in.dk).

Eating in Aarhus

Affluent Aarhus has plenty of great little restaurants. My listings are in the old town, within a few minutes' stroll from the cathedral.

IN AND NEAR THE LATIN QUARTER

The streets of the Latin Quarter are teeming with hardworking and popular eateries. The street called Mejlgade, along the eastern edge of downtown, has a smattering of youthful, trendy restaurants that are just far enough off the tourist trail to feel local. Look for a variety of fixed-price, three-course dinners—some affordable, others a splurge.

$$$$ Lecoq is a pricey favorite. Chef/owner Troels Thomsen and his youthful gang (proud alums from a prestigious Danish cooking school) serve up a fresh twist on traditional French cuisine in a single Paris-pleasant yet unassuming 10-table room. They pride themselves on their finely crafted presentation. Reservations are smart (daily 11:30-15:00 & 17:30-21:30, Graven 16, tel. 86 19 50 74, www.cafe-lecoq.dk).

$$$$ Den Rustikke is a French-style brasserie offering mostly French dishes (including affordable fixed-price meals), either in the rollicking interior or outside, under a cozy colonnade (daily 11:30-15:00 & 17:00-late, Mejlgade 20, tel. 86 12 00 95, www.denrustikke.dk).

$$$$ Pilhkjær is a bit more expensive and sedate, filling a cellar with elegantly casual atmosphere. The menu, which changes daily and can include fish, meat, or vegetarian offerings, is available only as a full-course meal—there's no à la carte option (Tue-Thu 17:30-22:30, Fri-Sat 17:30-23:30, closed Sun-Mon; at the end of a long courtyard at Mejlgade 28, tel. 86 18 23 30, www.pihlkjaer-restaurant.dk).

$$$ Carlton Brasserie, facing a pretty square, is a solid bet for good Danish and international food in classy (verging on stuffy) surroundings. The restaurant has tables on the square, with more formal seating in back (Mon-Sat from 12:00, closed Sun, Rosensgade 23, tel. 86 20 21 22).

A few short blocks farther from the action (past the Church of Our Lady), **$$$ Sota** is a local favorite for sushi, to eat in or take away. This sleek, split-level, Tokyo-Scandinavian hybrid is in a half-timbered old house (Mon-Thu 16:00-22:00, Fri-Sat 12:00-23:00, closed Sun, reservations recommended, Vestergade 48, tel. 86 47 47 88, www.sotasushibar.dk).

ALONG ÅBOULEVARDEN CANAL

The canal running through town is lined with trendy eateries—all overpriced unless you value making the scene with the locals (and all open daily until late). They have indoor and canalside seating with heaters and blankets, so diners can eat outdoors even when it's cold. Before settling in, cruise the entire strip, giving special consideration to **$$ Cross Café** (with red awnings, right at main bridge) and **$$ Ziggy,** both of which are popular for salads, sandwiches, burgers, and drinks; and **$$$ Grappa,** a classy Italian place with pastas and pizzas, as well as pricier plates. Several places along here serve basic breakfast buffets.

NEAR THE CATHEDRAL

These places, while a bit past their prime and touristy, are convenient and central.

$$$$ A Hereford Beefstouw, in the St. Clement's Brewery building facing the cathedral, is a bright, convivial, fun-loving, and woody land of happy eaters and drinkers. Choose from a hearty

JUTLAND

menu and eat amid shiny copper beer vats. If you're dropping by for a brew, they have enticing beer snacks and spicy little *ølpølse* sausages (hearty dinners such as steak, ribs, burgers, and fish; Mon-Thu and Sun 17:30-23:00, Fri-Sat 12:00-24:00, Kannikegade 10, tel. 86 13 53 25, www.beefstouw.com/aarhus).

$$$ **Teater Bodega** is the venerable best bet for traditional Danish—where local men go for "food their wives won't cook." While a bit tired and old-fashioned for Aarhus' trendy young student population, it's a sentimental favorite for old-timers. Facing the theater and cathedral, it's dressy and draped in theater memorabilia (open-face sandwiches at lunch only, Mon-Sat 11:30-21:30, Sun 12:00-20:00, Skolegade 7, tel. 86 12 19 17, www.teaterbodega.dk).

Aarhus Connections

BY PUBLIC TRANSPORTATION
From Aarhus by Train to: Odense (2/hour, 1.5 hours), **Copenhagen** (2/hour, 3.5 hours), **Ærøskøbing** (6-7/day, transfer to ferry in Svendborg, allow 5 hours total), **Billund/Legoland** (3/hour; 45-minute train to Vejle, then transfer to bus—described later, allow 2 hours total), **Hamburg,** Germany (2 direct/day, more with transfers, 5 hours).

You can take the train from Aarhus to **Hirtshals,** where you can catch the **ferry to Norway** on the Color Line (www.colorline.com) or Fjordline (www.fjordline.com). Trains depart Aarhus hourly and take about 2.5 hours (to meet the Color Line ferry, transfer at Hjørring and continue to Hirtshals Havn; note that rail passes don't cover the Hjørring-Hirtshals train, but do give a 50 percent discount; buy your ticket in Hjørring or on board).

ROUTE TIPS FOR DRIVERS
From the Ferry Dock at Hirtshals to Jutland Destinations: From the dock in Hirtshals, drive south (signs to *Hjørring, Ålborg*). It's about 2.5 hours to Aarhus. (To skip Aarhus, skirt the center and follow E-45 south.) To get to downtown **Aarhus,** follow signs to the center, then *Domkirke.* Park in the pay lot across from the cathedral. Signs all over town direct you to Den Gamle By open-air folk museum. From Aarhus, it's 60 miles to Billund/Legoland (go south on Skanderborg Road and get on E-45; follow signs to *Vejle, Kolding*). For **Jelling,** take the *Vejle N* exit and follow signs to *Vejle,* then veer right on the ring road (following signs to *Skovgade*), then follow Route 442 north. For **Legoland,** take the *Vejle S* exit for Billund (after *Vejle N*—it's the first exit after the dramatic Vejlefjord bridge).

Legoland

Legoland is Scandinavia's top kids' sight. If you have a child (or are a child at heart), it's a fun stop.

This huge park is a happy combination of rides, restaurants, trees, smiles, and 33 million Lego bricks creatively arranged into such wonders as Mount Rushmore, the Parthenon, "Mad" King Ludwig's castle, and the Statue of Liberty. It's a Lego world here, as everything is cleverly related to this popular toy. If your time in Denmark is short, or if your family has already visited a similar Legoland park in California, England, or Germany, consider skipping the trip. But if you're in the neighborhood, a visit to the mothership of all things Lego will be a hit with kids ages two through the pre-teens.

GETTING THERE

Legoland, located in the town of Billund, is easiest to visit by car (see "Route Tips for Drivers," earlier), but doable by public transportation. The nearest train station to Billund is Vejle. Trains arrive at Vejle from **Copenhagen** (2/hour, 2.5 hours), **Odense** (2/hour, 1 hour), and **Aarhus** (3/hour, 45 minutes). At Vejle, catch buses #43 or #143 to travel the remaining 25 miles to Billund (30-45 minutes). For train and bus details, see www.rejseplanen.dk.

ORIENTATION TO LEGOLAND

Cost: 359 DKK for adults, 339 DKK for kids ages 3-12. Advance tickets, often available at a discount, are sold online at www.legoland.dk (reduced-price family tickets also available), and at many Danish locations (stores, hotels, and TIs), including the Dagli' Brugsen store in Vandel, just west of Billund. Legoland generally doesn't charge in the evening (free after 19:30 in July and late Aug, otherwise after 17:30).

Hours: Generally April-Oct daily 10:00-18:00, later on weekends and for much of July-Aug, closed Nov-March and Wed-Thu in Sept-mid-Oct. Activities close an hour before the park, but it's basically the same place after dinner as during the day, with fewer tour groups. Confirm exact hours before heading out.

Information: Tel. 75 33 13 33, www.legoland.dk.

Crowd-Beating Tips: Legoland is crowded during the Danish summer school vacation, from early July through mid-August.

To bypass the ticket line, purchase tickets online in advance (simply scan them at the entry turnstile).

Money-Saving Deals: If a one-day visit is not enough, you can pay 488 DKK for a two-day ticket. If you hate waiting in lines, consider shelling out for a Q-bot, which allows you to book ahead and skip the queue for some popular attractions (available at select times).

Eating: Surprisingly, the park's restaurants don't serve Lego-lamb, but there are plenty of other food choices. Prices are high, so consider bringing a picnic to enjoy at one of the several spots set aside for bring-it-yourselfers.

BACKGROUND

Lego began in 1932 in the workshop of a local carpenter who named his wooden toys after the Danish phrase *leg godt* ("play well"). In 1949, the company started making the plastic interlocking building bricks for which they are world famous. Since then, Lego has continued to expand its lineup and now produces everything from Ninjago ninja warriors to motorized models, Clikits jewelry, board games, video games—many based on popular movies (*Lego Star Wars*, *Lego Harry Potter*, etc.)—making kids drool in languages all around the world. *The Lego Movie*, a hit animated feature released in 2014, kicked off a series of Lego-themed films, and *Beyond the Brick: A Lego Brickumentary* looks at the toy's enduring popularity. According to the company, each person on this planet has, on average, 62 Lego blocks.

VISITING LEGOLAND

Legoland is divided into eight different "worlds" with fun themes such as Adventure Land, Pirate Land, and Knight's Kingdom.

Pick up a brochure at the entrance and make a plan using the colorful 3-D map. You can see it all in a day, but you'll be exhausted. The Legoredo section (filled with Wild West clichés Europeans will enjoy more than Americans) merits just a quick look, though your five-year-old might enjoy roasting a biscuit-on-a-stick around the fire with  a tall, blond park employee wearing a Native American headdress.

A highlight for young and old alike is Miniland (near the entrance), where landscaped gardens are filled with carefully constructed Lego landscapes and cityscapes. Anyone who has ever picked up a Lego block will marvel at seeing representations of the world's famous sights, including Danish monuments, Dutch windmills, German castles, and an amazing version of the Norwegian harbor of Bergen. Children joyfully watch as tiny Lego boats ply the waters and Lego trains chug merrily along the tracks. Nearby, kids can go on mellow rides in child-size cars, trains, and boats. A highlight

of Miniland is the Traffic School, where young drivers (ages 7-13) learn the rules of the road and get a souvenir license. (If interested in this popular attraction, make a reservation upon arrival.)

More rides are scattered throughout the park. While the rides aren't thrilling by Disneyland standards, most kids will find some-

thing to enjoy (parents should check the brochure for strictly enforced height restrictions). The Falck Fire Brigade ride in Lego City invites family participation as you team up to put out a (fake) fire. The Temple is an Indiana Jones-esque Egyptian-themed treasure hunt/shoot-'em-up, and the Dragon roller coaster takes you in and around a medieval castle. Note that on a few rides (including the Pirate Splash Battle), you'll definitely get wet. Special

walk-in, human-sized dryers help you warm up and dry off.

The indoor museum features company history, high-tech Lego creations, a great doll collection, and a toy exhibit full of mechanical wonders from the early 1900s, many ready to jump into action with the push of a button. A Lego playroom encourages hands-on fun, and a campground is across the street if your kids refuse to move on.

Nearby: Those looking for water fun with a tropical theme can check out the Aquadome (one of Europe's largest water parks), located outside Legoland in Billund at the family resort of Lalandia (www.lalandia.dk).

SLEEPING NEAR LEGOLAND

$$$$ Legoland Hotel adjoins Legoland (family rooms and deals, tel. 79 51 13 50, www.hotellegoland.dk, reservation@legoland.dk).

$$$$ Legoland Holiday Village offers cabins, camping, and motel rooms that sleep up to eight people (Ellehammers Allé 2, tel. 79 51 13 50, www.legoland-village.dk, reservation@legoland.dk).

$$ Hotel Svanen is close by, in Billund (Nordmarksvej 8, tel. 75 33 28 33, www.hotelsvanen.dk, billund@hotelsvanen.dk).

JUTLAND

Nearby: In a forest just outside of Billund, Erik and Mary Sort run **$ Gregersminde,** a B&B with a great setup: six double rooms (some with shared bath), plus a cottage that sleeps up to six people. Guests enjoy a huge living room, a kitchen, lots of Lego toys, and a kid-friendly yard (breakfast extra, rental bikes, leave Billund on Grindsted Road, turn right on Stilbjergvej, go a half-mile to Stilbjergvej 4B, tel. 61 27 33 23, www.gregersminde.dk, info@gregersminde.dk).

Jelling

On your way to or from Legoland, consider a short side-trip to the tiny village of Jelling (pronounced "YELL-ing"), a place of immense importance in Danish history. Here you'll find two rune stones, set next to a 900-year-old church that's flanked by two enormous, man-made burial mounds. The two stones are often called "Denmark's birth certificate"—the first written record of Denmark's status as a nation-state. An excellent (and free) museum lies just across the street.

Two hours is ample for a visit. If pressed for time, an hour is enough to see the stones and take a quick look at the museum. Note that the museum is closed on Monday.

Jelling is too small for a TI, but the museum staff can answer most questions. If you're here around lunchtime, Jelling is a great spot for a picnic. There are several central eateries and a café and WC inside the museum, and another WC in the parking lot near the North Mound.

Getting There: Drivers can easily find Jelling, just 10 minutes off the main Vejle-Billund road (see "Route Tips for Drivers" under "Aarhus Connections"). Train travelers coming from Copenhagen or Aarhus must change in Vejle, which is connected to Jelling by hourly trains (direction: Herning) and bus #211.

Jelling Walk

Denmark is proud of being Europe's oldest monarchy and of the fact that Queen Margrethe II, the country's current ruler, can trace her lineage back 1,300 years to Jelling. This short, self-guided walk explores this sacred place.

• *Begin your visit at the...*

Kongernes Jelling Museum: Inside this modern, light-filled building you'll find informative exhibits, historical models of the area, and replicas of the rune stones. Kids will love the room in the back on the ground level where they can write their name in the runic alphabet—and the gift shop bristling with wooden swords and Viking garb (free, June-Aug Tue-Sun 10:00-17:00, Sept-May Tue-Sun 12:00-16:00, closed between Christmas and New Year's and on Mon year-round, café, tel. 75 87 23 50, http://natmus.dk/kongernes-jelling).

• *Cross the street and walk through the graveyard to examine the actual...*

Rune Stones: The stones stand just south of the church. The modern bronze-and-glass structure is designed to protect the stones from the elements while allowing easy viewing.

The smaller stone was erected by King Gorm the Old (a.k.a. Gorm the Sleepy), who ruled Denmark for 40 years in the ninth

century. You probably don't read runic so I'll translate: *"King Gorm made this monument in memory of Thyra, his wife, Denmark's salvation."* These are the oldest recorded words of a Danish king, and the first time that the name Denmark is used to describe a country and not just the region.

The **larger stone** was erected by Gorm's son, Harald Bluetooth, to honor his parents, commemorate the conquering of Denmark and Norway, and mark the conversion of the Danes to Christianity. (Today's Bluetooth wireless technology takes its name from Harald, who created the decidedly non-wireless connection between the Danish and Norwegian peoples.)

Harald was a shrewd politician who had practical reasons for being baptized. He knew that if he declared Denmark to be a Christian land, he could save it from possible attack by the predatory German bishops to the south. The inscription reads: *"King Harald ordered this monument made in memory of Gorm, his father, and in memory of Thyra, his mother; that Harald who won for himself all of Denmark and Norway and made the Danes Christian."*

This large stone has three sides. One side reveals an image of Jesus and a cross, while the other has a serpent wrapped around a lion. This is important imagery that speaks to the transition from Nordic paganism to Christianity. These designs carved into the rock were once brightly painted.

• *Go around the back of the church and climb the steps to the 35-foot-high, grass-covered...*

North Mound: According to tradition, Gorm was buried in a chamber inside this mound, with his queen Thyra interred in the smaller mound to the south. But excavations in the 1940s turned up no royal remains in either mound. (In the 1970s, what is believed to be Gorm's body was discovered below the church.) Scan the horizon and mentally remove the trees. Imagine the commanding view this site had in the past. Look north to stones that trace the outline of a ship. Below you lies a graveyard with typically Danish well-manicured plots.

• *Now descend the stairs to the...*

Church: Within the sparse interior, note the ship model hanging from the ceiling, a holdover from a pre-Christian tradition seeking a safe journey for ship and crew. The church, which dates from around 1100, is decorated with restored frescoes. A zigzag motif is repeated in the modern windows and the inlaid floor. The metal "Z" in the floor marks the spot where Gorm's body lies.

More Jutland Sights

NORTHEAST OF BILLUND
Himmelbjerget and Silkeborg

If you're connecting the Billund and Jelling area with Aarhus, consider this slower but more scenic route north through the idyllic Danish Lake District. (With less time, return to Vejle and take the E-45 motorway.)

Himmelbjerget, best seen by car, lies in the middle of Jutland near the town of Silkeborg. Both are about an hour northeast of Billund (22 miles west of Aarhus). Silkeborg is accessible by train from Aarhus with a change in Skanderborg.

Denmark's landscape is vertically challenged when compared to its mountainous neighbors Norway and Sweden. If you have a hankering to ascend to one of the country's highest points, consider a visit to the 482-foot-tall **Himmelbjerget,** which translates loftily as "The Heaven Mountain." That may be overstating it, but by Danish standards the view's not bad. One can literally drive to the top, where a short trail leads to an 80-foot-tall brick tower. Climb the **tower** for a commanding view. Clouds roll by above a patchwork of green and gold fields while boats ply the blue waters of the lake below. You may see the vintage paddle steamers make the hour-long trip between Himmelbjerget and Silkeborg in season (the dock is accessed by a short hike from the tower down to the lake).

Silkeborg, in the center of the Danish Lake District, has an excellent freshwater aquarium/exhibit/nature park called **AQUA** that's worth a visit, especially if you're traveling with kids (tel. 89 21 21 89, www.visitaqua.dk). Also in Silkeborg, modern-art lovers will enjoy the **Museum Jorn Silkeborg,** featuring colorful abstract works by Asger Jorn—a prominent member of the 1960s' COBRA movement—plus other Danish and foreign art (tel. 86 82 53 88, www.museumjorn.dk).

SOUTHWEST OF BILLUND
▲Ribe
A Viking port 1,000 years ago, Ribe, located about 30 miles southwest of Billund, is the oldest, and possibly the loveliest, town in Denmark. It's an entertaining mix of cobbled lanes and leaning medieval houses, with a fine **cathedral** boasting modern paintings under Romanesque arches. The **TI** is on the main square (Torvet 3, tel. 75 42 15 00, www.visitribe.com). **$ Weis Stue,** a smoky, low-ceilinged, atmospheric inn across from the church, rents primitive rooms with a shared bath and serves good meals (no breakfast, tel. 75 42 07 00, www.weis-stue.dk). Take the free **Night Watchman** tour (daily May-mid-Oct, www.visitribe.com).

WEST OF BILLUND
North Sea Coast
If beautiful beaches and WWII-era bunkers sound appealing, consider this side trip, worth ▲▲ on a nice day. Just an hour or so west from Legoland is a land of rolling dunes, wide sandy beaches and big waves. It's often windy and the water can be brisk but the Danes who flock here in the summer don't mind. You can make a strategic strike to Blåvand and back in half a day but allow a whole day to fully experience the coast. Bring your swimsuit!

Blåvand ("BLOW-van") is a popular beach destination a little over an hour west of Billund (take highway 30, then 475 to Varde, then follow highway 471). Turn left at Oksby on Tane Hedevej to reach the **Tirpitz Museum.** This striking structure, designed by Danish "starchitect" Bjarke Ingels, is built into the dunes and connected by tunnel to a German bunker that was part of Hitler's Atlantic Wall that stretched from Norway down to Spain. Look for the exhibit on amber (the "Gold of the North" washes up on local beaches) and an amazing amber model of the Sydney Opera House, which was designed by Dane Jørn Utzon (tel. 72 10 84 85, http://vardemuseerne.dk/museum/tirpitz). To reach the wide beach, backtrack through Oksby and follow Fyrvej to the lighthouse.

Just 20 minutes north is the low-key beach town of **Vejers Strand,** where the main drag dead-ends at the beach. **$$$$ Knudedyb,** a famous local restaurant, offers good seafood and on-site smoked fish (reservations smart, tel. 75 27 67 67). **$$$ Klithjem Badehotel** provides nice rooms just steps from the sea (two-night minimum but you might get lucky, closed Oct-April, tel. 40 18 17 26, www.klithjembadehotel.dk).

The dunes along the coast hide many other bunkers. Along with Blåvand, you'll find an easy-to-access observation post and troop bunker at **Hvide Sande,** a harbor town one hour north that straddles the entrance to a wide bay. After crossing the bridge, park in the lot on the right where you'll find a TI, plus some shops and restaurants. Cross the road and climb the Troldbjerg Hill, heading toward a large mast and a flagpole to find the sights.

More evocative and isolated are the bunkers 20 minutes further north at Houvig Strand. Along the way you'll pass dozens of summer houses, many with thatched roofs and Danish flags flapping in the breeze. Turn left at the *Houvig Strand* sign, and park in the lot, where a path leads through the dunes to the beach. One bunker is just in front of you and several others lie a 10-minute walk to the right. Be careful exploring these tilting concrete structures up close, as shifting sands covering rusty metal rebar can make them treacherous. From Houvig Strand it's a 90-minute drive back to Billund via Ringkøping.

PRACTICALITIES

This section covers just the basics on traveling in this region (for much more information, see *Rick Steves Scandinavia*). You'll find free advice on specific topics at www.ricksteves.com/tips.

MONEY

In Denmark, credit cards are widely accepted, even for small purchases, but you can generally pay with cash if you prefer. If you need cash, Denmark uses the Danish kroner (DKK): 1 krone equals about $0.16. To convert prices in kroner to dollars, divide by six (e.g., 15 DKK = about $2.50, 100 DKK = about $16). Check www.oanda.com for the latest exchange rates.

The standard way for travelers to get kroner is to withdraw money from an ATM using a debit card, ideally with a Visa or MasterCard logo. Before departing, call your bank or credit-card company: Confirm that your card(s) will work overseas, ask about international transaction fees, and alert them that you'll be making withdrawals in Europe. Also ask for the PIN number for your credit card—you may need it for Europe's "chip-and-PIN" payment machines (see below; allow time for your bank to mail your PIN to you). To keep your valuables safe while traveling, wear a money belt.

Dealing with "Chip and PIN": Most credit and debit cards now have chips that authenticate and secure transactions. European cardholders insert their chip card into the payment slot, then enter a PIN. (Until recently, most US cards required a signature.) Any American card with a chip will work at Europe's hotels, restaurants, and shops—although sometimes the clerk may ask for a signature. But some self-service payment machines—such as those at train stations, toll roads, or unattended gas pumps—may not accept your card, even if you know the PIN. If your card won't work, look for a cashier who can process the transaction manually—or pay in cash.

Dynamic Currency Conversion: If merchants or hoteliers offer to convert your purchase price into dollars (called dynamic currency conversion, or DCC), refuse this "service." You'll pay more in fees for the expensive convenience of seeing your charge in dollars. If an ATM offers to "lock in" or "guarantee" your conversion rate, choose "proceed without conversion." Other prompts might state, "You can be charged in dollars: Press YES for dollars, NO for kroner." Always choose the local currency.

STAYING CONNECTED

The simplest solution is to bring your own device—mobile phone, tablet, or laptop—and use it just as you would at home (following the tips below, such as connecting to free Wi-Fi whenever possible).

To call Denmark from a US or Canadian number: Whether you're phoning from a landline, your own mobile phone, or a Skype account, you're making an international call. Dial 011-45 and then the local number. (The 011 is our international access code, and 45 is Denmark's country code.) If dialing from a mobile phone, you can enter + in place of the international access code—press and hold the 0 key.

To call Denmark from a European country: Dial 00-45 followed by the local number. (The 00 is Europe's international access code.)

To call within Denmark: Just dial the local number.

To call from Denmark to another country: Dial 00 followed by the country code (for example, 1 for the US or Canada), then the area code and number. If you're calling European countries with phone numbers that begin with 0, you'll usually have to omit that 0 when you dial.

Tips: If you bring your own mobile phone, consider signing up for an international plan; most providers offer a global calling plan that cuts the per-minute cost of phone calls and texts, and a flat-fee data plan.

Use Wi-Fi whenever possible. Most hotels and many cafés offer free Wi-Fi, and you'll likely also find it at tourist information offices (TIs), major museums, and public-transit hubs. With Wi-Fi you make free or inexpensive domestic and international calls via a calling app such as Skype, FaceTime, or Google+ Hangouts. When you can't find Wi-Fi, you can use your cellular network to connect to the Internet, send texts, or make voice calls. When you're done, avoid further charges by manually switching off "data roaming" or "cellular data."

Without a mobile device, you can make calls from your hotel and get online using public computers (there's usually one in your hotel lobby or at local libraries). Most hotels charge a high fee for international calls—ask for rates before you dial. For more on

Sleep Code

Hotels are classified based on the average price of a typical en suite double room with breakfast in high season.

$$$$	**Splurge:** Most rooms over 1,100 DKK
$$$	**Pricier:** 900-1,100 DKK
$$	**Moderate:** 700-900 DKK
$	**Budget:** 500-700 DKK
¢	**Backpacker:** Under 500 DKK
RS%	**Rick Steves Discount**

Unless otherwise noted, credit cards are accepted, and free Wi-Fi is available. Comparison-shop by checking prices at several hotels (on each hotel's own website, on a booking site, or by email). For the best deal, always book directly with the hotel. Ask for a discount if paying in cash; if the listing includes **RS%,** request a Rick Steves discount.

phoning, see www.ricksteves.com/phoning. For a one-hour talk on "Traveling with a Mobile Device," see www.ricksteves.com/travel-talks.

SLEEPING

I've categorized my recommended accommodations based on price, indicated with a dollar-sign rating (see sidebar). To ensure the best value, I recommend reserving rooms in advance, particularly during peak season. Once your dates are set, check the specific price for your preferred stay at several hotels. You can do this either by comparing prices on sites such as Hotels.com or Booking.com, or by checking the hotels' own websites. To get the best deal, contact my family-run hotels directly by phone or email. When you go direct, the owner avoids any third-party commission, giving them wiggle room to offer you a discount, a nicer room, or free breakfast. If you prefer to book online or are considering a hotel chain, it's to your advantage to use the hotel's website.

For complicated requests, send an email with the following information: number and type of rooms; number of nights; arrival date; departure date; and any special requests. Use the European style for writing dates: day/month/year. Hoteliers typically ask for your credit-card number as a deposit. In general, hotel prices can soften if you do any of the following: offer to pay cash, stay at least three nights, or travel off-season.

Even though most hotels in Denmark base their prices on demand, it is possible to find lower prices during the summer and on weekends. Check hotel websites for deals. To find an apartment or room in a private home, try Airbnb, Booking.com, and the HomeAway family of sites (HomeAway, VRBO, and VacationRentals).

Restaurant Price Code

I've assigned each eatery a price category, based on the average cost of a typical main course. Drinks, desserts, and splurge items (steak and seafood) can raise the price considerably.

$$$$ **Splurge:** Most main courses over 150 DKK
$$$ **Pricier:** 100-150 DKK
$$ **Moderate:** 50-100 DKK
$ **Budget:** Under 50 DKK

In Denmark, a *pølsevogn* or other takeout spot is **$**; a sit-down café is **$$**; a casual but more upscale restaurant is **$$$**; and a swanky splurge is **$$$$**.

EATING

I've categorized my recommended eateries based on price, indicated with a dollar-sign rating (see sidebar).

Restaurants are often expensive. Alternate between picnics (outside or in your hotel or hostel); cheap, forgettable, but filling cafeteria or fast-food fare ($20 per person); and atmospheric, carefully chosen restaurants popular with locals ($40 per person and up).

The *smörgåsbord* (known in Denmark as the *store koldt bord*) is a revered Scandinavian culinary tradition. Seek it out at least once during your visit. Begin with the fish dishes, along with boiled potatoes and *knäckebröd* (crisp bread). Then move on to salads, egg dishes, and various cold cuts. Next it's meatball time! Pour on some gravy as well as a spoonful of lingonberry sauce. Still hungry? Make a point to sample the Nordic cheeses and the racks of traditional desserts, cakes, and custards.

For lunch, you'll find *smørrebrød* shops turning open-face sandwiches into an art form. Shops will wrap these Danish sandwiches up for a perfect picnic in a nearby park. For a quick, cheap meal, try a Danish hot dog (*pølse*), sold in *pølsevogne* (sausage wagons). Ethnic eateries—Turkish, Greek, Italian, and Asian—offer a good value and a break from Danish fare.

To avoid high restaurant prices for alcohol, many Danes—and tourists—buy their wine, beer, or spirits at any supermarket or corner store, and then drink at a public square; this is legal and openly practiced. A local specialty is *akvavit*, a strong, vodka-like spirit distilled from potatoes and flavored with anise, caraway, or other herbs and spices—then drunk ice-cold. *Salmiakka* is a nearly black licorice-flavored liqueur, and *Gammel Dansk* can be described as Danish bitters for the adventurous.

Service: Good service is relaxed (slow to an American). When you're ready for the bill, ask for the *regningen*. Throughout Denmark, a service charge is included in your bill, so there's no need to leave an additional tip. In fancier restaurants or any restaurant where you enjoy great service, round up the bill (about 5-10 percent of the total check).

TRANSPORTATION

By Train: In Denmark, the train system is excellent and nearly always a better option than buses. Faster trains are more expensive than slower "regional" trains. To see if a rail pass could save you money, check www.ricksteves.com/rail. If you're buying tickets as you go, note that prices can fluctuate. To research train schedules and fares, visit the Danish train websites: www.dsb.dk or www.rejseplanen.dk. Or check out Deutsche Bahn's excellent all-Europe timetable: www.bahn.com.

By Car: It's cheaper to arrange most car rentals from the US. For tips on your insurance options, see www.ricksteves.com/cdw, and for route planning, consult www.viamichelin.com. Bring your driver's license. Local road etiquette is similar to that in the US. Ask your car-rental company for details, or check the US State Department website (www.travel.state.gov, select "International Travel," then "Country Information," then search for your destination and click "Traffic Safety and Road Conditions"). Use your headlights day and night; it's required in most of Scandinavia. A car is a worthless headache in any big city—park it safely (get tips from your hotelier).

By Boat: Ferries are essential for hopping between the mainland and Denmark's islands, such as Ærø (drivers should reserve in advance for weekends and summer, www.aeroe-ferry.dk). Note that short-distance ferries may take only cash, not credit cards. Advance reservations are also recommended when using overnight boats in summer or on weekends to link Copenhagen to Oslo (www.dfdsseaways.com). Other worthwhile ferry routes connect northern Denmark to Norway; see www.fjordline.com and www.colorline.com.

By Plane: SAS is the region's dominant airline (www.flysas.com). Well-known cheapo airlines EasyJet (www.easyjet.com) and Ryanair (www.ryanair.com) fly into Scandinavia.

HELPFUL HINTS

Emergency Help: To summon the **police** or an **ambulance**, call 112. For passport problems, call the **US Embassy** (in Copenhagen: passport services by appointment only, tel. 33 41 74 00, https://dk.usembassy.gov).

If you have a minor illness, do as the locals do and go to a pharmacist for advice. Or ask at your hotel for help—they'll know of the nearest medical and emergency services. For other concerns, get advice from your hotelier.

Theft or Loss: To replace a passport, you'll need to go in person to an embassy (see above). Cancel and replace your credit and debit cards by calling these 24-hour US numbers collect: Visa—tel. 303/967-1096, MasterCard—tel. 636/722-7111, American Express—tel. 336/393-1111. In Denmark, to make a collect call to the US, dial 800-100-10; press zero or stay on the line for an operator. File a police report either on the spot or within a day or two; you'll need it to submit an insurance claim for lost or stolen rail passes or electronics, and it can help with replacing your passport or credit and debit cards. Precautionary measures can minimize the effects of loss—back up your photos and other files frequently. For more information, see www.ricksteves.com/help.

Time: Europe uses the 24-hour clock. It's the same through 12:00 noon, then keep going: 13:00, 14:00, and so on. Denmark, like most of continental Europe, is six/nine hours ahead of the East/West Coasts of the US.

Holidays and Festivals: Europe celebrates many holidays, which can close sights and attract crowds (book hotel rooms ahead). For info on holidays and festivals in Denmark, check the Scandinavia Tourist Board website: www.goscandinavia.com. For a simple list showing major—though not all—events, see www.ricksteves.com/festivals.

Numbers and Stumblers: What Americans call the second floor of a building is the first floor in Europe. Europeans write dates as day/month/year, so Christmas 2020 is 25/12/20. Commas are decimal points and vice versa—a dollar and a half is 1,50, and there are 5.280 feet in a mile. Europe uses the metric system: A kilogram is 2.2 pounds; a liter is about a quart; and a kilometer is six-tenths of a mile.

RESOURCES FROM RICK STEVES

This Snapshot guide is excerpted from the latest edition of *Rick Steves Scandinavia,* which is one of many titles in my ever-expanding series of guidebooks on European travel. I also produce a public television series, *Rick Steves' Europe,* and a public radio show, *Travel with Rick Steves.* My website, www.ricksteves.com, offers free travel information, a forum for travelers' comments, guidebook updates, my travel blog, an online travel store, and information on European rail passes and our tours of Europe. If you're bringing a mobile device on your trip, you can download my Rick Steves Audio Europe app, featuring dozens of self-guided audio tours of the top sights in Europe and travel interviews about Europe. You can get Rick Steves Audio Europe via Apple's App Store, Google Play, or the Amazon Appstore. For more information, see www.ricksteves.com/audioeurope.

ADDITIONAL RESOURCES
Tourist Information: www.goscandinavia.com
Passports and Red Tape: www.travel.state.gov
Packing List: www.ricksteves.com/packing
Travel Insurance: www.ricksteves.com/insurance
Cheap Flights: www.kayak.com or www.google.com/flights
Airplane Carry-on Restrictions: www.tsa.gov
Updates for This Book: www.ricksteves.com/update

HOW WAS YOUR TRIP?
If you'd like to share your tips, concerns, and discoveries after using this book, please fill out the survey at www.ricksteves.com/feedback. Thanks in advance—it helps a lot.

INDEX

INDEX

Our website enhances this book and turns

Explore Europe

At ricksteves.com you can browse through thousands of articles, videos, photos and radio interviews, plus find a wealth of money-saving travel tips for planning your dream trip. And with our mobile-friendly website, you can easily access all this great travel information anywhere you go.

TV Shows

Preview the places you'll visit by watching entire half-hour episodes of Rick Steves' Europe (choose from all 100 shows) on-demand, for free.

ricksteves.com

your travel dreams into affordable reality

Radio Interviews

Enjoy ready access to Rick's vast library of radio interviews covering travel

tips and cultural insights that relate specifically to your Europe travel plans.

Travel Forums

Learn, ask, share! Our online community of savvy travelers is a great resource for first-time travelers to Europe, as well as seasoned pros. You'll find forums on each country, plus travel tips and restaurant/hotel reviews. You can even ask one of our well-traveled staff to chime in with an opinion.

Travel News

Subscribe to our free Travel News e-newsletter, and get monthly updates from Rick on what's happening in Europe.

Audio Europe™

Rick's Free Travel App

Get your FREE **Rick Steves Audio Europe**™ app to enjoy...

- Dozens of self-guided tours of Europe's top museums, sights and historic walks
- Hundreds of tracks filled with cultural insights and sightseeing tips from Rick's radio interviews
- All organized into handy geographic playlists
- For Apple and Android

With Rick whispering in your ear, Europe gets even better.

Find out more at ricksteves.com

Pack Light and Right

Gear up for your next adventure at ricksteves.com

Light Luggage

Pack light and right
with Rick Steves'
affordable, custom-
designed rolling carry-on
bags, backpacks, day
packs and shoulder bags.

Accessories

From packing cubes to
moneybelts and beyond,
Rick has personally
selected the travel
goodies that will help
your trip
go smoother.

Shop at ricksteves.com

Experience maximum Europe

Save time and energy

This guidebook is your independent-travel toolkit. But for all it delivers, it's still up to you to devote the time and energy it takes to manage the preparation and logistics that are essential for a happy trip. If that's a hassle, there's a solution.

Rick Steves Tours

A Rick Steves tour takes you to Europe's most interesting places with great

great tours, too!

with minimum stress

guides and small groups of 28 or less. We follow Rick's favorite itineraries, ride in comfy buses, stay in family-run hotels, and bring you intimately close to the Europe you've traveled so far to see. Most importantly, we take away the logistical headaches so you can focus on the fun.

travelers—nearly half of them repeat customers—along with us on four dozen different itineraries, from Ireland to Italy to Athens. Is a Rick Steves tour the right fit for your travel dreams? Find out at ricksteves.com, where you can also request Rick's latest tour catalog. Europe is best experienced with happy travel partners. We hope you can join us.

Join the fun

This year we'll take thousands of free-spirited

See our itineraries at ricksteves.com

A Guide for Every Trip

BEST OF GUIDES

Full color easy-to-scan format, focusing on Europe's most popular destinations and sights.

Best of England
Best of Europe
Best of France
Best of Germany
Best of Ireland
Best of Italy
Best of Spain

COMPREHENSIVE GUIDES

City, country, and regional guides with detailed coverage for a multi-week trip exploring the most iconic sights and venturing off the beaten track.

Amsterdam & the Netherlands
Barcelona
Belgium: Bruges, Brussels, Antwerp & Ghent
Berlin
Budapest
Croatia & Slovenia
Eastern Europe
England
Florence & Tuscany
France
Germany
Great Britain
Greece: Athens & the Peloponnese
Iceland
Ireland
Istanbul
Italy
London
Paris
Portugal
Prague & the Czech Republic
Provence & the French Riviera
Rome
Scandinavia
Scotland
Spain
Switzerland
Venice
Vienna, Salzburg & Tirol

HE BEST OF ROME

, Italy's capital, is studded with
n remnants and floodlit-fountain
s. From the Vatican to the Colos-
with crazy traffic in between, Rome
derful, huge, and exhausting. The
, the heat, and the weighty history

of the Eternal City where Caesars walked
can make tourists wilt. Recharge by taking siestas, gelato breaks, and after-dark
walks, strolling from one atmospheric
square to another in the refreshing evening air.

Rick Steves guidebooks are published by Avalon Travel,
an imprint of Perseus Books, a Hachette Book Group comp

POCKET GUIDES
Compact, full color city guides with the essentials for shorter trips.

Amsterdam
Athens
Barcelona
Florence
Italy's Cinque Terre
London
Munich & Salzburg

Paris
Prague
Rome
Venice
Vienna

SNAPSHOT GUIDES
Focused single-destination coverage.

Basque Country: Spain & France
Copenhagen & the Best of Denmark
Dublin
Dubrovnik
Edinburgh
Hill Towns of Central Italy
Krakow, Warsaw & Gdansk
Lisbon
Loire Valley
Madrid & Toledo
Milan & the Italian Lakes District
Naples & the Amalfi Coast
Normandy
Northern Ireland
Norway
Reykjavik
Sevilla, Granada & Southern Spain
St. Petersburg, Helsinki & Tallinn
Stockholm

CRUISE PORTS GUIDES
Reference for cruise ports of call.

Mediterranean Cruise Ports
Scandinavian & Northern European
Cruise Ports

Complete your library with...

TRAVEL SKILLS & CULTURE
Study up on travel skills and gain insight on history and culture.

Europe 101
Europe Through the Back Door
European Christmas
European Easter
European Festivals
Postcards from Europe
Travel as a Political Act

PHRASE BOOKS & DICTIONARIES

French
French, Italian & German
German
Italian
Portuguese
Spanish

PLANNING MAPS

Britain, Ireland & London
Europe
France & Paris
Germany, Austria & Switzerland
Ireland
Italy
Spain & Portugal

Avalon Travel
Hachette Book Group
1700 Fourth Street
Berkeley, CA 94710

Printed in Canada by Friesens.
Fourth Edition. First printing July 2018.
ISBN 978-1-63121-818-7

For the latest on Rick's talks, guidebooks, tours, public television series, and public radio show, contact Rick Steves' Europe, 130 Fourth Avenue North, Edmonds, WA 98020, 425/771-8303, www.ricksteves.com, rick@ricksteves.com.

Rick Steves' Europe
Managing Editor: Jennifer Madison Davis
Special Publications Manager: Risa Laib
Assistant Managing Editor: Cathy Lu
Editors: Glenn Eriksen, Julie Fanselow, Tom Griffin, Katherine Gustafson, Suzanne Kotz, Rosie Leutzinger, Carrie Shepherd
Editorial & Production Assistant: Jessica Shaw
Editorial Intern: Kevin Teeter
Researchers: Glenn Eriksen, Cameron Hewitt, Pål Bjarne Johansen, Suzanne Kotz
Contributor: Gene Openshaw
Graphic Content Director: Sandra Hundacker
Maps & Graphics: David C. Hoerlein, Lauren Mills, Mary Rostad

Avalon Travel
Senior Editor & Series Manager: Madhu Prasher
Editor: Jamie Andrade
Editor: Sierra Machado
Copy Editor: Maggie Ryan
Proofreader: Kelly Lydick, Patrick Collins
Indexer: Stephen Callahan
Production & Typesetting: Christine DeLorenzo, Kit Anderson, Lisi Baldwin, Rue Flaherty
Cover Design: Kimberly Glyder Design
Maps & Graphics: Kat Bennett, Mike Morgenfeld

Photo Credits
Front Cover: Nyhavn harbor waterfront, Copenhagen © Luisa Vallon Fumi | Dreamstime.com
Title Page: © Dominic Arizona Bonuccelli
Additional Photography: Dominic Arizona Bonuccelli, Tom Griffin, Sonja Groset, Cameron Hewitt, David C. Hoerlein, Lauren Mills, Jennifer Schutte, Rick Steves, Ian Watson, Wikimedia Commons (PD-Art/PD-US)
Additional Credits: p. 23, photo of Richard Karpen— courtesy of Jack Juliussen
Photos are used by permission and are the property of the original copyright owners

Let's Keep on Travelin'

Your trip doesn't need to end.

Follow Rick on social media!